Learning to Program with Alice

Learning to Program with Alice

Wanda Dann
Ithaca College

Stephen Cooper
Saint Joseph's University

Randy Pausch
Carnegie Mellon University

PEARSON

Prentice
Hall

Upper Saddle River, NJ 07458

Library of Congress Cataloging-in-Publication Data on File

Vice President and Editorial Director, ECS: *Marcia J. Horton*
Acquisitors Editor: *Tracy Dunkelberger*
Editorial Assistant: *Christianna Lee*
Executive Managing Editor: *Vince O'Brien*
Managing Editor: *Camille Trentacoste*
Production Editor: *Rose Kernan*
Director of Creative Services: *Paul Belfanti*
Creative Director: *Kenny Beck*
Cover Designer: *Kenny Beck*
Manufacturing Manager: *Alexis Heydt-Long*
Manufacturing Buyer: *Lisa McDowell*
Executive Marketing Manager: *Pamela Hersperger*
Marketing Assistant: *Barrie Reinhold*

© 2006 Pearson Education, Inc.
Pearson Prentice Hall
Pearson Education, Inc.
Upper Saddle River, NJ 07458

Pearson Prentice Hall is a trademark of Pearson Education, Inc.
The Alice Software System is © by Carnegie Mellon University.

Printed in the United States of America
10 9 8 7 6 5 4 3

ISBN 0-13-187289-3

Pearson Education Ltd., *London*
Pearson Education Australia Pty. Ltd., *Sydney*
Pearson Education Singapore, Pte. Ltd.
Pearson Education North Asia Ltd., *Hong Kong*
Pearson Education Canada Inc., *Toronto*
Pearson Educación de Mexico, S.A. de C.V.
Pearson Education—Japan, *Tokyo*
Pearson Education Malaysia Pte. Ltd.
Pearson Education, Inc., *Upper Saddle River, New Jersey*

To Brian, Wendy, Jerry, and Noah

Wanda Dann

To Sandi and Jeanna

Stephen Cooper

To Jai, Dylan, and Logan

Randy Pausch

Contents

Foreword

Introductory programming has always been a frustrating course for many students, and recent attempts to include object-oriented programming in the first semester have only compounded an already difficult learning experience. This is especially worrisome when recent surveys show a 23% decline in the number CS majors. We simply can't afford to discourage students by needlessly frustrating them in their first exposure to computing.

The Alice system represents a breakthrough in teaching object-oriented computing: in Alice, objects are easily visible, because they are reified as three-dimensional humans, animals, furniture, etc. The state of Alice objects is changed via method calls such as "move forward one meter" or "turn left a quarter turn"—these messages are easily and intuitively understood by students. Computation is displayed via animations of these state changes: one can hardly imagine a more visceral way to express the notion of embodying state in an object and using computation to change that state. One of Alice's real strengths is that it has been able to make abstract concepts concrete in the eyes of first-time programmers.

Any good teacher knows that if a student is not motivated to learn, all the pedagogy and technique in the world won't help: students learn best when they are internally motivated. While we can create that motivation via rewards and punishments (i.e. "grades") the Alice system uses a purer form of motivation: it bases programming in the activity of storytelling which is universally compelling: as we say in Los Angeles, "everybody wants to direct."

By using 3D graphics as the authoring medium, the Alice system speaks directly to a generation raised on videogames and PIXAR's films; the authors leverage that by using "storyboarding" as a metaphor for computer program design—storyboarding being one of the few "design activities" that can be immediately understood by a college freshman.

Coupled with the high-level concepts such as reifying objects, the Alice system provides a well-engineered drag-and-drop user interface, inspired by the Squeak system's editor, that allows students to drag program components around the screen and guarantees that the student cannot make a syntax error.

One could make the argument that Alice is one of the most novel systems to hit introductory computing in the last twenty years—and it's arriving just in time!

ALAN KAY

Dr. Kay is one of the earliest pioneers of object-oriented programming, personal computing and graphical user interfaces. His contributions have been recognized with the Charles Stark Draper Prize of the National Academy of Engineering (with Robert Taylor, Butler Lampson, and Charles Thacker), the A.M. Turing Award from the Association of Computing Machinery, and the Kyoto Prize from the Inamori Foundation.

Preface

"... what is the use of a book," thought Alice, "without pictures or conversation?"

This book and the associated Alice system take an innovative approach to introductory programming. There have been relatively few innovations in the teaching of programming in the last 30 years, even though such courses are often extremely frustrating to students. The goal of our innovative approach is to allow traditional programming concepts to be more easily taught and more readily understood. The Alice system is free and is available at www.alice.org.

What should a programming course teach?

While many people have strong opinions on this topic, we feel there is a strong consensus that a student in a programming course should learn the following:

- Algorithmic thinking and expression: being able to read and write in a formal language.
- Abstraction: learning how to communicate complex ideas simply and to decompose problems logically.
- Appreciation of elegance: realizing that although there are many ways to solve a problem, some are inherently better than others.

What is different about our approach?

Our approach allows students to author on-screen movies and games, in which the concept of an "object" is made tangible and visible. In Alice, on-screen objects populate a 3D micro world. Students create programs by dragging and dropping program elements (if/then statements, loops, variables, etc.) in a mouse-based editor that prohibits syntax errors. The Alice system provides a powerful, modern programming environment that supports methods, functions, variables, parameters, recursion, arrays, and events. We use this strong visual environment to support either an objects-first or an objects-early approach (described in the ACM and IEEE-CS Computing Curricula 2001 report) with an early introduction to events. In Alice, every object is an object that students can visibly see! We introduce objects in the very first chapter.

In our opinion, four primary obstacles to introductory programming must be overcome:

1. **The fragile mechanics of program creation, particularly syntax** The Alice editing environment removes the frustration of syntax errors in program creation and allows students to develop an intuition for syntax, because every time a program element is dragged into the editor, all valid "drop targets" are highlighted.

2. **The inability to see the results of computation as the program runs** Although textual debuggers and variable watchers are better than nothing, the Alice approach makes the state of the program inherently visible. In a sense, we offload the mental effort from the student's cognitive system to his or her perceptual system. It is much easier for a student to see that an object has moved backward instead of forward than to notice that the "sum" variable has been decremented, rather than incremented. Alice allows students to see how their animated programs run, affording an easy relationship of the program

construct to the animation action. Today's students are immersed in a world where interactive, three-dimensional graphics are commonplace; we try to leverage that fact without pandering to them.

3. **The lack of motivation for programming** Many students take introductory programming courses only because they are required to do so. Nothing will ever be more motivating than a stellar teacher, but the right environment can go a long way. In pilot studies of classes using Alice, students do more optional exercises and are more likely to take a second class in programming than control groups of students using traditional tools. The most common request we received regarding earlier versions of Alice was to be able to share creations with peers; we have added the ability to run Alice programs in a World Wide Web browser so students can post them on their Web pages. Although we have seen increased motivation for all students, we have seen especially encouraging results with underrepresented groups, especially female students.

4. **The difficulty of understanding compound logic and learning design techniques** The Alice environment physically encourages the creation of small methods and functions. More importantly, the analogy of making a movie allows us to utilize the concept of a storyboard, which students recognize as an established movie-making process. We illustrate design techniques using simple sketches and screen captures. Also, we encourage the use of textual storyboards, progressively refining them and essentially designing with pseudocode.

How to use this text

Of course, as an instructor, you should use this text as you see fit! We list four ways we imagine the book being used, but you may discover others:

As the only text in a short or semester-long course on programming. This would allow students to build relatively complex (say, 300-line) programs by the end of the semester or term. Such a course might be for non-majors who want to learn the concepts behind programming without needing to transition to a real-world language. Alternatively, this course can be used as a pre-CS1 course for students who might like to major in computing but lack previous programming experience. In our NSF-supported study (NSF-0126833), we found that students who jump right into a rigorous CS1 course with little or no previous programming have an extremely high attrition rate. The use of Alice in a pre-CS1 course has significantly reduced attrition for these students in our CS1 courses.

As the first portion of a traditional "Introduction to Programming" course, such as CS1. Both Seymour Papert's Logo and Rich Pattis' Karel the Robot have been used this way, and these systems have inspired us greatly. Unlike these systems, Alice is powerful enough to support students for several semesters (for example, seniors majoring in computer science at Carnegie Mellon routinely write 3,000-line programs in Alice). However, many introductory programming courses must both teach concepts and also prepare students to write programs in traditional languages, such as Java. By learning Alice first, students become acquainted with the fundamental concepts of programming, and can quickly learn the specific syntax rules of a particular "real" language as a transition. The Alice environment can ease the transition by displaying programs with a Java-like syntax, as shown in Figure P-1-1.

As the programming component of a "Computer Literacy" course. At many schools, computer literacy courses attempt to give non-majors a broad introduction to computers and/or "information technology." Many of these courses have removed their programming component and are little more than extended laboratories on "office productivity tools" such as spreadsheets and word processors. Alice has the potential to return a gentle programming component to computer literacy courses.

In a high school "Introduction to Programming" course. A course in Alice has great potential for a high school environment, where a high-interest, highly motivating environment is a teacher's best friend. This book could be used as part of a stand-alone course or as preparation for the College AP computing course.

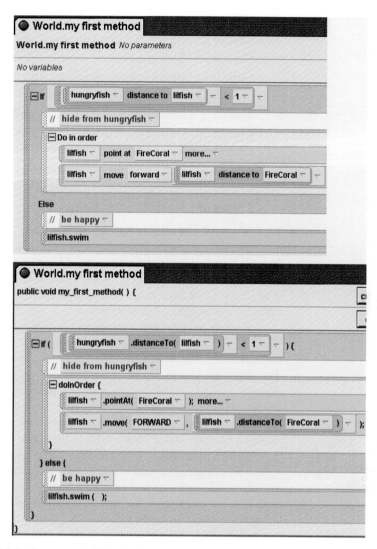

Figure P-1-1. Programs in Alice (top) can optionally be displayed with a Java-like syntax (bottom)

Instructional materials

An errata list, lecture notes, links to other instructional materials, and examples of course schedules can be found at http://www.aliceprogramming.net.

Structure of the book

Chapter 1 gives students some motivating reasons to want to write a computer program and addresses any fears they may have about programming (especially helpful for computer literacy courses). It then introduces some basic Alice concepts. A traditional, paper-based tutorial is presented in Appendix A. Computing and programming terminology (e.g., program, class, and object) are written in blue when first introduced and defined.

The remaining chapters each begin with a motivational overview of the chapter's topic and end with exercises, projects, and a summary. The list below is a (very) brief overview of the major concepts covered, chapter by chapter. Clearly, the major focus of the text material is to introduce the fundamental concepts of programming.

We recommend a rapid pace through the first three or four chapters of the book (Chapters 1 and 2 can easily be covered in just 2 or 3 class days.) Instructors should assign exercises selectively from the large number of exercises at the end of each chapter. (A large number of exercises were provided to allow the instructor to choose exercises most appropriate for their students.) Examples of larger, more free-form "projects" are provided at the end of later chapters. (A "project" is a more advanced exercise that takes more time.)

Projects are meant to turn on the creative spirit, not weigh the student down. Where feasible, we recommend "open-ended" projects. An open-ended project is one which asks students to design their own animation beginning with their own storyline and using objects of their choosing. We do require that a project meet certain requirements—for example, "an interactive world, containing two or more interactions with the mouse, at least three methods, using a decision statement, and having objects from two classes you have created by writing class-level methods and saving out the new classes." Alice lends itself particularly well to student demonstrations of their worlds to the rest of the class on the project due date.

Each chapter has a "Tips & Techniques" section. Collectively, these sections and Appendices A and B comprise a mini User's Guide to Alice. The Tips & Techniques cover animation in Alice rather than traditional fundamental concepts of programming presented in the major chapter material. The techniques explained in these sections are strategically placed throughout the text, laying the groundwork for using these techniques in programming examples that follow. Tips & Techniques provide a guide for those who want to learn more about animation with Alice. Appendix A is a "getting started" tutorial. Appendix B describes how to manage the interface. Use of the interface is also integrated with text examples for programming concepts, where needed. The Tips & Techniques sections enrich the flavor of the book with selected "how to" topics.

Topic selection and sequence of coverage

The topic selection and sequence of coverage is in the instructor's hands! The dependency chart in Figure P-1-2 should help you in selecting a path through the book.

From an overly simplistic perspective, Chapters 1–4 present topics in sequence and Chapters 5–11 are more independent and can be covered in many different sequences. A sequential coverage of Chapters 1–4 is an "Objects Early" approach. Skipping Chapter 3 is an "Objects First" approach. Examples in Chapters 4 and 5 were designed to be independent of Chapter 3. Thus, an Objects First approach can safely skip Chapter 3 and pick up these topics later as part of coverage of topics in Chapters 6 and 7. Another flexible sequencing option is to reverse Chapters 7 and 8 to allow coverage of recursion before *Loop* and *While* control structures.

In working with instructors in various college and university settings, we found that topic selection and sequences are often based on time constraints for a particular course structure, pedagogy, and philosophy of teaching. If you are limited to three or four weeks as part of a larger course, you may wish to assign exercises throughout with only one project at the end.

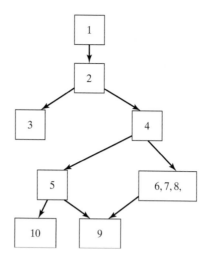

Figure P-1-2. Dependency Chart

Also, you can use Tips & Techniques sections as reading assignments, not requiring classroom presentation time. The following **Sequence Chart** illustrates some examples of sequences.

Sequence	strategy/time constraints	courses
1–2–3–4 (and possibly 5)	Objects Early (3–4 weeks)	Computer Literacy First 3 weeks of CS1
1–2–4–5–6–7–8	Objects First (short course)	Introduction to Programming Pre-CS1
1–2–4–5–6–8–7	Objects First, Recursion Early (short course)	Pre-CS1
1–2–3–4–5 and selected topics from 6–11	Objects Early (full semester)	Introduction to Programming Pre-CS1
1–2–4–5–6 and elected topics from 7–11	Objects First (full semester)	Introduction to Programming Pre-CS1

Notes concerning specific aspects of the text

If you are using this text to teach/learn Alice without discussing design, you may skip the first section of Chapter 2. However, textual storyboards and stepwise refinement will be used throughout the rest of the text to provide a framework in which to discuss design from an algorithmic, problem-solving perspective. You may choose to use a different design framework (perhaps the Unified Modeling Language or a more traditional version of pseudocode). This may be done safely, without impacting the content.

In Chapter 4, we note that Alice does not provide a complete implementation of inheritance. When a new class is created in Alice, it gets a copy of the properties and methods of the base class and is saved in a new 3D model file. Subsequent changes to the super class are not reflected in the subclass.

Inheritance is accomplished in object-oriented programming languages via two mechanisms: (a) adding methods (behavior), and (b) adding extra state information via the use of mutable variables. We separate discussion of these mechanisms, introducing added behavior in Chapter 4, but deferring discussion of additional state information until Chapter 10. Because mutable variables are not visible/visual in the way the rest of the Alice environment is, they are introduced much later in the text, after students have developed a mastery of several other programming concepts.

We have found that interactive programs are fun and highly motivating to students. From a pedagogical perspective, however, Chapter 5 may be skipped. Some exercises and projects in later chapters use an interactive style, but you may be selective in examples and assignments.

Alice

The latest version of the Alice software and online galleries of 3D models can be downloaded from http:www.alice org. The version of Alice on the disk supplied with this book is meant to run on a PC with the Windows ME, 2000, or XP operating system. If you are using a Macintosh or a PC with Linux, check the Web site http://www.alice.org for a version of Alice compatible with your system. The Alice website also provides instructions for installation, Frequently Asked Questions, links for receiving bug reports, and access to an online community forum for Alice educators.

The Alice system is 3D graphics and memory intensive. The Alice development team has a set of minimum and recommended requirements for running Alice. Please note that many older laptops do not meet these requirements. It is extremely important to try Alice on the specific machines you will be using, just to be sure.

Operating system requirements:
Windows ME, 2000, or XP

Minimum hardware requirements:
A Pentium running at 500 MHz or better
VGA graphics card capable of high (16 bit) color
128 MB of RAM
Video resolution of 1024×768
A sound card

Recommended hardware requirements:
A Pentium running at 1.0 GHz or better
16 MB 3D video card (see www.alice.org for more details)
256 MB of RAM

Alice works well with digital projection systems for classroom demonstrations. Projectors limited to 800×600 video resolution will work, although 1024×768 is best.

Acknowledgments

As noted above, Seymour Papert's Logo and Rich Pattis' Karel the Robot were great inspirations in using a visible micro world. Alan Kay and the Squeak team inspired us to create the mouse-based program editor, and we were also inspired by the syntax-directed editor work done by Tim Teitelbaum. We are indebted to George Polya, Mike Clancy, and Doug Cooper for our problem-solving approach.

Our deep gratitude goes to early testers and users of our text and instructional materials for their helpful comments and suggestions: Susan Rodger (Duke University), Rick Zaccone (Bucknell University), Bill Taffe (Plymouth State), Angela Shifflet (Wofford College), and William Taylor (Camden County College). In addition, we are thankful for the assistance of our students: Toby Dragon (Ithaca College), Kevin Dietzler (Saint Joseph's University), Patricia Hasson (Saint Joseph's University), and Kathleen Ryan (Saint Joseph's University).

The life and breath of the Alice software is dependent on a group of creative, energetic, and dedicated graduate students, undergraduate students, and staff members at Carnegie Mellon University. Without these people, Alice does not live and we could not have written this textbook. The primary authors of this version of Alice include Ben Buchwald, Dennis Cosgrove, Dave Culyba, Cliff Forlines, Jason Pratt, and Caitlin Kelleher; a more complete list is available at www.alice.org. Many artists at Carnegie Mellon have graciously placed their work into the gallery for the benefit of others. We list Sarah Hatton, Mo Mahler, Shawn Lawson and Tiffany Pomarico here, but the contributors run into the hundreds. Tommy Burnette, Kevin Christiansen, Rob Deline, Matt Conway, and Rich Gossweiller all made seminal contributions to earlier versions of Alice at the University of Virginia. We also thank the University for its support and encouragement of earlier versions of Alice.

This material is based upon work partially supported by the National Science Foundation under Grant Numbers 0302542, 0339734, and 0126833. Any opinions, findings, and conclusions or recommendations expressed in this material are those of the author(s) and do not necessarily reflect the views of the National Science Foundation.

We also thank the reviewers, who provided valuable comments and suggestions:

John Dougherty, Haverford College
Mark Guzdial, Georgia Institute of Technology
Susan Rodger, Duke University
Rick Zaccone, Bucknell University
Mary Ann Amy-Pumphrey, De Anza College
Richard Pattis, Carnegie Mellon University
Deb Deppeler, University of Wisconsin
Odis Hayden Griffin, Jr., Virginia Tech
William Taylor, Camden County College
Suzanne Westbrook, University of Arizona
Kendra Dinerstein, Utah State University
Leland Beck, San Diego State University
Elizabeth Boese, Colorado State University
Sally Peterson, University of Wisconsin

We thank Tracy Dunkelberger of Prentice Hall and Alan Apt for supporting this effort. Over the last ten years DARPA, NASA, Apple, Ford, Intel, Microsoft Research, and SAIC have contributed support for the development of the Alice system, for which we are most grateful.

WANDA DANN
STEPHEN COOPER
RANDY PAUSCH

Part I
Introduction to Alice

Chapter 1

Getting Started with Alice

"Let's pretend there's a way of getting through into it, somehow, Kitty. Let's pretend the glass has got all soft like gauze, so that we can get through. Why, it's turning into a sort of mist now, I declare! It'll be easy enough to get through—"

1-1 Introduction to Alice

Why learn about programming computers?

We are guessing that you are reading this book because either (a) you **want to learn about programming** computers, or (b) **you are taking a course where you are required** to learn about programming computers. In either case, let's begin by talking about why it might be valuable for you to learn how to write computer programs.

First, let's get one thing out of the way: **learning to program a computer does not turn you into a computer nerd**. We know there are lots of preformed ideas in people's heads about what computer programming is, and what kinds of people write computer programs. But we promise that you won't suddenly develop a desire to wear a pocket protector, stop taking showers, or start speaking in obscure computer-language abbreviations. Honest. **This book uses a system called Alice, which makes it possible to write computer programs in a totally different way than ever before**. Rather than typing obscure "computer language" into a machine in the hopes of getting it to do some sort of strange calculation, you'll have the opportunity to be the director of a play, where on-screen objects act out the script you create! But let's not get too far ahead of ourselves. Let's get back to why you might want to program a computer at all.

There are many reasons to learn to program a computer. For some people, computer programming is actually a great deal of fun—they enjoy it as an end unto itself. But for most people, writing computer programs is satisfying because it is a means to an end; they have something important to do, and the computer is a useful tool for them. In fact, the applications of computers are becoming so pervasive in our society that if you were born tomorrow you might be interacting with a computer from your very first day to your very last. Many hospitals put a small computer chip on a band around your ankle as a newborn, to make sure they know where you are at all times. On your last day, you are likely to have a computer monitoring your vital signs on your deathbed. In between, you're likely to live a lot longer and a lot healthier, because of computer advances aiding medical research, computer-controlled brakes and airbags in our cars, and computer modeling that allows us to design new drugs to fight diseases like AIDS. Computer programmers help to make all of these technological advances possible.

Computers, and the software that computer programmers write for them, have revolutionized the entertainment industry. Computer gaming is becoming increasingly popular. The Pew Internet and American Life Project reported (in 2003) that about 70 percent of college students play online computer games at least once a week. Movies in the *Star Wars* series, and the special effects in them, are only possible because of computers. By the way, one of the undergraduate authors of the Alice system graduated and went to work at ILM (Industrial Light and Magic), who do the special effects for *Star Wars* films. So the next time you watch *The Phantom Menace*, look for Tommy Burnette in the credits!

Computers help us communicate with each other by maintaining complex cellular telephone networks, they aid marine research by tracking animal migratory patterns, and they allow us to explore space. None of these things would be possible without computers.

Of course, many of the people who write the software for these projects are professionals who have spent years studying programming. But even people who are not planning to be professionals can benefit greatly from even a single course in programming. Modern applications, like spreadsheets and word processors, give end users the opportunity to save time and effort by using "macros" or other programming-like features that tell the computer to do something long and tedious, instead of having the user do it. Also, if you have even a little experience with programming, you're much more likely to become the "go to" person in an office where computers are used, which can help you get ahead in your career.

Most importantly, even one course in computer programming can be useful as a way of **learning a new way to think**, much as taking a drawing course is a way to learn how to **look at the world differently**. Learning to think in new ways is always extremely valuable. Many of us talk about how we'd like to improve our general problem-solving skills. "Problem solving" is really just finding an answer to a question or figuring out how to perform a task. Computer programming is a pure, distilled form of problem solving. So, learning to program a computer will truly help you learn a new way to think—enabling you to find answers to questions and figure out how to make things work.

How you will learn to program with this book and Alice

This book and the associated Alice system will teach you to program a computer, but in a fundamentally different and more enjoyable way than ever before. In terms of tone, we have worked very hard to make learning to program as painless as humanly possible. Most programming, especially in introductory computing courses, has the feeling of mundane calculation: add up a bunch of numbers, and print out their sum and average. Often, students find these courses frustrating because of all the obscure technical details they must get right before anything will work at all. Students often talk about singing songs in ritual attempts to appease the computer gods. We felt there had to be a better way.

This book uses a completely different approach that is only recently possible due to the increased power of desktop computers and the development of novel software that uses that power, especially for 3D graphics. The Alice system, which is provided freely as a public service by Carnegie Mellon University,[1] provides a completely new approach to learning to program. Originally developed as part of a research project in Virtual Reality,[2] Alice lets you be the director of a movie, or the creator of a video game, where 3D objects in an on-screen virtual world move around according to the directions you give them. Rather than using obscure computer terms, you use natural English language words, like "move forward" or "turn right." Best of all, you can't make mistakes! Well, of course you can **always** make some mistakes,

---

[1]We also gratefully thank the University of Virginia, where an earlier version of Alice was developed.

[2]We gratefully acknowledge the support of the National Science Foundation, DARPA, Intel, and a number of other sponsors who have supported the Alice project: a complete list is available at www.alice.org.

such as telling one of your objects to move forward when you **meant** to move it backward. You can't, however, make the kind of "computer mistake" that most students get frustrated by—where you type something wrong and you can't figure out why the program won't run at all.

If the term "computer programmer" makes you think of some poor drudge hunched over a computer keyboard in a darkened room—don't worry! You'll almost never even touch the keyboard when using the Alice system. You will create programs by dragging words and objects around on the screen using the mouse. Then, when you press the **"Play"** button (circled in Figure 1-1-1), the objects in the 3D world on your screen will come to life and act out the script you have written for them! So, in a sense, **being a "computer programmer" using Alice is really like being a movie director, a puppeteer, or a choreographer**—anyone who gives people instructions about what to do in a precise but limited vocabulary.

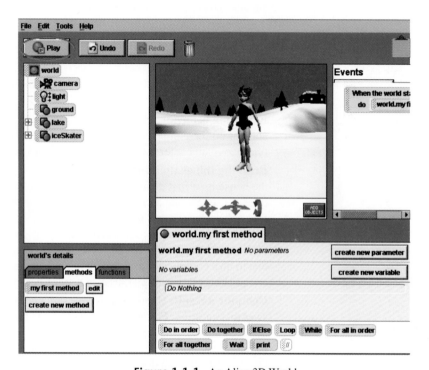

Figure 1-1-1. An Alice 3D World

After you've learned how to use Alice, you'll understand all the fundamental ideas involved in programming. Then, you will be in great shape to use one of the "real world" languages where you have to type with the keyboard and get all the commas and semicolons in the right place. You will know how to program, and all you'll have to learn are the particular grammar "rules" (sometimes called the "syntax"[3]) of languages like Java, C++, C[#], or whatever.

The basics of computer programming

A computer program is really nothing more than a set of instructions that tell the computer what to do. Of course, there are many ways of telling the computer to do something, so how you do it can matter. Believe it or not, computer programmers often use words like "elegant" to describe well-written programs. We recommend that you think of a computer program not

---

[3]Not to be confused with *sin tax*, a tax on things like cigarettes or alcohol.

only as a way to tell the computer what to do, but also as a way to tell another human being what you want the computer to do.

A computer program is not only "a way to tell the computer what to do."

A computer program is a way to tell another human being what you want the computer to do.

That makes it a lot easier to talk about whether something is "elegant." A program is elegant if other human beings can easily understand and appreciate the intentions of the original programmer. For this reason, one basic part of writing a computer program is to include documentation (comments in the program, a web page for reference, or an accompanying written document) that helps another human being understand what you were trying to do.

The key to computer programming is to get a handle on the fundamental ideas. At its heart, programming is really very simple. All computer programs are made from very simple ideas:

A list of instructions: For example, "Beat eggs, mix in flour, sugar, and shortening, pour into baking pan, then bake at 375 degrees for 45 minutes." Computer scientists call this sequential processing.

Ifs: For example, "IF it is raining, take an umbrella." Computer scientists call this conditional execution.

Repeating behavior: For example, "Stomp your foot five times" or "WHILE there are cookies on the plate, keeping eating cookies." (That last part actually sounded kind of fun!) Computer scientists call this looping, or iteration.

Breaking things up into smaller pieces: For example, "The way we're going to clean the house is to first clean the kitchen, then clean the bathroom, then clean each of the three bedrooms one at a time." Okay, so that doesn't sound like as much fun as eating the cookies, but it's still a pretty easy concept. Computer scientists call this problem decomposition, or stepwise refinement, or top-down design, but it's really an ancient philosophical approach called reductionism. Regardless of what you call it, it means that to do a complicated task, break it down into a list of simpler tasks. The result of accomplishing all the simpler tasks is that the complicated task is accomplished.

Compute a result: Here we perform a sequence of steps to obtain a result that is an answer to a question. For example, "Look in the phone book and find the number for Rebecca Smith," or "Put this baby on a scale and tell me how many pounds she weighs." Actually, each of these actions embodies a question: "What is Rebecca's phone number?" or "How much does the baby weigh?" A question is known as a function in computer programming. Asking a question so as to compute a result (find an answer) is known as calling a function.

Computer programming is really just using these ideas in various combinations. What can make things hard is complexity. The truth is that most computers "understand" only about 100 different instructions. The millions of programs that run on computers use these same 100 instructions in different orders and combinations. So where is the complexity? Think about it like this: In a chess game, there are only six kinds of chess pieces, and each piece moves in a simple pattern. Chess is a complicated game because of all the possible combinations of moves.

To put this another way, writing a computer program is like putting on a stage play with 200 actors, 500 costumes, and 5 live camels that appear in Act II, Scene IV. Things can get complicated just because that's a lot to keep track of! This book will teach you some tricks for managing complexity and for planning out how to write programs before you actually try to make them work. In fact, **learning how to think about arranging a sequence of instructions to carry out a task (how to design a program) is probably the most valuable part of learning to program**. You may have heard the term object-oriented programming. This textbook and the Alice system are based on the use of objects. In an Alice program, the objects are things you can actually see.

Why is it called Alice?

First of all, Alice is not an acronym: it isn't A.L.I.C.E and it doesn't stand for anything. The team named the system "Alice" in honor of Charles Lutwidge Dodson, an English mathematician and logician who wrote under the pen name Lewis Carroll. Carroll wrote *Alice's Adventures in Wonderland* and *Through the Looking Glass*. Just like the people who built Alice, Lewis Carroll was able to do complex mathematics and logic, but he knew that the most important thing was to make things simple and fascinating to a learner.

In the same way that Alice was hesitant when she first stepped through the looking glass, you may have some doubts about learning to program. Please take that first step, and we promise that **learning to program a computer will be easier than you might think**.

1-2 Alice concepts

Learning to program in Alice means that you will create virtual worlds on your computer and populate them with some really cool objects in creative scenes. Then, you will write programs (sort of like movie scripts or video game controllers) to direct your own production of animations in those worlds. In this section, we begin with an overview of the Alice software and the interface to help you get started. This section works hand-in-hand with the Getting Started exercises in Appendix A. We suggest that you read this section and work through the Getting Started exercises while sitting at a computer where you can try things out as you read.

Concept: Virtual world

Video games and simulations can be either two or three dimensional (2D or 3D). You may have used a 2D graphic simulator in a driver education course. Pilots, as part of their training, use flight simulators. The advantage of simulations is obvious—when a fighter plane crashes under the hands of the novice pilot, neither the pilot nor the aircraft is actually in danger. A video game or simulation implemented in 3D is called a virtual world. Using a virtual world lends a sense of reality to the simulator and increases its effectiveness.

To see the difference between 2D and 3D, compare the images in Figures 1-2-1 and 1-2-2. Figure 1-2-1 shows a movie set mock-up front and back. Clearly the structure is 2D because it has width and height, but no depth. Figure 1-2-2 shows front and back camera shots of the tortoise and hare out for their daily exercise run. The tortoise and hare are objects in a 3D virtual world, having width, height, and depth, so camera shots captured from different angles show objects that give a sense of being real.

Figure 1-2-1. 2D mock-up, front and back view

Figure 1-2-2. 3D world with the tortoise and hare, front and back view

An Alice virtual world begins with a template for an initial scene. The templates are shown in the opening window when Alice is started. The templates can be seen in Figure 1-2-3, where we have selected an initial scene composed of a blue sky and a grassy-green ground surface.

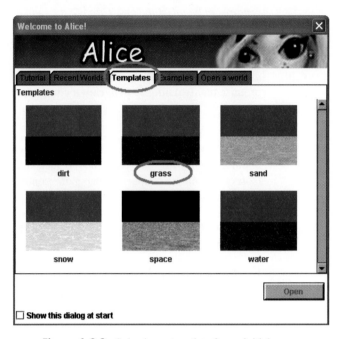

Figure 1-2-3. Selecting a template for an initial scene

Concept: Objects and 3D models

Part of the fun of using Alice is to use your imagination to create new worlds. We begin with a simple scene and add objects. In the world shown in Figure 1-2-2, the objects added are a tree, fence, tortoise and hare. Some objects provide a setting (trees, houses, starry skies, and such). Other objects (people, animals, space ships, and others) play the role of actors in your script (that is, they move around and perform various actions during the animation).

To make it easy to create a new world and populate it with all kinds of objects, the Alice developers have provided a huge number of 3D models. In a way, a 3D model is like a blueprint used to design a house. The blueprint provides a model of what the house will look like, the location and size of each room in the house, and some instructions for the housing contractor to follow in actually building the house. Likewise, an Alice 3D model tells Alice how to create a new object in the scene. The 3D model provides instructions on how to draw the object, what color it should be, what parts it should have, its size (height, width, and depth), and many other details.

The installation of Alice on your computer includes a Local gallery that contains a selection of 3D models. Additional models can be found in the Web gallery (http://www.alice.org) and on the CD provided with this book. Easy access to the 3D models in a gallery collection is provided by the scene editor, shown in Figure 1-2-4. If you have the CD in your CD ROM, a CD gallery folder will also appear in the folder. Examples and exercises in this book use models from both the Local and the Web galleries. If you want to use a 3D model that does not appear in the Local gallery, you can find it on the CD or the Web gallery.

Alice is not a 3D graphics drawing program. This is why generous galleries of 3D models are provided. It is not possible, though, to think of everything someone may want for a virtual world. To help you build people objects of your own, custom builder tools (*hebuilder* and

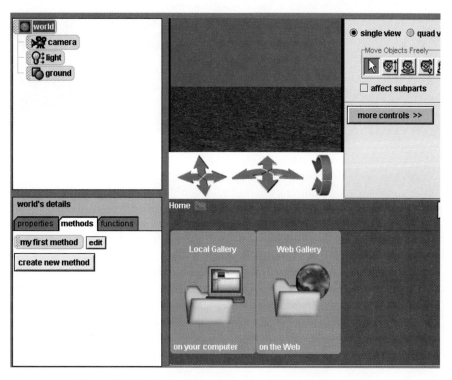

Figure 1-2-4. Scene editor with Local and Web gallery folders

shebuilder) are available in the People folder of the Local gallery. Details on using these tools are provided in Appendix B.

Concept: Three dimensions and six directions

Objects in an Alice world are three dimensional. Each object has width, height, and depth, as illustrated in Figure 1-2-5. (In this world, the astronaut has been added (People gallery folder) to the space world template.) The height is measured along an imaginary line running vertically from top to bottom, the width along an imaginary line running horizontally from left to right, and the depth along an imaginary line running from front to back.

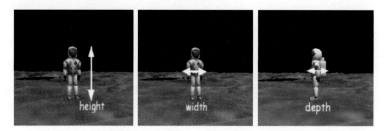

Figure 1-2-5. Three dimensions

In terms of these three dimensions, an object "knows" which way is *up* or *down* relative to itself. Also, the object understands the meaning of *left* and *right* and *forward* and *backward*, as seen in Figure 1-2-6. This amounts to six possible directions in which an object may move. That is, an object has six degrees of freedom to move around in a world. It is important to notice, for example, that directions are *left* and *right* with respect to the astronaut object, not the camera's point of view. We call the six degrees of freedom (possible directions of motion) the

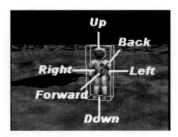

Figure 1-2-6. Object orientation: six degrees of freedom

object's orientation. When you mouse-click an object in an Alice world, a yellow bounding box is displayed, as seen in Figure 1-2-6. The bounding box highlights the selected object.

Concept: Center of an object

Each object in Alice has a unique "center." The center point isn't calculated. Instead, it is a feature of each object that is set by a graphic artist when the 3D model is first created. Usually, the center point of an object is at the center of its bounding box—or as near to the center of mass as the graphic artist could determine. The center point provides a reference for a pivot or spin type of movement. So, an object like a tire or a bird will spin around its center. Figure 1-2-7 illustrates the center of a bird object. We used a wire frame display to show that the center of the bird is located in the interior of its body.

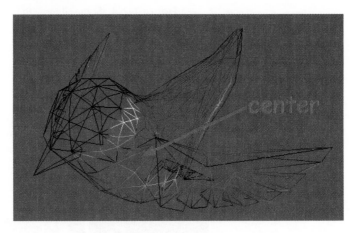

Figure 1-2-7. Center at the center of mass

Not all objects have their center located at their center of mass. Those that generally sit or stand on the ground or a table have their center located at the bottom of their bounding box. For people objects, the center point is between their feet, as shown in Figure 1-2-8. This is because a person's feet are on the ground and the distance of the person above the ground is zero (0) meters.

Other kinds of objects that do not have a center at the center of mass are those that are "held" when used, such as a baseball bat. The center point of a baseball bat is where it would be held, as illustrated in Figure 1-2-9. The center is on the handle so that when you rotate it, it will "swing" about that point.

Concept: Distance

One object's distance to another is measured from its center. For example, the bird's distance downward to the ground in Figure 1-2-10 is measured from the bird's center.

Figure 1-2-8. Center of an object that stands on the ground

Figure 1-2-9. Center of an object that is held

Figure 1-2-10. Distance downward to the ground is measured from the center

Concept: Position

The center of an object is the point used as its "position" in a world. Alice automatically puts the center of the ground at the center of the world. In Figure 1-2-11, a set of coordinate axes is positioned at the center of the ground. In the properties list for the ground (located in the details panel at the lower left of Figure 1-2-11), you can see that the center of the ground is located at (0, 0, and 0).

Like the ground, any object in the world is located relative to the center of the world. The bird in Figure 1-2-12 is located at position (–3.41, 1.59, 6.15). That is, the center of the bird is 3.41 meters left, 1.59 meters above, and 6.15 meters forward of the center of the world.

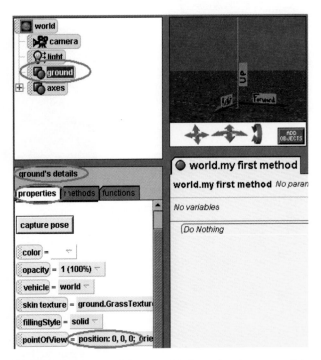

Figure 1-2-11. The center of the ground is located at the center of the world

Concept: Animation

In Alice, you will build virtual worlds and create animations by moving the objects in a world in the same way that objects are moved in a flight simulator or a video game. You will use many of the same techniques to give the illusion of motion as are used by animators to create animated cartoons for film studios such as Disney® and Pixar®. Animation is a fantasy of vision, an illusion. To generate this illusion, the filmmaker and artist collaborate to create a sequence of artwork frames (drawings or images) where each has a slightly different view of a scene. The scene is drawn with objects, and then redrawn with the objects positioned in a slightly different place. The scene is drawn again and the objects moved just a bit more, over and over and over! Figure 1-2-13 illustrates a sequence of frames in Alice.

In animation production, frames are photographed in sequence on a reel of film or captured by a digital video camera. The film is run through a projector or viewed on a monitor, displaying many pictures in rapid sequence and creating an illusion of motion. Alice creates a similar effect on your computer screen. There is no need to worry about being a great artist. Alice takes care of all the computer graphic work to create the sequence of frames. You act as the director to tell Alice what actions the objects are to perform. Alice creates (renders) the animation.

Getting started with Alice

We encourage you to experiment with the Alice system in much the same way as you would explore a new cell phone. You take it out of the box and try out all its cool features—sort of a "poke and prod" kind of procedure. In the same way, you can learn how to use the Alice system.

Appendix A provides a tutorial-style Getting Started set of self-paced exercises with detailed instructions on how to start a new Alice world, where to find the galleries of 3D models, how to change the color of the ground, and how to add objects to a new world and properly position them in a scene. If you have not already done so, go and do these exercises now!

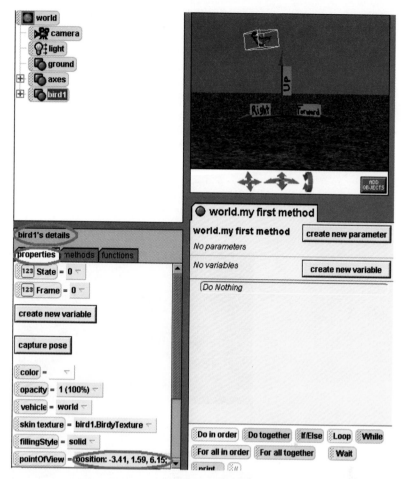

Figure 1-2-12. The bird's position relative to the center of the world

Figure 1-2-13. A sequence of frames to create an animation

Tips & Techniques 1
Special Effects: Text and 2D Graphic Images

While it is beyond the scope of this text to cover all of Alice's special capabilities, we will show you some of its features as we work through examples. At the end of each chapter, Tips & Techniques sections will present fun ways to build great animations with special effects. Although these Tips & Techniques sections are not essential to learning fundamental programming concepts, they are important to read because some of these techniques are used in example worlds. Tips & Techniques provide a guide for those who want to learn more about animation. The tables on the inner front and back covers summarize the Tips & Techniques and where they are used. Additional details of using Alice are also provided in Appendix B, where you can learn how to search the gallery and how to export a world to the Web. The Tips & Techniques sections along with Appendix A and Appendix B can be considered a mini User's Guide for Alice.

An important aspect of an animation is communicating information to the person viewing the animation (the user). Text, sound, and graphic images help you communicate. The following sections show how to add text and graphic images to your world.

3D text

To add a 3D text object to a world, click on the Create 3D Text thumbnail in the Local Gallery, as seen in Figure T-1-1.

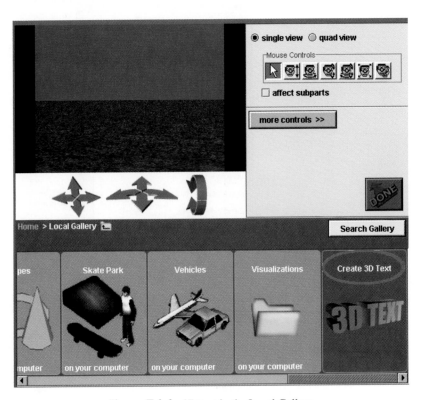

Figure T-1-1. 3D text in the Local Gallery

A text dialog box pops up for entering text, as in Figure T-1-2. The dialog box allows font, bold, and italic selections, and a text box where words can be typed.

When the Okay button is clicked, Alice adds a text object to the world and an entry for the object in the Object tree. The name of the object is the same as the text displayed, as seen in Figure T-1-3.

The text object can be positioned using mouse controls in the same way as any other object. To modify the text in the object string, click on the text in the properties list of the details panel. Then, enter a new string of text in the popup dialog box, illustrated in Figure T-1-4.

Note that modifying the string in the text object does not modify the name of the object. The name is still as it was when the text object was originally created, as seen in Figure T-1-5.

Figure T-1-2. A text dialog box

Figure T-1-3. The text object is added to the scene and object tree

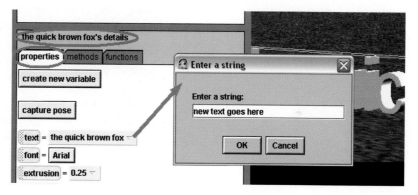

Figure T-1-4. Modifying text

Figure T-1-5. The name of text object remains the same

Graphic images (Billboards)

Although Alice is a 3D system, it is possible to display flat 2D images in a scene. Flat 2D images can be created in any paint tool and saved in GIF, JPG, or TIF formats. To add a 2D image (Alice calls it a billboard) to your world, select **Make Billboard** from the **File** menu, as seen in Figure T-1-6. In the selection dialog box, navigate to the stored image and then click the **Import** button.

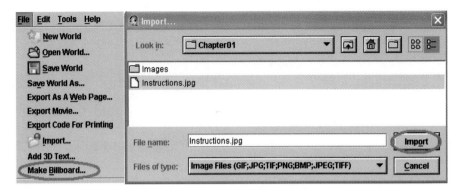

Figure T-1-6. Importing a billboard

Alice will add the flat image to the world. The billboard in Figure T-1-7 illustrates one of the uses of billboards—providing information to the user about how to play a game or simulation. In this example, a billboard provides instructions for how to use the keyboard to control the motion of an object. (Keyboard control examples are used in Chapter 5.)

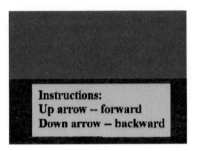

Figure T-1-7. A billboard to provide information

Exercises

The exercises below are to verify that you have learned and are comfortable using the Alice software. The goal in each exercise is to create an initial scene for a world. Alice will periodically prompt you to save your world. (Instructions on how to save a world are provided in the Getting Started exercises in Appendix A.) A name for your world is suggested by the name of the exercise. For example, the world in Exercise 1 could be named *Island.a2w*.

The objects in each world are created from the 3D models in the Alice gallery. Most models are located in the Local Gallery included in the Alice installation. If the model is not in the Local gallery, look for the model in the CD gallery or the online Web gallery (www.alice.org).

1. *Island*

   Create an island scene. Start by choosing a water world template. (Alternatively, start with a green grass world and change the ground color to *blue*.) Add an island object (from the Environments gallery folder). Use the scene editor to position the island a bit to the right of the center of the scene. Now, add a goldfish to the scene. You may find that the goldfish is invisible because it is located behind the island or is not properly positioned. Use the scene editor and its quad view to arrange the goldfish so it looks like it is swimming in the water to the left of the island. Use the camera controls to zoom out so the island and the goldfish are both in the camera's view.

2. *Winter*

   Add two snowmen (People gallery folder) to a snowy scene. Use a snow template initial world. Then, create a snowman stack by using the scene editor's quad view to position one snowman on top of the other (vertically), as shown below.

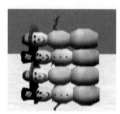

3. *Snowpeople Pile*

   Build a "wall" of four snowpeople by tipping them over on their sides and piling them on top of one another. (Use methods, mouse controls, and quad view.) Four snowpeople (alternating between snowman and snowwoman) might be used to produce a wall that looks like this:

4. *Tea Party*

   As a tribute to Lewis Carroll, create a Tea Party for Alice Liddell and the white rabbit. In addition to AliceLiddell (People) and the whiteRabbit (Animals), the party should include a table (Dining Table in Furniture folder on CD or Web gallery) and three chairs (Furniture), a teapot, a toaster, and a plate (Kitchen). Use method instructions, the mouse, and quad view to properly position objects like the teapot and creamer on the table. The picture below is provided as an example. Use your imagination to make a better scene, if you wish.

5. *Soldiers on Deck (Challenging)*

   Add a carrier (Vehicle) and four toy soldiers (People) to a new world. Line up the soldiers for a formal ceremony—two on each end of the carrier deck, as shown below.

Right-click on each soldier and use methods (from the popup menu) to move the arms of the soldiers to salute each other. Or, use the mouse controls in the scene editor to move the arms into position. (Use the "affect subparts" checkbox to allow the mouse to move their arms.) Raise the left arm of each soldier (at about a 45-degree angle with the horizontal plane). The result should be a scene where all four soldiers are saluting. This is not an animation—all you are trying to do is set up the scene.

Hint: If you check the "affect subparts" checkbox to allow the mouse to move subparts of an object, remember to uncheck the box before using the mouse for some other purpose!

Summary

At the end of each chapter, we will present a summary and a list of important concepts. The purpose of a summary is to pull together the information and ideas presented in the chapter into a meaningful whole. The purpose of a list of important concepts is to provide a quick review and study guide.

In this chapter, a computer program was presented as a sequence of instructions that tell the computer what to do. Importantly, a computer program is also a way to tell another human being what you want the computer to do. Learning to think about arranging a sequence of instructions to carry out a task (how to design a program) is probably the most important part of learning to program.

Alice is a 3D animation software tool that can be used to learn how to design and write computer programs. Alice allows you to quickly create cartoon-like animations of objects in a 3D virtual world. The objects are three dimensional, having width, height, and depth. Each object has an orientation that provides a sense of direction. That is, an object "knows" which way is up, down, left, right, forward, and backward relative to itself.

Important concepts in this chapter

- A computer program is a sequence of instructions that tell the computer what to do. It is also a sequence of instructions that tells another human being what you want the computer to do.
- Learning to program is actually learning how to think about arranging a sequence of instructions to carry out a task.
- In Alice, the animation of 3D objects takes place in a virtual world.
- Alice provides a huge number of 3D models. The 3D models are available on the CD accompanying this textbook, as well as on the Alice website at http://www.alice.org
- An Alice object has six degrees of freedom to move around in a virtual world. We call the six degrees of freedom (possible directions of motion) the object's orientation.
- An Alice object has a unique center set by the graphic artist when the 3D model is first created. The center of the ground in an Alice world is located at the position (0, 0, 0).

Chapter 2

Program Design and Implementation

"Then you should say what you mean,"
the March Hare went on.
"I do," Alice hastily replied; "at least—at least
I mean what I say—that's the same thing,
you know.'
"Not the same thing a bit!" said the Hatter.
"You might just as well say that 'I see what
I eat' is the same thing as 'I eat what I see'!"

In this chapter we begin an introduction to programming. A program is a set of instructions that tells the computer what to do. Each instruction is an action to be performed. Writing a program to animate 3D objects in a virtual world is naturally all about objects and the actions objects can perform. From a practical viewpoint, writing a program is somewhat like working with word problems in math. We first read the word problem (a description of the situation) and decide how to go about solving it (what steps need to be done). Then, we solve the problem (write a solution) and test our answer to make sure it is correct. Similarly, in writing an animation program we first read a scenario (a description of the story, game, or simulation—often called the problem statement) and decide how to go about creating the animation (design a storyboard). Then we write the program code (implement) and test it by running the animation.

As in Alice's conversation with the March Hare (see above), you must say exactly what you mean when you write a program. The best way to write a program is to begin by reading a scenario (the description of the story, game, or simulation) and then design a list of actions for the program.

Section 2-1 begins with scenarios and storyboards as a methodology for designing programs. Visual storyboards were chosen because they are the design tool used by professional animators in film studios. Textual storyboards were chosen because they provide an algorithmic (step-by-step) structure. The lines of text in a textual storyboard are similar to pseudocode—a loose version of the instructions that will eventually become program code.

Section 2-2 presents the basics of creating a simple program in Alice. The idea is to use a storyboard as a guide for writing the program (list of instructions) in Alice's mouse-based editor. We can focus on a step-by-step solution because Alice will automatically take care of all the details of syntax (statement structure and punctuation). In an animation, some actions must take place in sequence and others simultaneously. This means the program code must be structured to tell Alice which actions to *Do in order* and which to *Do together*.

2-1 Scenarios and storyboards

Creating a computer program that animates objects in a virtual world is a four-step process: read the scenario (a description of the problem or task), design (plan ahead), implement (write the program), and test (see if it works). This section introduces the first two steps.

Reading the scenario and designing a plan of action are important steps in constructing programs for animation. A design is a "plan ahead" strategy and takes practice to master. While the programs presented in the first few chapters of this text are reasonably clear-cut, we think it is advisable to start building good designs early on. Then, when programs begin to get more complicated, the time invested in learning how to design good program solutions will pay great dividends.

Read the scenario

Before we can discuss how to create a design, we need to know what problem is going to be solved or what task is going to be performed. A scenario is a problem (or task) statement that describes the overall animation in terms of what problem is to be solved or what lesson is to be taught. (Many computer scientists use the term requirements specification. In Alice, the term scenario is easier to relate to the world scene, objects, and actions.) Cartoons and feature-length animated films begin with a scenario created by professional writers, sometimes called the "story." As used here, in addition to the traditional meaning, a story can be a lesson to teach, a game to play, or a simulation.

In an Alice world, a scenario gives all necessary details for setting up the initial scene and then planning a sequence of instructions for the animation. That is, a scenario provides answers to the following questions:

1. What story is to be told?
2. What objects are needed? Some objects will play leading roles in the story while other objects will be used to provide background scenery.
3. What actions are to take place? The actions in the story will eventually become the instructions in the program.

Scenario example

Let's consider an example scenario: After traveling through space, a robot-manned craft has just made a breathless landing on the surface of a moon. The robot has already climbed out of the lunar Lander and has set up a camera so earthbound scientists at the NASA center in Houston can view this historic event. Through the camera (the scene in our world), we can see the robot, the lunar Lander and some nearby rock formations. Suddenly an alien peeks out from behind a rock and looks at the robot. The robot is surprised and rotates its head all the way around. The robot walks over to take a closer look and the alien hides behind the rocks. Finally, the robot looks at the camera, signals danger, and says "Houston, we have a problem!"

From this scenario, we have answers to questions:

- What story is to be told? This scenario tells a humorous story about a robot's first encounter with an alien on a distant moon.
- What objects are to be used? The objects are the robot, a lunar Lander, and an alien. The background scenery should depict a moon surface in a space world.
- What actions are to take place? The actions include the alien peeking out from behind a rock, the robot turning its head around and moving toward the alien, the alien hiding behind the rocks, and the robot sending a message back to earth.

Design

A storyboard is the design approach we will use to create a solution to a problem or plan a list of actions to perform a task, as specified in the scenario. At Pixar, Disney, and other major animation studios, animators break down a long scenario into sequences of many short scenarios. For each scenario, a storyboard is created to depict the sequence of scenes. The storyboard may consist of dozens of scene sketches, drawn by animation artists or generated by computer animation specialists using computer software. Figure 2-1-1 illustrates storyboard sketches

Figure 2-1-1. Storyboard sketches from *Geri's Game*, courtesy of Pixar®

from *Geri's Game*, an animated short film by Pixar® written and directed by Jan Pinkava. The film won an Oscar for Best Animated Short Film. In this film, the title character plays a game of chess against himself.

The storyboard approach to design that breaks a problem or task down into smaller subproblems or tasks is not unique to computer programmers and animators. Playwrights, for example, break their plays down into individual acts and the acts into individual scenes! Engineers break down complicated systems (e.g., jet airplanes and claw hammers) or devices (e.g., microcircuits) into component parts to make the problem more manageable.

Visual storyboards

A visual storyboard breaks down a scenario into a sequence of major scenes with transitions between scenes. Each sketch is a representation or a snapshot of a scene (state) in the animation. Each snapshot is associated with objects in certain positions, colors, sizes, and poses. When one or more transitions (changes) occur in the animation, the transition leads to the next scene (state).

The snapshots are numbered in sequence and labeled with necessary information. For short animations, the breakdown might be presented on one large sheet of paper. For more complex designs, a separate sheet of drawing paper might used for each scene, allowing the animation artist to easily rearrange or discard scenes without starting over.

To create a visual storyboard we borrow a technique from professional animators—a sequence of hand-drawn scenes. A visual storyboard template is shown in Figure 2-1-2. Each snapshot is labeled with a Scene Number and contains a sketch or picture showing where the objects are in the scene. The description tells what action is occurring. If sound is appropriate in the animation, the description will include a list of sounds that will be played during the scene. If a comic-book style is desired, text may be included to show the words or phrases that will be displayed in a text bubble. Sound and/or text are used only if needed.

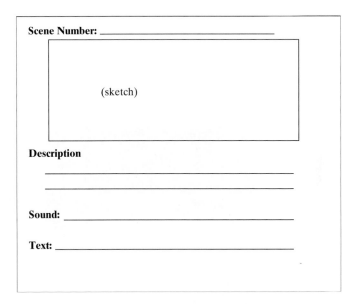

Figure 2-1-2. Storyboard template

For our purposes, preparing storyboard sketches is not intended to be a highly artistic task. Simple circles, squares, and lines can be used to represent the objects that will appear in the scene. If necessary, shapes can be labeled with the name of the object or color coded.

To illustrate the creation of a storyboard, the sample scenario for the robot's first encounter will be used. Figure 2-1-3 shows a simple scene where the alien peeks up from behind

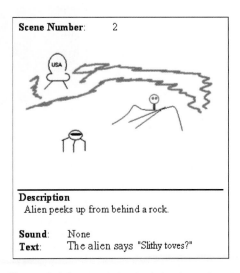

Figure 2-1-3. Hand-sketched visual storyboard

a rock. Simple sketches were used to create the lunar Lander, robot, and alien. Brown lines were drawn to create rocks in front of the alien. The grey squiggly lines represent the surface of the moon. Using simple figures, hand-sketched storyboards are quick and easy to create.

For illustrations in this book, we use Alice's scene editor to add objects to a world and then patiently arrange the objects in various poses. As each successive scene is created, a screen capture is made and copied to a document. Figure 2-1-4 illustrates screen captures in a storyboard for the beginning of the robot's first encounter animation. (We used the spiderRobot and the alienOnWheels from the SciFi folder in the gallery.) Naturally, screen captures for a storyboard are fancier than hand-drawn sketches, but they take longer to put together.

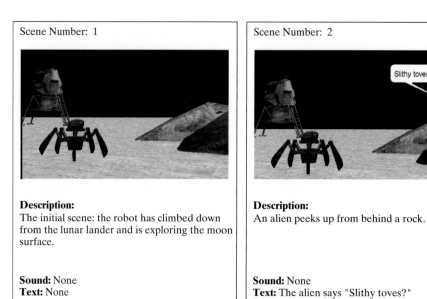

Scene Number: 1

Description:
The initial scene: the robot has climbed down from the lunar lander and is exploring the moon surface.

Sound: None
Text: None

Scene Number: 2

Description:
An alien peeks up from behind a rock.

Sound: None
Text: The alien says "Slithy toves?"

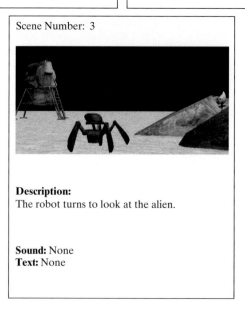

Scene Number: 3

Description:
The robot turns to look at the alien.

Sound: None
Text: None

Figure 2-1-4. Screen captures of storyboard scenes

Textual storyboards

While professional animation artists use visual storyboards as part of their project development process, not everyone has the patience to make dozens of sketches. A textual storyboard is a good alternative. It looks something like a "to-do list" and allows us to prepare a planned structure for writing program code. To take advantage of the strengths of each, both visual and textual storyboards are used throughout this book.

Textual storyboard example

A textual storyboard for the first encounter animation is shown next. Notice that a textual storyboard may summarize several scenes from a visual storyboard. For instance, the textual storyboard shown here summarizes scene number 1, scene number 2, and scene number 3 from the visual storyboard in Figure 2-1-4. This storyboard represents only the first few actions. It will be completed in the next section.

```
Do the following steps in order
   alien moves up
   alien says "Slithy toves?"
   robot's head turns around
   robot turns to look at alien
   Do the following steps together
     robot moves toward the alien
     robot legs walk
   etc.
```

The lines of text in a textual storyboard provide an ordered list of actions. The lines are written in an outline format and indentation makes the storyboard easy to read. Notice that two lines are in italics. These lines organize the actions—some actions are to be done in order (one at a time), others are to be done together (at the same time). The first four actions are performed in order (the alien moves up, alien says "Slithy toves?", robot's head turns around, robot turns to look at the alien). The next action, where the robot moves toward the alien to take a closer look, is actually a composite of actions performed simultaneously (the robot moves forward at the same time as the robot's legs simulate a walking action).

In computing terminology, a textual storyboard is called an algorithm—a list of actions to perform a task or solve a problem. The actions in a textual storyboard are very close to (but not quite) actual program code and so they are often known as pseudocode.

Evaluate and revise

Once a storyboard has been designed, it is a good idea to take an objective look to decide what might be changed. Evaluate the storyboard by answering these questions:

- Does the action flow from scene to scene, as the story unfolds?
- Do any transitions need to be added to blend one scene to the next?
- Did you overlook some essential part of the story?
- Is there something about the story that should be changed?

The important idea is that the storyboard is not final. We should be willing to review our plans and modify them, if necessary. In creating a program design, we go through the same kinds of cycles as an artist who has an idea to paint on a canvas. The painter often sketches a preliminary version of what the painting will look like. This is a way of translating the abstract idea into a more concrete vision. Then, the painter looks at the preliminary version and may change it several times before actually applying oils to the canvas. Likewise, an engineer who designs a bridge or an airplane (or anything else) goes through many design-modify-create phases before the final product is constructed. All creative people go through these design-modify-create cycles.

2-2 A first program

In Section 2-1, you learned how to carefully read a scenario and design an animation to carry out a task, play a game, or create a simulation. Now you are ready to look at how an animation program can be written. This step is called implementation. We recommend that you read this section while sitting at a computer: start up Alice and repeat the steps shown in the example in this section.

What is a program?

As you know, a program is a list of instructions (actions) to accomplish a task. You can think of an Alice program as being somewhat like a script for a theatrical play. A theatrical script tells a story by describing the actions to be taken and the words to be delivered by actors on stage. In a similar manner, an Alice program prescribes the actions to be taken and the sound and text to be used by objects in a virtual world.

Create an initial scene

An ancient Chinese proverb advises that "The longest journey begins with a single step." Let's begin our journey by implementing the robot first encounter animation described in Section 2-1. Recall that a robot-manned spacecraft has just landed on a moon. The robot encounters an alien that curiously peeks out from behind the rocks. The surprised robot walks toward the alien to check it out and then sends a message back to earth: "Houston, we have a problem!"

The first step in implementing the animation program is to create the initial scene. A space template is selected and then a spiderRobot, alienOnWheels, and lunarLander (from the SciFi folder in the gallery) are added to the world. Rocks (from the Nature folder on the CD or Web gallery) are added and positioned in front of the alien to hide the alien from view. The initial scene is shown in Figure 2-2-1.

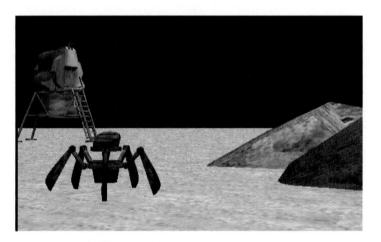

Figure 2-2-1. First encounter initial scene

Worlds on the CD

The CD accompanying this book contains the worlds for all examples in the chapters. The worlds have all the objects for the world, properly positioned in the initial scene. The CD worlds do not have the program code—the code is provided in the narrative of each chapter section. We recommend that you sit at a computer, load the CD world for the example and reconstruct the program as you read the chapter. This experience will help you learn how to write programs and will also help you get started in creating your own animations.

Program code editor

Once the initial scene has been set up, the instructions that make up the program code must be written. Alice provides a program code editor—the large yellow pane at the lower right of the main Alice window, as shown in Figure 2-2-2. The instructions for a program are entered in the editor. (From now on, we refer to the program code editor as "the editor.")

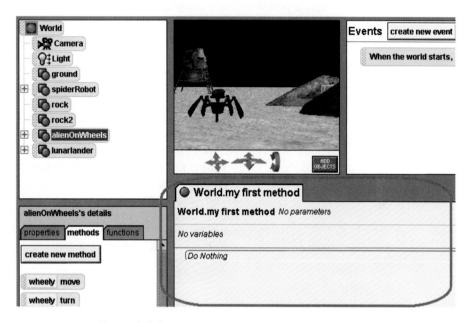

Figure 2-2-2. Program code editor (the large yellow pane)

World.my first method

As seen in Figure 2-2-2, the tab for the editing area is labeled *World.my first method*. A method is a segment of program code (a small set of instructions) that defines how to perform a specific task. Alice automatically uses the name *World.my first method* for the first editing pane. Actually, any name can be made up and used for a method name. We will use the name *World.my first method* for this example. The robot world scenario is simple enough to be programmed in just one method, *World.my first method*. When the **Play** button is pressed, Alice will execute *World.my first method* by carrying out the instructions that we write there.

What instructions are needed?

Let's take another look at the storyboard presented earlier.

```
Do the following steps in order
  alien moves up
  alien says "Slithy toves?"
  robot's head turns around
  robot turns to look at alien
  Do the following steps together
    robot moves toward the alien
    robot legs walk
  etc.
```

Actually, this storyboard is incomplete because (in the interests of space) we did not finish the story. The scenario described a sequence of actions: (a) the alienOnWheels moves up from behind the rocks, (b) the alienOnWheels says "Slithy toves?", (c) the spiderRobot's head turns around, (d) the spiderRobot turns to look at the alienOnWheels, (e) the spiderRobot moves toward the alienOnWheels to get a closer look, (f) the alienOnWheels hides behind a rock, (g) the spiderRobot looks at the camera, and (h) the spiderRobot says "Houston, we have a problem!" Let's complete the textual storyboard by adding the remaining actions, as shown next.

```
Do the following steps in order
  alien moves up
  alien says "Slithy toves?"
  robot's head turns around
  robot turns to look at alien
Do together
  robot moves toward the alien
  robot legs walk
alien moves down
robot turns to look at the camera
robot's head turns red (to signal danger)
robot says "Houston, we have a problem!"
```

Translating a storyboard to program code

To translate a storyboard to program code, begin with the first step of the storyboard and translate it to an instruction. Then translate the second step to an instruction, then the third, and so forth until the entire storyboard has been translated to instructions. The instructions used in program code are the same built-in methods you learned in the Getting Started exercises in Appendix A. To display the alienOnWheels' available methods, first click the alienOnWheels object in the Object tree and then click the methods tab in the details area, as seen in Figure 2-2-3.

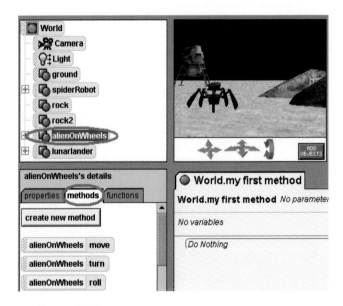

Figure 2-2-3. Built-in methods for writing program code

In our example, we want to translate the storyboard to program code. We begin with the first step, making the alienOnWheels peek up from behind the rocks. One of the alienOn-Wheels' methods is *move*—we can use this method to make the alienOnWheels move upward. The next step is to have the alienOnWheels say, "Slithy toves?" The alienOnWheels has a *say* method that can be used for this purpose. In a similar manner, each action in the storyboard will be translated to instructions, using the built-in methods of the objects in the world.

Sequential versus simultaneous actions

From our storyboard, it is clear that the first four actions must occur one after another, in sequence. We can tell Alice to *Do* these instructions *in order*. Other actions occur simultaneously. For example, the spiderRobot moves forward at the same time as the spiderRobot's legs walk. Alice must be told to *Do* these actions *together*. *Do in order* and *Do together* are part of the Alice language. We call them control statements, because we use them to tell Alice how to carry out the instructions in a program.

Do in order

To tell Alice to do instructions in sequential order, a *Do in order* block is dragged into the editor, as shown in Figure 2-2-4.

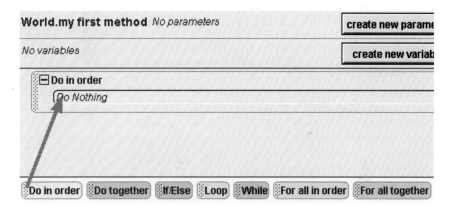

Figure 2-2-4. Dragging a *Do in order* tile into the editor

The first four instructions can now be placed within the *Do in order* block. First, the alienOnWheels is selected in the Object tree. Then, the alienOnWheels's *move* method tile is selected and dragged into the *Do in order*, as shown in Figure 2-2-5. The *move* method requires arguments—which *direction* and how far (*distance*) the alienOnWheels should move. (An argument is an item of information that must be supplied so Alice can execute the action.) In this example, the alienOnWheels is hidden behind the rocks and we want the alienOnWheels to move upward so the direction is *up*. The rocks are not very tall, so we will try a distance of 1 meter. (If this distance is not enough or is too much, we can adjust it later.) The method name and its arguments are the components of an instruction.

The resulting instruction is shown in Figure 2-2-6.

The second instruction is to have the alienOnWheels say, "Slithy toves?" Select alienOn-Wheels in the Object tree and drag in the *say* method tile. Select *other* as the argument, as shown in Figure 2-2-7. A popup dialog box provides a text area where you can enter the words you want to appear. Type "Slithy toves?" without the quotes, as illustrated in Figure 2-2-8 and then click OK.

The first two instructions are shown in Figure 2-2-9. When this program is run (it is perfectly fine to try out the effect of just one or two Alice instructions by clicking on the **Play** button), the alienOnWheels will move up from behind the rocks and then say, "Slithy toves?"

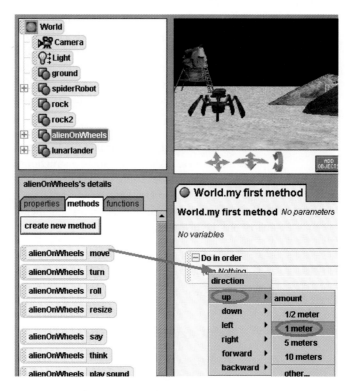

Figure 2-2-5. Adding a *move* instruction

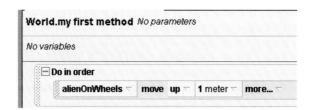

Figure 2-2-6. The completed *move* instruction

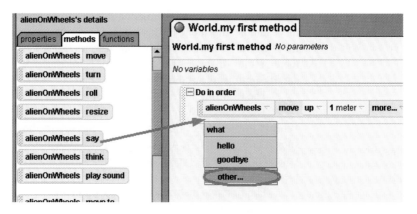

Figure 2-2-7. Adding a *say* instruction for alienOnWheels

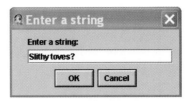

Figure 2-2-8. Entering a string

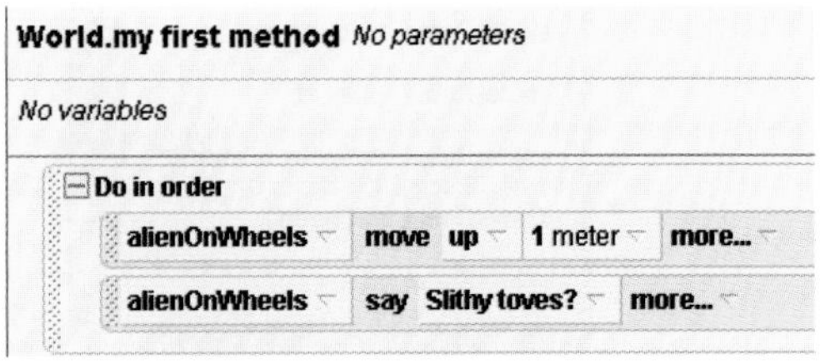

Figure 2-2-9. First two instructions

For the third instruction, the spiderRobot's head is to turn around a full revolution (to express surprise). How can we turn the spiderRobot's head? Clicking the + next to spiderRobot in the Object tree causes its subparts to be displayed. Click on the + next to spider Robot's neck in the Object tree. Then clicking on the spiderRobot's head in the Object tree allows access to instructions for moving its head. Drag the *turn* method tile into the editor and select *left* as the direction and *1 revolution* as the amount of turn, as shown in Figure 2-2-10.

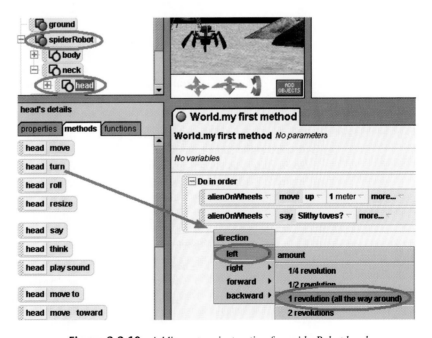

Figure 2-2-10. Adding a *turn* instruction for *spiderRobot head*

In the fourth instruction, the spiderRobot will *turn to face* the alienOnWheels. The spiderRobot *turn to face* method tile is dragged into the editor and alienOnWheels is selected as the target argument, as illustrated in Figure 2-2-11.

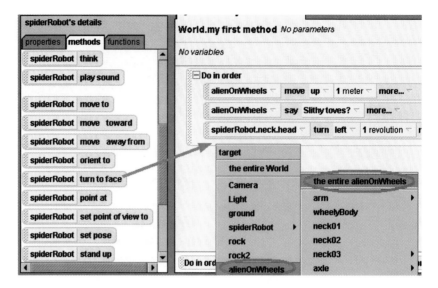

Figure 2-2-11. Adding a *turn to face* instruction

The program code with the first four instructions completed is shown in Figure 2-2-12.

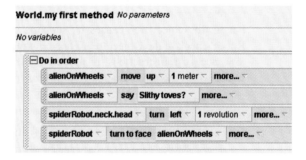

Figure 2-2-12. *Do in order* with first four instructions

Do together

The next step in the storyboard requires two things to occur at once: the spiderRobot moving forward at the same time as its legs move up and down. A *Do together* tile is dragged into the *Do in order*, as shown in Figure 2-2-13. Notice the horizontal (green in the editor) line in Figure 2-2-13. A green line indicates where the *Do together* instruction will be dropped.

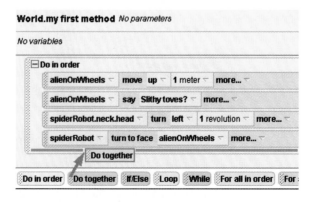

Figure 2-2-13. Adding a *Do together* (inside the *Do in order*)

The result of this modification, illustrated in Figure 2-2-14, is that the *Do together* block is nested within the *Do in order* block. Nesting means that one program statement is written inside another. Note that nesting the *Do together* inside the *Do in order* just happens to be the best way to animate this example. A *Do together* does not have to be inside a *Do in order*. These two coding blocks can work together or can work separately in many different combinations.

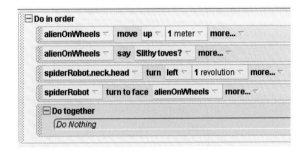

Figure 2-2-14. *Do together* nested within a *Do in order*

Now, methods can be dragged into the *Do together* block to simultaneously have the spiderRobot move forward and walk. The *move* forward instruction is easy. Just add a spiderRobot *move* instruction with forward as the *direction* and 1 meter as the *distance*, as illustrated in Figure 2-2-15.

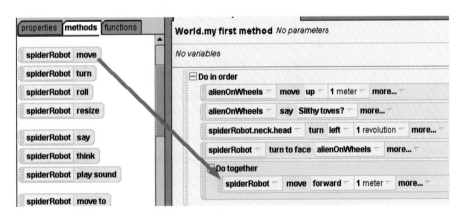

Figure 2-2-15. Adding a *move* instruction inside the *Do together*

The spiderRobot has several legs. To simplify our program, we will animate the walking action of just two legs (backLeft and frontRight). A leg walks by turning at a joint (similar to bending your knee). Let's begin by creating an instruction to turn the backLeftLegUpperJoint. First select the backLeftUpperJoint subpart of the backLeftLegBase subpart of the spiderRobot in the Object tree and then drag the *turn* method tile into the *Do together* block, as shown in Figure 2-2-16.

Note that popup menus allow you to select arguments for the *direction* and the *amount* of turn. Select *forward* as the direction and *other* as the amount. When *other* is selected as the amount, a number pad (looks like a calculator) pops up on the screen. We chose 0.1 revolutions, clicking the buttons on the number pad to make our selection. How did we know to use *0.1* revolutions as the amount? Well, we didn't. We just tried several different amounts until we finally found one that worked to give the best bending motion for the leg joint. This is an

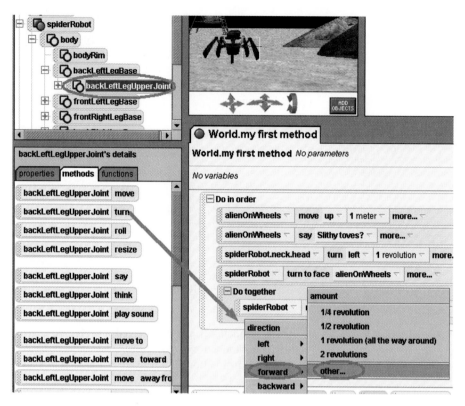

Figure 2-2-16. Dragging in a *turn* instruction for the backLeftLegUpperJoint

example of a trial-and-error strategy. While we always recommend good planning strategies, sometimes trial and error is useful.

Naturally, when a leg joint is turned in one direction it must turn back again (to maintain balance). The two *turn* instructions for the backLeft leg are shown in Figure 2-2-17.

Figure 2-2-17. Instructions to *turn forward* and *backward*

Using the same technique, instructions are created to turn the frontRight leg. The completed walking instructions are shown in Figure 2-2-18.

Figure 2-2-18. Instructions to simulate a walking motion for the spiderRobot

Bugs

You will recall that the four steps in creating an animation program are: read, design, implement, and test. Now that several lines of code have been written (implemented), it is a good idea to test whether what you have written thus far works the way you thought it would. You do not have to wait until the entire program is completed. To test the instructions written thus far, the **Play** button is clicked. The alienOnWheels pops up from behind the rocks and then says "Slithy toves?" The spiderRobot's head turns around and then the spiderRobot turns to face the alienOnWheels. So far so good, but when the spiderRobot moves forward, the legs do not walk. That is, the leg joints do not appear to turn at all!

The reason the leg joints do not turn is that the program has a bug. (Errors in computer programs are generally referred to as bugs. When we remove bugs from a program, we debug the program.) The problem is, in the code shown above, the leg joint *turn* instructions are written inside a *Do together*. Of course, if the joints both forward and backward at the same time, they effectively cancel each other and the spiderRobot's legs do not walk at all! To fix this problem, it is necessary to place the backLeft leg-joint-turn instructions within a *Do in order* block and also the frontRight leg-joint-turn instructions within a *Do in order* block, as illustrated in Figure 2-2-19.

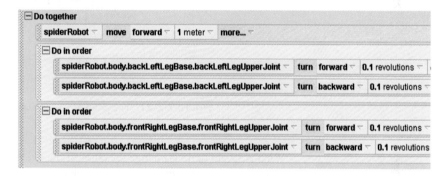

Figure 2-2-19. Revised instructions for walking the spiderRobot's legs

Now the spiderRobot's backLeft and frontRight legs walk! There is one other useful observation to make. Animation instructions, by default, require one second to run. Normally, within a *Do together* block, each of the instructions should take the same amount of time. Since it takes one second for the spiderRobot to move forward 1 meter, the walking action of each leg should also take one second. However, there are two steps in bending the leg joint (forward and then backward). Each step in bending the leg joint should require one-half second. To change the duration, click on *more ...* (at the far right of the instruction where the duration is to be changed), select the *duration* menu item, and select *0.5 seconds*, as shown in Figure 2-2-20.

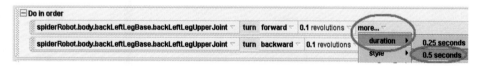

Figure 2-2-20. Changing the *duration* of an instruction

Using a property

We still need to complete the final four actions described in the storyboard (alienOnWheels moves down, the spiderRobot turns to face the camera, spiderRobot's head turns red, and spiderRobot says "Houston, we have a problem!"). You have already used a *move, turn to face,* and *say* instruction—so these will be easy to create. The only new instruction is the one that requires the spiderRobot's head to turn red (a danger signal). To make this happen, we use the color property of the spiderRobot's head. To view the list of properties of the spiderRobot's head, select the spiderRobot's head in the Object tree and select the properties tab in the details area (lower left of the Alice window), as shown in Figure 2-2-21.

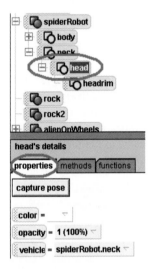

Figure 2-2-21. The properties of the spiderRobot's head

What we want to do is change the color of the spiderRobot's head after it turns to face the camera. Of course, the properties can be changed when the initial world is created. But, we want to change the color property while the animation is running. (The technical term for "while the animation is running" is "at runtime.") An instruction must be created to set the color. Figure 2-2-22 demonstrates dragging in the color property tile to create a set instruction. The color tile in the properties list for the spiderRobot's head is dragged into the *Do in order* block. Then, the *color* red is selected from the popup menu of available colors.

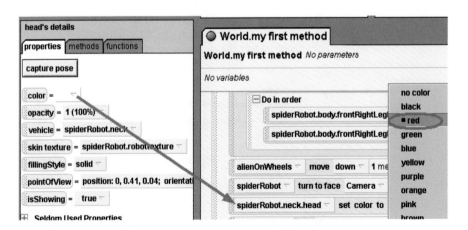

Figure 2-2-22. Changing the *color* of the spiderRobot's head

The final code for the entire animation is listed in Figure 2-2-23.

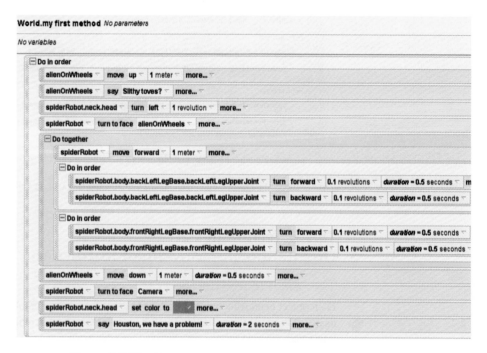

Figure 2-2-23. The program code for the entire first encounter animation

Comments

Now that we have written our first program, it is time to look at a useful component in programs—comments. Comments are NOT instructions that cause some action to take place. This means that Alice can ignore comments when running a program. However, comments are considered good programming "style" and are extremely useful for humans who are reading a program. Comments help the human reader understand what a program does. This is particularly helpful when someone else wants to read your program code to see what you wrote and how you wrote it.

Comments in Alice are created by dragging the green // tile into a program and then writing a description of what a sequence of code is intended to do. Figure 2-2-24 illustrates *World.my first method* with a comment added. Where it is not obvious, a comment should be included at the beginning of a method to explain what the method does. This kind of comment is like writing a topic sentence in a paragraph—it summarizes what is going on.

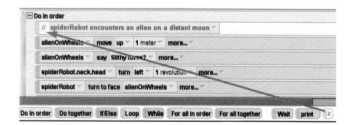

Figure 2-2-24. An overview comment for *World.my first method*

Also, small sections of several lines of code that collectively perform some action can be documented using a comment. An additional comment has been added in Figure 2-2-25.

Figure 2-2-25. A comment for a small section of code

This comment explains that this small section of the code is to have the spiderRobot move forward as its legs walk.

Tips & Techniques 2
Orientation and Movement Instructions

The *orient to* method

Each object in an Alice world has its own coordinate system that provides a sense of direction—its orientation. To illustrate the way the coordinate system provides orientation for an object, we implanted a visible set of axes (Shapes) into the monkey (Animals) shown in Figure T-2-1.

Figure T-2-1. The monkey's orientation

When two objects must move together, the orientation of the two objects must be synchronized. In the world shown in Figure T-2-2, we want the monkey to stay on top of toyball (Sports) as the ball moves forward for a short distance.

The code we wrote to make the monkey and ball move forward together is shown in Figure T-2-3.

Imagine our surprise when the ball moved in one direction and the monkey moved in a different direction, ending up well away from the ball, suspended in midair. Why did this happen? Well, the ball is an example of an object for which we can't tell (just by looking at it) which direction is forward and which direction is backward. Evidently, in positioning the ball and the monkey in the scene, we positioned the ball so its forward direction was not the same as the forward direction for the monkey, as illustrated in Figure T-2-4. So, when the ball and the monkey each move forward, they move in different directions.

Figure T-2-2. The monkey jumps on top of a toyball

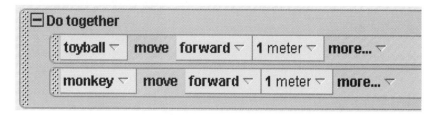

Figure T-2-3. Code to move toyball and monkey forward together

Figure T-2-4. The monkey and toyball move forward in different directions

The way to solve this problem is to synchronize the orientation of the two objects. In this example, we will use a *toyball.orient to(monkey)* instruction, as shown in Figure T-2-5.

The result is shown in Figure T-2-6. Now, the toy ball has the same orientation (the same sense of direction) as the monkey. This means that the two objects will move in the same direction when a *move forward* instruction is given to each.

The *orient to* instruction may seem a bit weird, but it simply tells Alice that the first object should take on the same sense of direction as the second object. So, if we orient two objects to

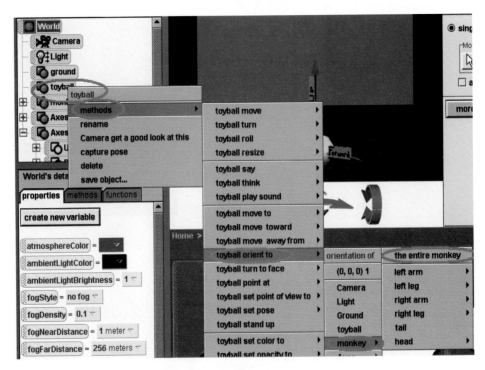

Figure T-2-5. Cascading menus for *orient to*

Figure T-2-6. Now the monkey and the toyball have the same orientation

have the same orientation, then the two objects are synchronized—they have the same sense of up, down, left, right, forward, and backward.

The *vehicle* property

Another way to synchronize the movements of two objects is to take advantage of a special property called *vehicle*. As an illustration of the vehicle property, consider a circus act where a chicken (Animals) rides on the back of a horse (Animals), as seen in Figure T-2-7. As part of the circus act, the horse trots around in a circular path and the chicken rides on the back of the horse.

To synchronize the movement of the chicken and the horse, you can make the horse be a *vehicle* for the chicken. To create this special effect, select chicken in the object tree and then

Figure T-2-7. Circus act, chicken riding on horse

select the properties tab (under the object tree at the lower left of the window). Then click on the white tile to the right of the word vehicle. A list of possible vehicles is shown in a popup menu, from which horse can be selected, as illustrated in Figure T-2-8. Now, when the horse moves, the chicken will move with it.

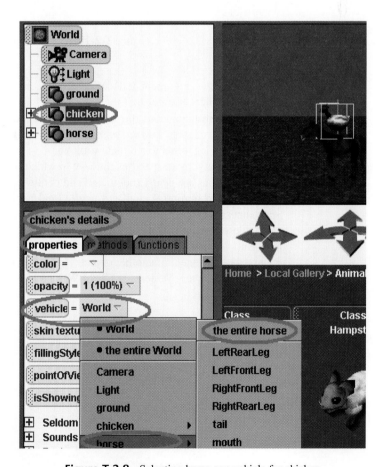

Figure T-2-8. Selecting horse as a vehicle for chicken

Arguments: *duration, style, asSeenBy*

Movement instructions (e.g., *move, turn, roll*) end with the editing tag "*more...*", as in Figure T-2-9.

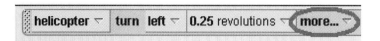

Figure T-2-9. The *more . . .* editing tag

When *more . . .* is clicked, a popup menu allows you to select from a list of three arguments, *duration, style,* and *asSeenBy*—as shown in Figure T-2-10.

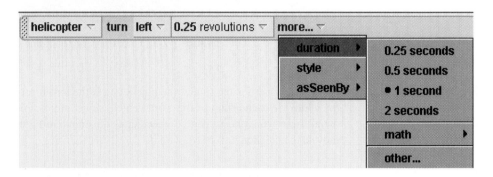

Figure T-2-10. Popup menu for *more . . .*

The *duration* argument tells Alice an amount of time (in seconds) for animating the movement. (Alice assumes that the amount of time for a movement is 1 second.) A zero (0) duration is an instantaneous movement. Negative values are not used. In the First Encounter example in this chapter, a *duration* argument was used to shorten the amount of time for turning the robot's leg joints to simulate walking.

The *style* argument specifies the way in which one movement instruction blends into the next. The options are *gently* (begin and end gently), *abruptly* (begin and end abruptly), *begin gently* (and end abruptly), and *end gently* (and begin abruptly). To get the right degree of "smoothness" for a movement, it is often worthwhile to experiment with *style*.

As described in Chapter 1, each object in Alice has its own sense of direction (orientation). But, you can use the *asSeenBy* argument to tell Alice to use an orientation of one object to guide the movement of another object. This is best explained by using an example. Suppose we have a helicopter (Vehicles in CD or Web gallery) on a pilot training mission, as shown in Figure T-2-11.

Figure T-2-11. Training mission

The code in Figure T-2-12 is intended to roll the helicopter left and then move it upward.

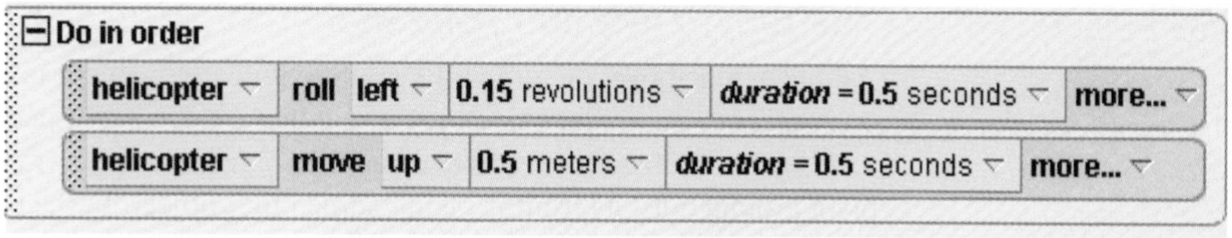

Figure T-2-12. Code to *roll* and then *move* upward

Running the animation, we see that the result is not what we had in mind. When the helicopter moves upward, it does so from its own sense of direction, as in Figure T-2-13.

Figure T-2-13. Up—from the helicopter's sense of direction (orientation)

What we had wanted, however, was an upward movement with respect to the ground. To correct this problem, we clicked on *more . . .* and then selected *asSeenBy* → *ground*, as in Figure T-2-14.

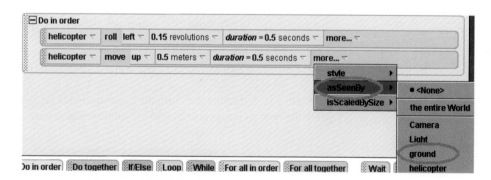

Figure T-2-14. Selecting *asSeenBy* Ground

The resulting code, shown in Figure T-2-15, gives the desired movement.

Figure T-2-15. The modified code

The *turn to face* and *point at* methods

As discussed above, the *asSeenBy* argument in a movement instruction uses the orientation of one object to guide the movement of another object. Two special methods are also useful for making an object turn to "look at" another object. A *turn to face* method causes one object to pivot around until its front is facing some other object. In the previous section of this chapter, *turn to face* was used to have the spiderRobot turn to look at the alienOnWheels.

A second method, *point at*, can be used to align two objects from the center of one to the center of another. It is easiest to explain *point at* in an example. In Figure T-2-16, the rowers in the lifeboat (Vehicles) want to row toward the lighthouse (Beach) on the island (Environments). An obvious first step is to have the boat and the rowers turn to look at the lighthouse on the island.

Figure T-2-16. The lighthouse, island, and boat initial scene

The *point at* method may be used to aim the boat at the lighthouse location. Then, movement instructions may be used to move the boat toward the island and the lighthouse, as in Figure T-2-17.

Figure T-2-17. Code to aim the boat toward the lightHouse

While this instruction does turn the lifeboat toward the lighthouse, it also has the effect of tipping the boat so it seems to be sinking on one end, as seen in Figure T-2-18.

Figure T-2-18. The lifeboat tips on the *point at* instruction

The *point at* instruction aligns the center of the lifeboat with the center of the lighthouse, which is higher in elevation than the boat, as shown in Figure T-2-19. As a result, the boat tips.

Figure T-2-19. Alignment from center to center

You may, or may not, want the boat to tip. To provide some control of the *point at* instruction, additional arguments are available in the *more...* popup menu, as seen in Figure T-2-20. Selecting *true* for the *onlyAffectYaw* argument allows an object to point at another object without tipping (pitching). Yaw is technical term meaning a left-right turning motion, and pitch is a tipping, rocking-chair kind of motion. (When *onlyAffectYaw* is *true,* the *point at* instruction works the same as a *turn to face* instruction.) Note that in target games and flight animations *onlyAffectYaw* should be *false* (so as to align on the diagonal with a target object).

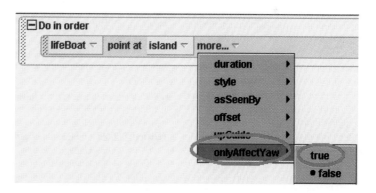

Figure T-2-20. Selecting *onlyAffectYaw* → *true*

The *move to* and *move toward* methods

Two special instructions are useful for moving an object in relation to the location of another object. The *move to* instruction moves an object to a specific location in the world. Although we can tell Alice to move an object to a location by entering number coordinates, much of the time we use the *move to* instruction with the position of another object as the target location. (Alice knows the center location of every object in the scene and can move another object to the same location.) In the lighthouse and lifeboat example, we could write the code in Figure T-2-21.

When this code is run, the boat moves to the center of the island, as seen in Figure T-2-22. Of course, the center of the island is located at its center of mass. So, the boat plows right into the middle of the island!

Figure T-2-21. Code to *move to* the island

Figure T-2-22. Result of a *move to* the island

To gain more control of the move (and perhaps avoid a collision), we could use the *move toward* instruction. The *move toward* instruction allows you to specify exactly how many meters to move toward the target. For example, we could move the lifeboat toward the island 3 meters, as in the Figure T-2-23.

Figure T-2-23. Code to *move toward* the island

Figure T-2-24. Result of a *move toward* the island

Now, when the lifeboat moves, it moves 3 meters toward the island but does not collide with the island, as illustrated in Figure T-2-24. (In our example world, the boat is more than 3 meters from the island.)

Exercises

2-1 Exercises

1. *Creating Storyboards*
   Create a visual and a textual storyboard (two storyboards) for each of the following scenarios:

   (a) A child's game: Alice, the white rabbit, and the Cheshire cat enjoy a game of musical chairs in a tea party scene. One of the characters yells "switch" and they all run around the table to stand beside the next chair. After the switch, a chair is tipped over and the character standing next to it is eliminated from the game (moves away from the table).

   (b) A video game: A jet fighter plane is returning to the carrier deck after a training mission. The plane makes a half-circle around the carrier to get into position for landing and then gradually descends. The carrier is in motion, so the plane has to continually adjust its descent to finally land on the deck. After the plane touches down on the carrier, it continues to move across the deck to finally come to a halt.

   (c) An Olympic simulation: An ice skater is practicing her skating routine for the Olympic trials. She will perform a sequence of jumps and spins, while classical music is playing.

2-2 Exercises

2. *First Encounter—Extended*

   (a) The worlds used for chapter examples throughout this book can be found on the CD. Each world provided on the CD has the initial scene already set up with the background scenery and the objects, as shown in the example. In this chapter, the example world is a first encounter, where a robot meets an alien on a distant moon. Start Alice. Then, copy the *FirstEncounter.a2w* world to your computer. In Alice, use **File|Open** to open the world. Follow along with the reading in the chapter and recreate the program as described in the chapter.

   (b) In the code presented in this chapter, only two legs (backLeft and frontRight) were animated in a walking action. Add code to animate a walking action for the other legs. Be sure to save the world.

3. *Snowpeople*
   Create a snow people world as shown the scene below. Several snow people are outdoors on a snow-covered landscape.

A snowman is trying to meet a snowwoman who is talking with a friend (another snowwoman.) The snowman tries to get her attention. He turns to face the snowwoman and says "Ahem." She turns to look at the snowman and he blinks his eyes at her. She blushes (her head turns red). But, alas, she is not interested in meeting him. She gives him a "cold shoulder" and turns back to talk with her friend. He hangs his head in disappointment and turns away.

4. *Circling Fish*
Create an island world with a fish in the water. (You may wish to reuse the island world created in an exercise for Chapter 1.) Position the fish and the camera point of view so the scene appears as illustrated below. Write a program that has the fish swim around in a circle in front of the island. Next, have the fish swim around the island. You may wish to have the fish move *asSeenBy* the island (*asSeenBy* is described in Tips & Techniques 2). Finally, have the fish jump out of the water and then dive down into the water. The final scene should look somewhat like the initial scene, with the fish back in roughly the same position as where it started.

5. *Tortoise Gets a Cookie*
Create a world having a tortoise (Animals), a stool (Furniture in CD or Web gallery), and a cookie (Kitchen/Food), as shown below. Put the cookie on top of the stool. (Cookies are the tortoise's favorite snack food.) Position the tortoise and the stool side by side and then use a *move* method to move the tortoise 2 meters away from the stool. (This way, you know exactly how far the tortoise is from the stool.) Use a *turn to face* method to be sure the tortoise is facing the stool. Write a program to move the tortoise to the stool to get the cookie. Have the tortoise show its thanks (for the cookie) by looking at the camera and waving an arm.

6. *Magnet Fun*
Create a world where Mana (People) has a magnet (Objects) held out in her left hand. Add five metallic objects (Objects folder in Local, CD, or Web gallery) of your

choice to the world and one by one have Mana point the magnet at each object. As Mana points the magnet toward an object, have the object move to the magnet. Have the last object be very large (perhaps a car from the Vehicles folder) so when Mana points at it, she instead is pulled toward the object while saying something like "Whoa!" or "Yikes!"

Hints: See Tips & Techniques 2 for information on how to (1) use the *vehicle* property for help in making the magnet move in coordination with Mana's hand, and (2) use the *move toward* instruction to make an object move toward another object. Also, you may wish to review the notion of center of an object, as described in Chapter 1, Section 2.

Summary

This chapter introduced the fundamental concepts of programming in Alice. We began with reading the scenario and designing a storyboard. A scenario helps us set the stage—that is, it tells us what objects will be used and what actions they will perform. A storyboard breaks down a scenario into a sequence of scenes that provide a sense of the order in which actions will take place.

Some actions in a program will take place in sequence (one after the other) and some actions simultaneously (at the same time). Once prepared, a storyboard is used as a guide for implementation (writing the program code). Testing code (running the program) is an important step in finding and removing bugs (errors in the program).

Comments are used to document methods, where the purpose of the method or a small section of a method is not immediately obvious. Comments are considered good programming "style."

Important concepts in this chapter

- A scenario is a problem statement that describes the overall animation in terms of what problem is to be solved, what lesson is to be taught, what game played, or what simulation demonstrated.
- A storyboard can be visual or textual.
- A visual storyboard is a sequence of hand-drawn sketches or screen captures that break down a scenario into a sequence of major scenes with transitions between scenes.
- Each sketch represents a state of the animation—sort of a snapshot of the scene—showing the position, color, size, and other properties of objects in the scene.
- A textual storyboard is somewhat like a to-do list, providing an algorithmic list of steps that describe sequential and/or simultaneous actions.

- A program consists of lines of code that specify the actions objects are to perform.
- The characters you see in an Alice world are known as objects. We write program statements to make the objects move by dragging their action instructions (methods) into the editor.
- In Alice, program code is structured in *Do in order* and *Do together* blocks to tell Alice which instructions are to be executed in order and which are to be executed simultaneously.
- Complicated animations may be constructed from simple compositions of *Do in order* and *Do together* blocks of code. Knowing what each means and knowing how to combine them (by nesting one inside the other) is powerful; it provides an easy way to put together more complicated actions.

Chapter 3
Programming: Putting Together the Pieces

"Let me think: was I the same when I got up this morning? I almost think I can remember feeling a little different. But if I'm not the same, the next question is, 'Who in the world am I? Ah, THAT'S the great puzzle!"

In this chapter, you will see how to put together different kinds of program code "pieces" to make the program do what you want it to do. The pieces of program code will include:

instruction—a statement that executes to make objects perform a certain action

control structure—a statement that controls the execution of a block of instructions

function—asks a question about a condition or computes a value

expression—a math operation on numbers or other kinds of values

You have already seen instructions such as:

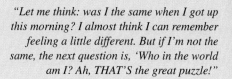

You have also been using the *Do in order* and *Do together* control structures. The *Do in order* structure tells Alice to run the instructions sequentially, one after the other. The *Do together* structure tells Alice to run the instructions all at the same time.

This chapter presents two additional execution controls: conditional execution (*If/Else*) and repetition. This is where programming gets exciting, because you gain control of how the program is executed. Conditional execution makes use of functions and expressions to check a current condition in the world. For example, "Is the color of the spiderRobot's head red?" Obviously, this is a question and a function is used to ask the question. Often, checking a condition requires that two or more objects be compared. For example, we might check whether "the distance of the spiderRobot from a rock is greater than 1 meter." An expression is used to compare whether the distance between the two objects is greater than 1 meter.

Section 3-1 uses short examples to show how to use built-in functions in Alice. We also look at simple arithmetic operations (addition, subtraction, multiplication, and division) in expressions.

Section 3-2 introduces conditional execution in the form of an *If/Else* statement. An *If/Else* statement involves making a decision based on a current condition in the world. A simple repetition control structure is also introduced, in the form of a *Loop* statement. A *Loop* statement repeats the execution of a section of program code a specific number of times.

3-1 Built-in functions and expressions

As you know, information about the world and objects within the world is stored in properties. We can use a function to ask questions about these properties. Also, we can perform arithmetic operations on the values of these properties by using expressions. The focus of this section is on how to use properties, functions, and expressions to allow a program to work with information about a world and its objects.

Built-in functions

Not all properties of objects are available in its properties list. Only properties most commonly used in setting up your world (for example, *color* and *opacity*) are listed. Other properties of objects (such as *height, width,* and *position*) can be determined, however, by asking Alice for the information. The Alice system provides a set of built-in *functions*—statements you can use to ask about properties of objects and relationships of objects to one another. Also, utilitarian kinds of questions can be asked of the world—about things like the position of the mouse and some math operations.

To better understand why we want to use functions, let's look again at the First Encounter world, shown in Figure 3-1-1. As you view this scene, you interpret what you see. For

Figure 3-1-1. Initial scene from the First Encounter world

example, you pick up visual clues in the scene that lead you to believe that the spiderRobot is closer to the camera than the rocks. An artist calls this perspective. Of course, it is difficult to know exactly how far away the rocks are from the spiderRobot. Likewise, it is difficult to know how far the spiderRobot is away from the lunarLander. The camera angle simply does not provide enough information.

This is where functions come into play. Functions can be used to get the information we need. Alice provides several functions that can be used for each object in a world. We call these built-in functions. To view a list of built-in functions about an object in a world, select the object in the Object tree and view the functions in the details area. In this example, you can view a list of built-in functions for the spiderRobot by selecting spiderRobot in the Object tree and then its functions tab, as in Figure 3-1-2.

At the right of the functions list, a scroll bar allows you to scroll the window down to view all the available functions for the spiderRobot. The built-in functions are divided into subcategories:

Proximity—how close the object is to some other object in the world (such as *distance to, distance above*). (The functions in Figure 3-1-2 are **proximity** functions.)

Size—dimensions such as height, width, and depth, and how these compare to the dimensions of another object in the world

Spatial relation—orientation compared to another object in the world (such as *to left of, to right of*)

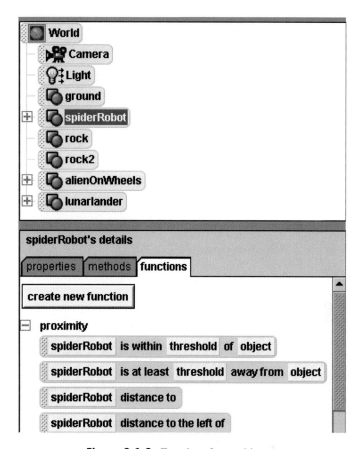

Figure 3-1-2. Functions for an object

Point of view—position in the world

Other—miscellaneous items such as the name of a subpart of the object

In our daily conversations, when a question is asked, we expect to receive an answer. In Alice, the answer is the value of the property you are asking about. What types of values can you expect? That depends on what question the function is asking. For example, the proximity function spiderRobot *is within threshold of object* (*is within threshold* means "is within a given distance") will return a *true* or *false* value. But the function, spiderRobot *distance to,* returns a number (*distance to* means "the distance in meters to another object").

In Alice, values can be of several different types. Four common types of values are:

number (for example, 5 or −19.5)

Boolean value (*true* or *false*)

string (for example, "*hello world*")

object (for example, a *spiderRobot*)

In the first program for the First Encounter world, the spiderRobot wants to get a closer look at the alien. So the spiderRobot moves forward 1 meter as the legs walk. The code is repeated in Figure 3-1-3.

We don't know exactly how far the spiderRobot is away from the rock where the alienOnWheels is hiding. The 1 meter distance for the move forward instruction is just a guess. The problem is that we don't know exactly how far to move the spiderRobot forward. One way to find out is to use trial and error—that is, try different distances until we find one that works best. Another technique to find the distance is to use a function to ask a question: "What is the

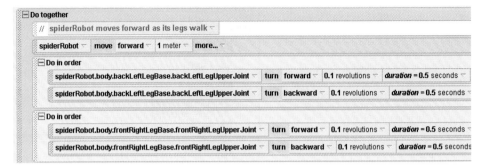

Figure 3-1-3. Code to move the spiderRobot forward as the legs walk

spiderRobot's distance to the rock (where the alienOnWheels is hiding)?" Alice will return the distance (in meters). Then the spiderRobot can be moved forward that distance.

To use the *distance to* function, just drag the spiderRobot's *distance to* tile into the editor and drop it on top of the 1 meter distance. Then, select rock as the target object , as shown in Figure 3-1-4.

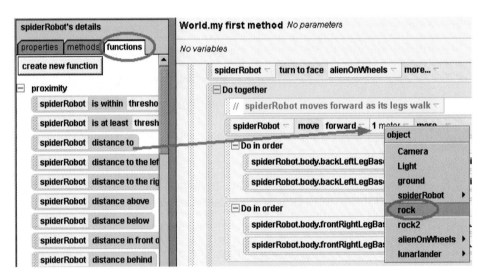

Figure 3-1-4. Dragging the *distance to* function into the editor

The resulting code is:

Collision

After making such a change to our program, the program should be tested. In this example, when the program is run the spiderRobot walks right into the middle of the rock! This is called a collision. In some animations, a collision is exactly what is desired. In this example, though, we do not want the spiderRobot to collide with the rock. The reason a collision occurs is that *distance to* is measured from the center of one object to the center another object. In this example, *distance to* is measured from the spiderRobot's center to the rock's center, as shown in Figure 3-1-5.

Figure 3-1-5. The *distance to* function is measured center-to-center

Expressions

How can a collision be avoided between these two objects? One way is to adjust the distance that the spiderRobot moves so it doesn't move the entire distance. Adjusting the distance requires the use of an arithmetic expression to subtract a small value from the distance. In this example, the rock is bigger than the spiderRobot. If the width of the rock is subtracted from the distance between the two objects, a collision can be avoided.

Alice provides math operators for common math expressions: add (+), subtract (−), multiply (*), and divide (/). A math expression is obtained by selecting *math* from the popup menu of number value in an instruction. For example, to use a math expression to adjust the distance the spiderRobot moves, click the down icon at the far right of the *distance to* tile in the *move* instruction, then select *math* → spiderRobot *distance to* rock − 1, as illustrated in Figure 3-1-6.

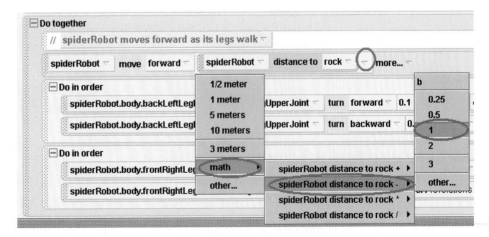

Figure 3-1-6. Using a math expression

The resulting instruction subtracts 1 meter from the distance. Actually, we want to subtract the width of the rock from the distance (not 1 meter). But, we had to choose something from the popup menu so we arbitrarily chose 1 meter. This is okay to do because we can now substitute the rock's width for the 1 meter value, as shown in Figure 3-1-7.

Figure 3-1-7. Substituting the rock's *width* function for the arbitrary 1 meter value

Now, the spiderRobot moves forward so it gets close to the rock without a collision. The completed code is shown in Figure 3-1-8.

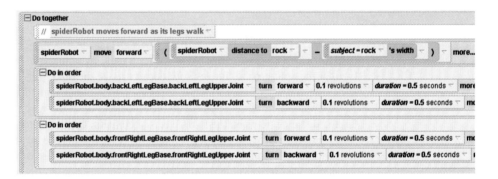

Figure 3-1-8. Code to move spiderRobot forward and avoid collision with the rock

Technical Note: The distance expression used in the *move* instruction of this example works very well. We should note, however, that this expression is purposely a primitive form of collision detection. To be more technically correct, a collision detection would be computed by subtracting the sum of half the spiderRobot's width and half the rock's width from the total distance (spiderRobot *distance to* rock), as shown in the following code.

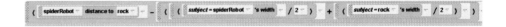

3-2 Simple control structures

In order to create a program that does more than just execute a few simple instructions, you will need to use control structures. A control structure is a programming statement that allows you to control the order in which instructions are executed. You have already seen two control structures: *Do in order* and *Do together*. This section introduces two more execution control structures: conditional execution and repetition. Conditional execution is where some condition is checked and a decision is made about whether (or not) a certain section of the program code will be executed. Repetition is where a section of the code is run a number of times.

Conditional execution

A conditional execution control statement depends on a decision. Sometimes life is "one decision after another." If the grass isn't wet, we can mow the lawn. If the dishwasher is full of dirty dishes, we run the dishwasher. If we are taking the dog out for a walk, we put a leash on the dog. Programming, too, often requires making decisions. Decisions are useful when writing programs where some instructions are expected to run only under certain conditions.

When a decision is being made, a question is asked about a current condition in the world. For example, "Is the space ship visible?" or "is the color of the hat red?" Clearly the answer is either *true* or *false*. *True* and *false* values are known as Boolean values, named after the 19th century English mathematician, George Boole, who was the first (as far as we know) to be interested in expressions that can evaluate only to either *true* or *false*.

In Alice, an *If/Else* statement is used as a conditional execution control structure. (For convenience, we refer to an *If/Else* statement as an *If* statement.) Figure 3-2-1 illustrates the processing of an *If* statement. The statement checks to see whether a condition is *true*. If the condition is *true*, one set of program instructions is run. If the condition is *false*, a separate set of program instructions is run. The section of code that is executed (or not) depends on the value of the condition.

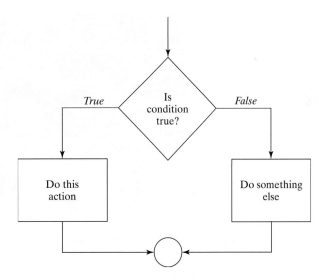

Figure 3-2-1. How an *If* statement is processed

An *If* statement is created in Alice by dragging the *If/Else* tile into the editor. A popup box allows you to select the initial condition (*true* or *false*), as shown in Figure 3-2-2.

The green color of this block is a visual clue that an *If* statement is being used in the program. The *If* statement has two parts (an *If* part and an *Else* part). Although an initial condition (*true* or *false*) is selected from the popup menu, Alice allows you to create your own conditional expression on top of the condition tile. A conditional expression is a function that will evaluate (at runtime) to either *true* or *false*. If the answer is *true*, the *If* part is executed and the *Else* part is skipped. But, if the answer is *false*, then the *If* part is skipped and the *Else* part is executed.

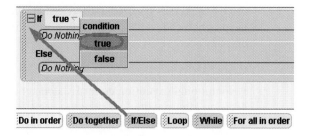

Figure 3-2-2. Using an *If* statement

A simple example

To illustrate the usefulness of an *If* statement, let's continue with First Encounter world. As mentioned before, our sense of perspective can be misleading about distances and sizes of objects in a world. The spiderRobot walks over to the rock to get a closer look at the alienOnWheels, but then the alienOnWheels moves down (out of our sight). From this camera angle, as seen in Figure 3-2-3, the rock appears to be taller than the robot, but we cannot be sure. So we can not tell whether the spiderRobot is actually able to see over the rock. If the spiderRobot is shorter than the rock, it could move its neck up to look over the rock. Otherwise, the spiderRobot can still see the alienOnWheels and no additional action is necessary.

Figure 3-2-3. The spiderRobot moves closer, but the alienOnWheels hides behind the rock

The problem is, how do we know which is taller (the spiderRobot or the rock)? One solution is to use an *If* statement with the built-in *is shorter than* question. The storyboard is:

```
If spiderRobot is shorter than rock
    Do in order
      spiderRobot neck move up
      spiderRobot neck move down
Else
  Do nothing
```

Translating the storyboard into program code is straightforward. First an *If* statement is created by dragging the *If/Else* tile into the editor and selecting *true* as the default condition, as was demonstrated previously in Figure 3-2-2. Then, the spiderRobot's *is shorter than* function is dragged into the editor in place of *true*, and rock is selected as the target object, as shown in Figure 3-2-4.

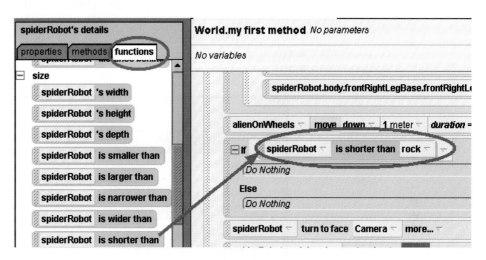

Figure 3-2-4. Using a function to check a condition in an *If/Else*

Finally, spiderRobot.neck *move* instructions are added in a *Do together* block for the *If* part of the *If/Else* statement. The *Else* part of the *If/Else* statement is *Do Nothing*. The resulting code is shown below.

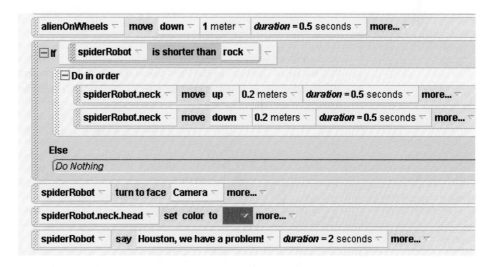

When this code is run, a function is used to ask the question: "Is the spiderRobot shorter than the rock?" The answer is either *true* or *false* (a Boolean result). Then, a decision is made on the basis of the answer. If the answer is *true* the spiderRobot's neck moves up and down (to peek behind the rock). Otherwise, the *Else* section kicks in and nothing happens. That is, the spiderRobot's neck is not moved up and down. We could have written instructions to make the spiderRobot do something different in the *Else* part—like spin the head around—but we wanted to show that *Do Nothing* is an acceptable alternative to an action.

Relational operators

In the example above, we used a built-in function to compare the heights of the spiderRobot and the rock. We frequently take advantage of built-in functions to check a condition in an *If* statement. Sometimes, though, we want to write our own condition using a relational operator. Alice provides six relational operators grouped together in the math category of the World's built-in functions, as shown in Figure 3-2-5. The operators work the same as they do in mathematics. We added labels to the screen capture in Figure 3-2-5 to indicate the meaning of each operator. For example, "==" means "is equal to" and "!=" means "is not equal to."

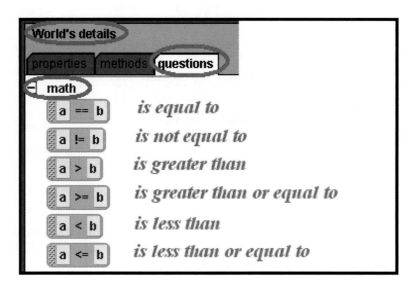

Figure 3-2-5. Relational operators

As an example of using a relational operator to write your own condition, let's assume that we know the rock in the First Encounter world is 2 meters tall (2 meters is about 6 feet). We could write an *If* statement that checks the spiderRobot's height against 2 meters. We want to write a statement for the following storyboard:

```
If the spiderRobot's height is less than 2 meters
    Do in order
        spiderRobot's neck move up
        spiderRobot's neck move down
```

The condition of the *If* statement is "spiderRobot's height is less than 2 meters." The condition must be written as a Boolean expression (is either *true* or *false*). Let's write an *If* statement for this storyboard, creating our own Boolean expression with a relational operator.

First, drag the *If* tile into the editor, as in the examples above. Then, complete the following two-step process:

1. Drag the World function "less than" tile ($a < b$) on top of the *true* tile in the *If* statement. A popup menu allows you to select values for a and b, as shown in Figure 3-2-6.

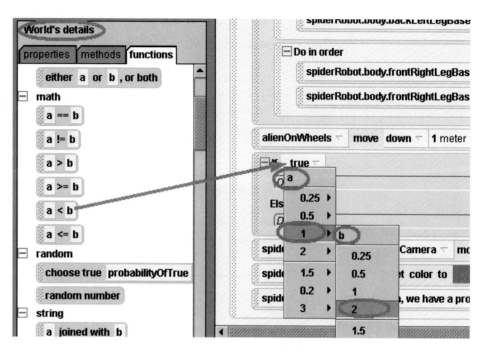

Figure 3-2-6. Creating your own Boolean expression

From the popup menu, select 1 for *a* and 2 for *b*. The resulting expression looks like this:

Actually, we want to drag in the tile representing the spiderRobot's height to use as the value for *a*, but we chose 1 from the popup menu as a placeholder to complete this first step. We will fix it in the next step.

2. Now, drag in the spiderRobot *'s height* function to replace the 1 (that was put there as a placeholder). Inside the *If* part, a *Do in order* block and instructions to make the spider-Robot's neck move up and down are added. The *Else* part of the statement is left as *Do nothing*. If the condition (spiderRobot's *height* < 2) is *false*, no action will be taken. The resulting code is shown below.

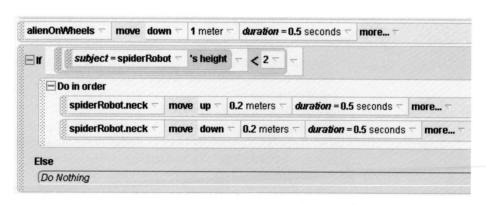

The need for repetition

In the example world created in Chapter 3, Section 1, the spiderRobot moves forward to the rock (an expression computes the distance—several meters), and the spiderRobot's legs simulate a walking action (turning the leg joints) only once. (The code is shown in Figure 3-2-7.) When the program is run, the walking action is not realistic because the robot moves forward a relatively long distance but the legs take only one step.

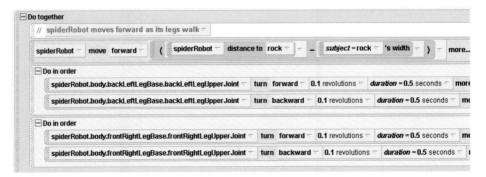

Figure 3-2-7. The spiderRobot moves forward several meters but legs take only 1 step

It would be more realistic if the spiderRobot legs walked a step with each meter that the spiderRobot moves forward. In other words, if the spiderRobot moved forward 3 meters, then the leg walking action would occur 3 times. If the spiderRobot moved forward 4 meters, then the leg walking action would occur 4 times, and so forth.

We could revise the program code to move spiderRobot forward 1 meter and the legs would take one step. (You may recall that this is what was in the original code in Chapter 2, Section 2). Then, the code would (once again) look like the code shown in Figure 3-2-8.

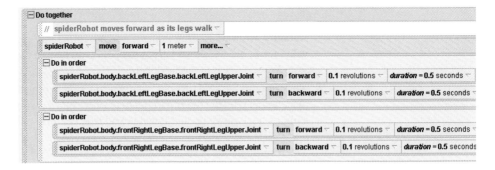

Figure 3-2-8. The spiderRobot moves forward 1 meter and legs walk once

The problem is that the spiderRobot is now moving forward only 1 meter. We want the spiderRobot to move forward several (3 or 4) meters. It would be rather tedious to create this set of instructions 3 or 4 times. Also, think about what would happen if we wanted the robot to move forward say 20 meters!

A possible solution is to use the clipboard. The clipboard is a wonderful tool for copying a set of instructions from one place to another in the editor. (See Appendix B for instructions on how to use the clipboard.) In this situation, however, dragging the same set of instructions from the editor to the clipboard and then from the clipboard back into the editor several times is still a bit tedious.

Repetition with a loop

What we want is a way to make our job easier by using a repetition control construct, called a *Loop* statement. A *Loop* statement, found in many programming languages, is a simple and easy way to repeat an action a counted number of times. To create a loop in a program, the *Loop* tile is dragged into the editor (drag it into the editor, before the *Do together* block).

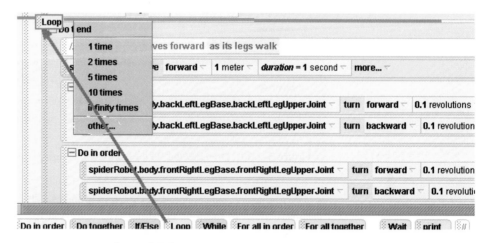

Figure 3-2-9. Dragging a *Loop* statement into the editor

When the Loop tile is dragged into the editor, a popup menu offers a choice for the count (the number of times the loop will execute). Alice uses the term "end" to describe the end of the count. We selected *other* and then entered the number 3. Note that a loop can execute only a whole number of times. (A whole number is a number with no fractional part.)

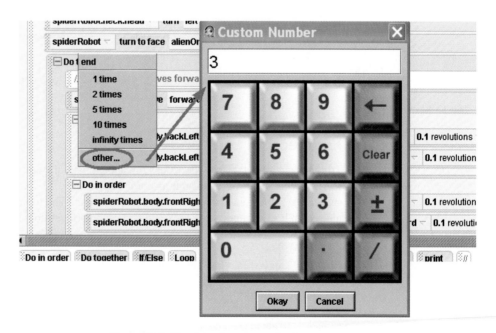

Figure 3-2-10. Selecting a count for the *Loop* statement

Finally, drag the *Do together* block into the *Loop* statement, as shown in Figure 3-2-11.

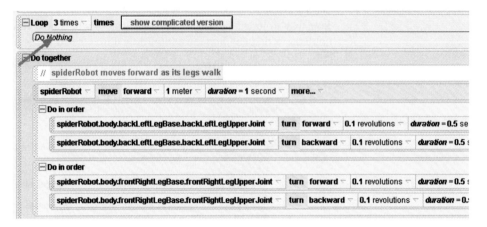

Figure 3-2-11. Dragging the *Do together* block of instructions into the *Loop* statement

The resulting *Loop* statement is shown in Figure 3-2-12. The blue-green block encloses all the instructions in the loop construct. The comment has been updated to show that the walking steps will be repeated 3 times.

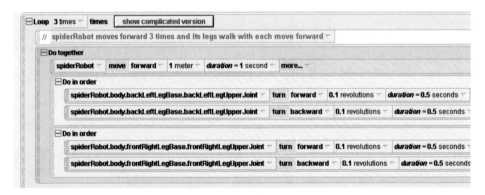

Figure 3-2-12. The completed *Loop* statement

Tips & Techniques 3
Engineering Look and Feel

The phrase "look and feel" describes the appearance of objects. We often describe look and feel in terms of properties, such as *color* and *texture*. As an example, we might say that a sweater is "yellow and has a smooth velvety texture." The topics in this section provide information on how to modify the look and feel of a world and objects within it.

Texture maps

Objects displayed in Alice are covered with texture maps to provide a sense of realness. For example, consider the plate (Kitchen) on a table (Furniture on CD or Web gallery) scene, shown in Figure T-3-1.

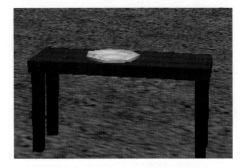

Figure T-3-1. A plate on the table

A texture map named *ground.GrassTexture* covers the ground surface, and a texture map named *plate.TextureMap* covers a plate, as can be seen in Figure T-3-2.

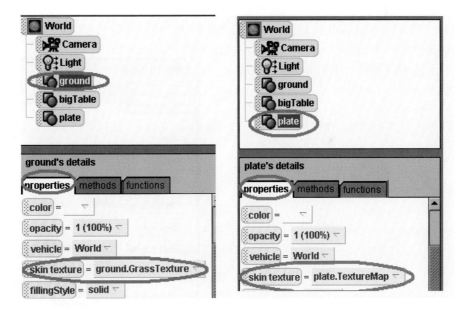

Figure T-3-2. Texture maps used as skin

A graphic file (.gif, .bmp, .jpg, or .tif) can be used to give an object a different look. The Internet is a good to place to look for graphic files—just be sure the images are not copyrighted! As an example, let's change the appearance of the plate to look like a cookie instead. Two steps are required. The first step is to import a texture map that we intend to use for that object. In this example, we selected the plate object, clicked the **import texture map** button, and then selected *cookie.gif* to be used as the texture. (The *cookie.gif* file is not part of Alice. We created the graphic image using a paint program.) Figure T-3-3 illustrates the importing step. The second step is to set the skin property to use the new texture map, as in Figure T-3-4. The result is seen in Figure T-3-5.

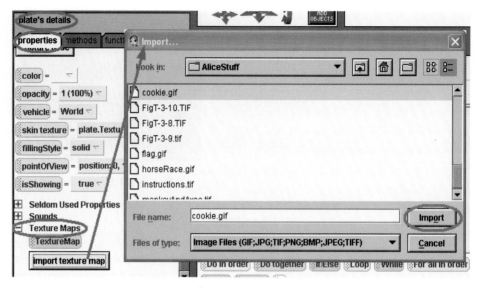

Figure T-3-3. Importing a texture map

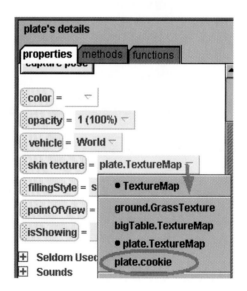

Figure T-3-4. Changing the texture map for the skin

Figure T-3-5. Cookie plate

Special effect: fog

In some worlds you may want to create a fog-like atmosphere. Consider the scene in Figure T-3-6. A knight (Medieval) is searching for a dragon (Medieval) in a forest (trees in Nature folder). We would like to give the impression that the dragon is hiding from the knight. In most stories involving dragons, the weather is dreary and grey. Some sort of fog would make the knight's job (of finding the dragon) much more challenging.

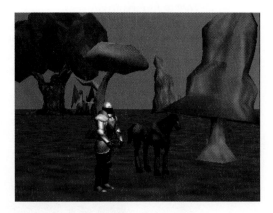

Figure T-3-6. No fog

To add fog, click on *World* in the object-tree and select properties, as shown in Figure T-3-7. Then, click on the image to the right of *fogStyle* and select *density*. Density refers to the thickness of the fog. To adjust the fog density, click the *fogDensity* tile and adjust the density value to achieve the desired effect. A larger density value produces a thicker fog.

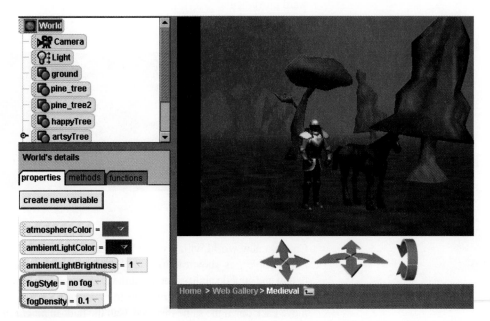

Figure T-3-7. The *fogStyle* and *fogDensity* properties are used to create a foggy scene

Exercises

3-1 Exercises

1. *Robot to Lunar Lander*

   Use the First Encounter world to recreate the program code as described in Chapter 3, Section 1. After the spiderRobot moves to the rock, have the spiderRobot turn to face the lunarLander and then move forward half the distance between the spiderRobot and the lunarLander.

2. *Dog to Fire Hydrant*

   Create a world with a dog (wolf from Animals) and a fire hydrant (City), as shown in the scene below. (We used a wolf as a dog.) Write an instruction that puts together a *distance to* function and a math expression to move the dog to the fire hydrant. The dog should stop short of colliding with the hydrant.

3. *Hop*

   Create a world with a crate (Objects) and a kangaroo (Animals). Write a program to make the kangaroo hop to the top of the box, turning the kangaroo's legs backward and forward to make it look like a hop. Use the *height* function to guide the forward and upward movements.

4. *Volleyball Jump*

   Create a new world with a volleyball net, a volleyball (Sports), and the skater girl and girl (People), as shown below. Each person in the world is likely to have a different height and athletic ability. Let's assume each person can jump up 1/4 of his or her height to hit the volleyball. Write instructions to make each person jump up this distance and then move back down the same distance. Call the built-in *height* function and use an expression to compute the distance the person should move up and down.

3-2 Exercises

5. *SpiderRobot's Walk*

   In Section 3-2, program code was presented to make the spiderRobot walk forward 3 times in a loop. Recreate the program code and test the *Loop* statement with a count of 2, 4, and then 5. Which count works best? Why?

6. *Blimp and Dragon*

   Create a scene as shown below with a blimp (Vehicle) and a dragon (Medieval). In this fantasy scene, the dragon has found a blimp and is curious. The dragon flies around the blimp to check it out. Write a program to have the dragon move to the blimp and then fly around it (lengthwise) three times.

7. *Snowman to Stool*

   This exercise uses a number function as the count for a *Loop*. Create a world with a snowman and a stool, as seen below. Use a *Loop* to make the snowman (People) move to the stool (Kitchen), one meter at a time. Use a *distance to* function to determine the number of times the loop repeats. (The *distance to* function might return a fractional distance such as 3.75 meters. The *Loop* statement truncates the fractional number to the integer 3 and will repeat 3 times.) We recommend that you test your solution by moving the snowman and the stool to different locations on the screen and running the program with each change, so you can whether it works no matter where the snowman and the stool are located.

Summary

In this chapter, we looked at how to put together the "pieces" of program code. The "pieces" that we use to create our programs include the following:

instruction—a statement that executes to make objects perform a certain action

control structure—a statement that controls the execution of instructions

function—asks a question about a condition or computes a value

expression—a math operation on numbers or other kinds of values

Alice provides built-in functions for the World and for objects within it. Functions can have different types of values (for example, number, Boolean, or object). Expressions allow you to compute a value or perform a comparison of some property of two objects. One use of functions and expressions in an animation program is to help avoid collisions (when an object moves into the same position as another object).

We can use the built-in functions and Boolean expressions (expressions that have a *true* or *false* value) to check the current condition in the world and make decisions about whether (or not) a section of the program will be executed. In Alice, the conditional execution control structure is the *If/Else* statement. An *If* statement has two parts: the *If* part and the *Else* part. In the *If* part, a condition is checked and a decision is made depending on the condition. If the condition is *true*, the *If* part of the *If/Else* statement is executed. Otherwise, the *Else* part of the statement is executed. It is possible that the *Else* part of the statement may be *Do nothing*, in which case no action is taken. (It is also possible for the *If* part of the statement to be *Do nothing*—but this is an awkward way of thinking about a condition.)

A simple repetition control structure is the *Loop*. A *Loop* statement allows you to repeat a section of program code a counted number of times.

Important concepts in this chapter

- Functions can be used in Alice to ask questions about properties of the World or properties of an object within it. Functions can also be used to compute a value.
- When a function is called, it returns a particular type of value.
- A Boolean function returns either *true* or *false*.
- An expression may use an arithmetic operation (addition, subtraction, multiplication, division) to compute a numeric value.
- Another kind of expression compares one object to another, using relational operators $\left(==, \, != , \, >, \, >=, \, <, \, <= \right)$. The result is *true* or *false*.
- A conditional execution control structure (in Alice, an *If/Else* statement) is used to make a decision about whether a particular section of the program will be executed.
- A repetition control structure is used to repeat a section of program code again and again. A simple repetition control in Alice is the *Loop* statement.

Part II
Object-Oriented and Event-Driven Programming Concepts

Chapter 4

Classes, Objects, Methods, and Parameters

"The Queen of Hearts, she made some tarts,
All on a summer day:
The Knave of Hearts, he stole those tarts,
And took them quite away!"

Instructions for Making a Strawberry Tart
1 crust, baked
3 cups strawberries, hulled
1 pkg. strawberry gelatin
$1\frac{1}{2}$ cups of water
2 Tbs. corn starch
Place strawberries in the crust.
Mix gelatin, water, and corn starch in a small pan.
Stir, while heating to a boil.
Let cool and then pour over strawberries.
Chill.

When you created your own animations in earlier chapters, you may have started to think about more complicated scenarios with more twists and turns in the storyline, perhaps games or simulations. Naturally, as the storyline becomes more intricate, so does the program code for creating the animation. The program code can quickly increase to many, many lines—sort of an "explosion" in program size and complexity. Animation programs are not alone in this complexity. Real-world software applications can have thousands, even millions, of lines of code. How does a programmer deal with huge amounts of program code? One technique is to divide a very large program into manageable "pieces," making it easier to design and think about. Smaller pieces are also easier to read and debug. Object-oriented programming uses classes, objects, and methods as basic program components, which will help you organize large programs into small manageable pieces. In this chapter and the next, you will learn how to write more intricate and impressive programs by using objects (instances of classes) and writing your own methods.

Classes

A class defines a particular kind of object. In Alice, classes are predefined as 3D models provided in the gallery, categorized into groups such as Animals, People, Buildings, Sets and Scenes, Space, and so on. Figure 4-0-1 shows some of the classes in the Animals folder. Notice that the name of a class begins with a capital letter.

Figure 4-0-1. Classes of 3D Models in the Animals folder

Each class is a blueprint that tells Alice exactly how to create and display an object from that class. When an object is created and displayed, we call this instantiating the class because an object is an instance of that class.

Objects

In Figure 4-0-2, Person and Dog are classes. Joe, stan, and cindy are instances of the Person class while spike, scamp, and fido are instances of the Dog class. Notice that the name of an object begins with a lowercase letter. This naming style helps us to easily distinguish the name of a class from the name of an object. All objects of the same class share some commonality. All Person objects have properties such as two legs, two arms, height, and eye color. Person objects can perform walking and speaking actions. All Dog objects have properties including four legs, height, and fur-color, and have the ability to run and bark. Although each object belongs to a class, it is still unique in its own way. Joe is tall and has green eyes. Cindy is short and has blue eyes. Spike has brown fur and his bark is a low growl, and scamp has golden-color fur and his bark is a high-pitched yip.

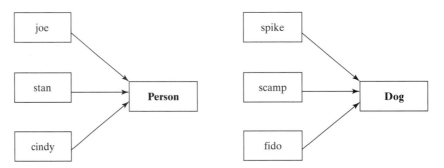

Figure 4-0-2. Organizing objects into classes

In Figure 4-0-3, larry, lila, and louis are all instances of the Lemur class (Animals) in Alice. We named the lemurs in this world, made them different heights, and changed the color of lila. Larry, lila and louis are all objects of the same Lemur character class and have many common characteristics. They also differ in that larry is the tallest, lila has rich, dark fur, and louis is the shortest.

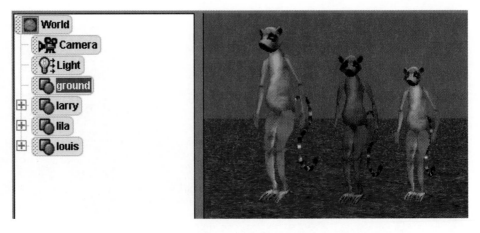

Figure 4-0-3. Objects of the Lemur class in Alice

Methods

A method is a coordinated sequence of instructions that will be carried out when requested. You have already used methods in your animations. Every object in an Alice world has a repertoire of instructions it knows how to do—*move, turn, turn to face*, etc. These instructions are actually primitive methods, built-in to the Alice software. The primitive methods can be organized into a method of your own—to carry out a small piece of the overall program. Each method performs its own job, but all the methods in a program work together to create the overall animation.

As your animation programs grow larger, it will become increasingly important to use many, many methods as a way of organizing the program. Methods divide a program into small manageable pieces that work together to create a meaningful whole. Just as paragraphs, sections, and chapters make a book easier to read, methods make a program easier to read. Methods also provide a number of advantages. For example, once a method is written it allows us to think about an overall task instead of all the small actions that were needed to complete the task. This is called abstraction.

Some methods need to be sent certain pieces of information to carry out an action. For example a *move* method needs a *direction (forward, backward, left, right, up,* or *down)* and a *distance* (in meters). A parameter acts like a basket to receive information that we send to a method. In a way, you can think of a method as somewhat like a recipe—a set of instructions that describe how to perform some action. (As an example, see the recipe at the beginning of this chapter for making a strawberry tart.) Parameters hold onto the specific items of information. In a recipe, a parameter could specify the amount of water. In a method, a parameter could specify the distance a spaceship is to move.

In Alice, you can define methods for an object acting alone or for two or more objects interacting with one another. This is similar to the way a director works with the cast of actors in a play. The director gives instructions sometimes to a single cast member and at other times to several cast members to coordinate their actions. Methods that specifically reference more than one object are world-level methods. Methods that define behaviors for a single object may be considered class-level methods.

In Section 4-1, our focus is on learning how to create and run your own world-level methods. This section will demonstrate how to call your own method. Calling a method causes Alice to animate the instructions in the method. We revise our storyboard design process to use a technique of breaking the overall task down into abstract tasks and then break each task down into smaller pieces and then define the steps in each piece. This design technique is known as stepwise refinement.

Section 4-2 launches a discussion of parameters. A parameter helps us send information to a method—a form of communication with the method. The information that gets sent to a method can be of many different types (e.g., a numeric value, an object, or some property value such as a color).

Section 4-3 presents an introduction to class-level methods. An advantage of class-level methods is that once new methods are defined, we can create a new class with all the new methods (and also the old methods) as available actions. This is a form of inheritance—the new class inherits methods from the old class.

4-1 World-level methods

In this section, an example will be used to demonstrate how to organize several primitive instructions into a method. Each method in a program performs its own job, but all the methods work together to create the overall animation. A method allows the programmer to think about a collection of instructions as if it was just one instruction—this is called abstraction. Furthermore, each individual method can be tested to be sure it works properly. Finding a bug in a few lines of code is much easier than trying to find a bug in hundreds of lines of code where everything is interrelated.

A problem

In the *FirstEncounter* world, a spiderRobot has traveled through space to land on the surface of a distant moon. The spiderRobot surprisingly encounters an alienOnWheels, investigates the alien, then sends a message back to earth. To construct this first animation program, we used a rather straightforward technique of designing a storyboard and then writing the program instructions all in *World.my first method*. The code for this program (as written in Chapter 2) is shown in Figure 4-1-1.

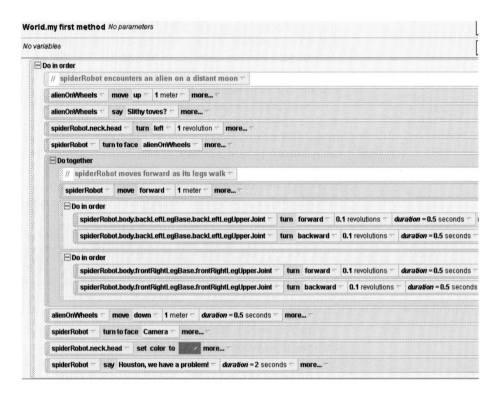

Figure 4-1-1. Program code for First Encounter world (as created in Chapter 2)

As we constructed this program, the code just seemed to grow and grow until we ended up with a large number of instructions all together. If we continue to write our programs this way, our program code is likely to grow to hundreds of lines of code all in one big block. The problem with many lines of code all in one big block is that it becomes difficult to read and even more difficult to find and remove bugs.

We need a way to better organize the instructions to make it easier to read and debug a program. One way to do this is to organize the instructions into smaller methods. Once the method is defined, we can tell Alice to run it from one main method. Another advantage of using small methods is that the methods can be called from several different places in the program, without having to copy all the instructions again and again into the editor. The following illustrates how to organize your program by using methods.

Creating your own method

If we had a chance to start again to write the First Encounter animation program, this time using methods, how would we begin? Well, the first step is to think about the animation in terms of large tasks, without all the details. For the First Encounter animation, we could write the storyboard like this:

```
Do in order
  surprise-spiderRobot and alienOnWheels surprise each other
  investigate-spiderRobot gets a closer look at alienOnWheels
  react-alienOnWheels hides and spiderRobot sends message
```

The next step is to break down each major task of our storyboard design into simpler steps. As an example, let's do this for the *surprise* task.

```
Do in order
  surprise-spiderRobot and alienOn Wheels surprise each other
  investigate-spiderRobot moves closer to alienOnWheels
  react-alienOn Wheels hides and spiderRobot sends message
```

```
surprise

Do in order
  alien moves up
  alien says "Slithy toves?"
  robot's head turns around
```

The steps in the *surprise* storyboard are the same as the first four instructions in the program we wrote in Chapter 2. But now we are thinking of these instructions as one abstract idea—the spiderRobot and alienOnWheels surprise each other. In a similar way, we can construct storyboards for the *investigate* and *react* tasks.

```
investigate

Do in order
  robot turns to look at alien
  Do together
    robot moves forward (toward the alien)
    robot's legs walk
```

```
react

Do in order
  alien moves down
  robot turns to look at the camera
  robot's head turns red (to signal danger)
  robot says "Houston, we have a problem!"
```

The process of breaking a problem down into large tasks and then breaking each task down into simpler steps is called stepwise refinement—a design technique used in many of the examples presented in the next few chapters. Now that we have organized our storyboard into three abstract tasks, the program can be constructed by writing a method for each task. Let's write a method for the task named *surprise*. (Notice that method names conventionally begin with a lowercase letter.) We know that when objects carry out instructions in an Alice world, they may be acting alone—that is, not affecting or being affected by other objects. On the other hand, objects are often interacting in some way with other objects. For a method where objects are interacting with other objects, we write a world-level method. The *surprise* method will involve both the spiderRobot and the alienOnWheels, so it will be a world-level method.

Although the instructions we will use are the same as those presented in Chapter 2, we will go through some of the steps of creating the animation once again (starting with the initial scene, containing no program code) so as to illustrate the process of writing our own method. In the object tree, the World object is selected and then the *methods* tab in the Details panel (located in the lower left of the screen). Then the **create new method** button (in the methods detail panel) is clicked. Figure 4-1-2 illustrates the **create new method** button selection. When the **create new method** button is clicked, a popup box allows you to enter the name of the new method. In this example, we entered *surprise*.

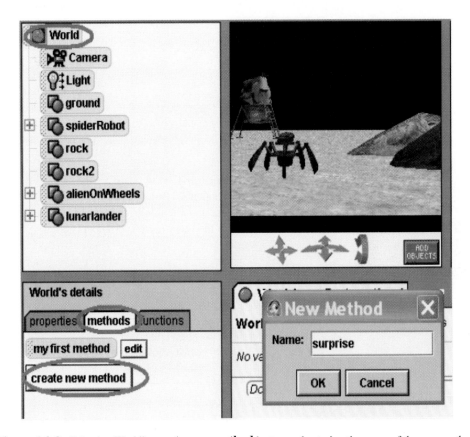

Figure 4-1-2. Selecting World's **create new method** button and entering the name of the new method

Alice automatically opens a new editor tab, where the code can be written for the new method. (See Figure 4-1-3.)

Note that the particular method being edited has its tab colored yellow, and that all other method tabs are greyed out. To switch back and forth between the editor tabs, click the edit button to the right of the method you want to work on (in the details panel on the left).

Now we can add instructions for the *World.surprise* method, using instructions similar to those in the program in Chapter 2, as in Figure 4-1-4.

Note: If the **Play** button is clicked at this time, the animation will NOT run. Although the *surprise* method has been defined, Alice has not been told to execute it. That is, the method has

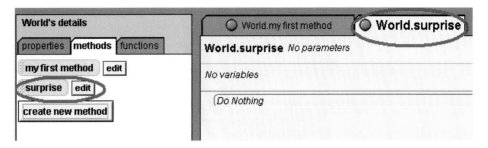

Figure 4-1-3. The new *World.surprise* code editor

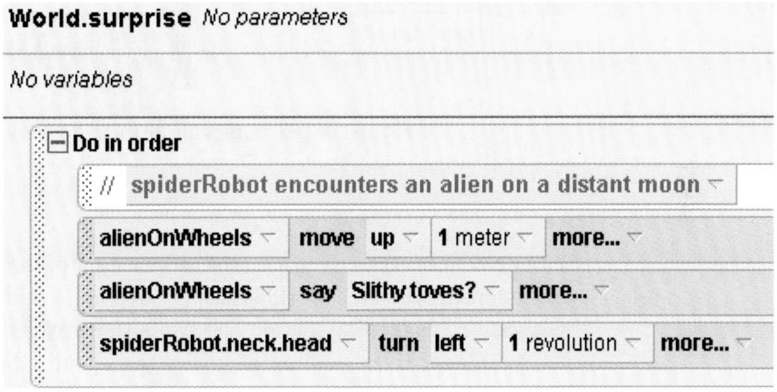

Figure 4-1-4. Defining the *World.surprise* method

not been called into action. (Another phrase commonly used for "calling a method" is "invoking a method"—but in this book we will use the phrase "calling a method.")

Calling a method

How is your new method called into action? You have no doubt discovered that when you (as the human "user") click on the Play button, Alice automatically executes *World.my first method*. You can see why this happens by looking carefully at the Events editor, located in the top right of the Alice interface as seen in Figure 4-1-5. The instruction in this editor tells Alice *When the world starts, do World.my first method*. We didn't put this instruction here—the Alice interface is automatically programmed this way. So, when the user clicks on the Play button, the world starts and *World.my first method* is called.

Figure 4-1-5. *When the world starts* is linked to *World.my first method*

Let's take advantage of this arrangement. All we have to do is drag the *World.surprise* method from where it is listed in the methods tab of the details panel into *World.my first method*, as illustrated in Figure 4-1-6. Now, whenever the Play button is clicked, *my first method* will run and the *World.surprise* method will be called.

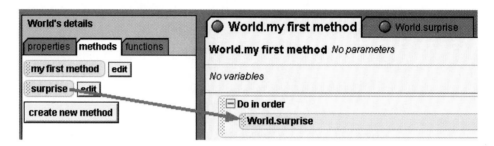

Figure 4-1-6. Dragging *World.surprise* into *World.my first method*

Technical Note: The Events editor (upper right of the Alice interface) can be used to modify what happens when the world starts. By default (meaning "unless you tell Alice otherwise"), the user presses the Play button and Alice starts executing *World.my first method*. Modifying this event in the Events editor tells Alice to execute a different method when the user clicks on the Play button.

To modify the *When the world starts* event, click on the right of the *World.my first method* tile in the Events editor. Then, select *surprise* from the drop down list, as seen in Figure 4-1-7. Now, when the world starts, the *World.surprise* method will run instead of *World.my first method*.

Figure 4-1-7. Modifying the *When the world starts* event

A second method

Now that the *World.surprise* method is complete, we can construct the second method, named *World.investigate*. *World.investigate* is a world-level method because both the spiderRobot and the alienOnWheels objects are directly referenced in the instructions. Following the same process as above for the *World.surprise* method, we created a *World.investigate* method as shown in Figure 4-1-8.

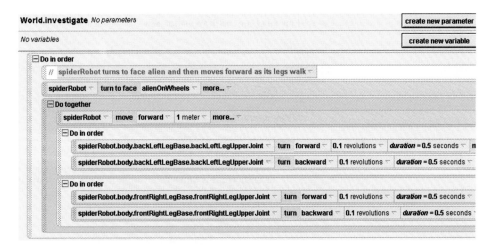

Figure 4-1-8. Defining the *World.investigate* method

The third method

Finally, a world-level method is created for the *react* task. As with the *World.surprise* and *World.investigate* methods, *World.react* is world-level because the spiderRobot and the alienOn-Wheels are both directly referenced in the instructions. The *World.react* method is shown in Figure 4-1-9.

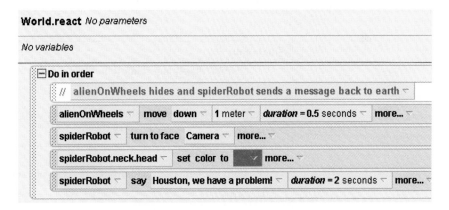

Figure 4-1-9. A world-level method, *react*

Now, we are ready to call each of the methods in *World.my first method*. The code is illustrated in Figure 4-1-10.

Compare the revised program code in Figure 4-1-10 to the code in Figure 4-1-1. One thing that you should notice immediately is that the revised code in Figure 4-1-10 has fewer lines of code. The overall program has been broken down into methods—small collections of instructions that carry out specific abstract tasks. *World.my first method* acts as a driver that calls the methods. This organization makes the program easier to read and understand. Also, writing and testing short methods makes it easer to debug your programs.

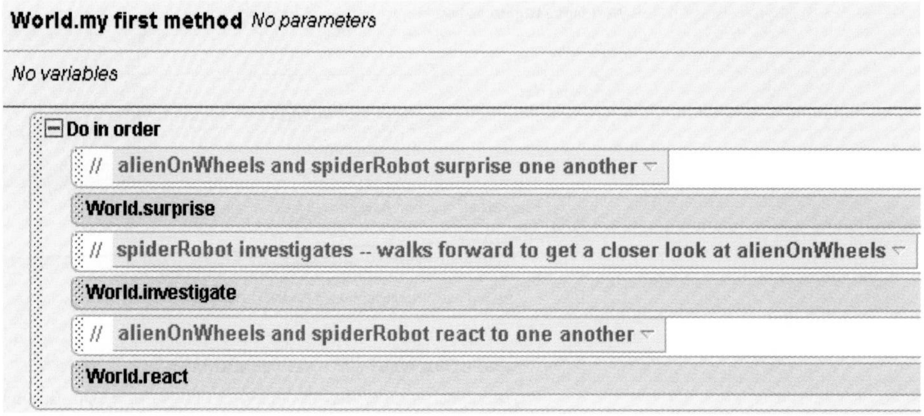

Figure 4-1-10. Revised *World.my first method*

One benefit of writing methods this way is that some methods may be called more than once. For example, the *World.investigate* method can be called multiple times to make the spiderRobot walk toward the alienOnWheels. This reduces the amount of program code and saves us time as we create our programs. Figure 4-1-11 illustrates two calls to the *World.investigate* method.

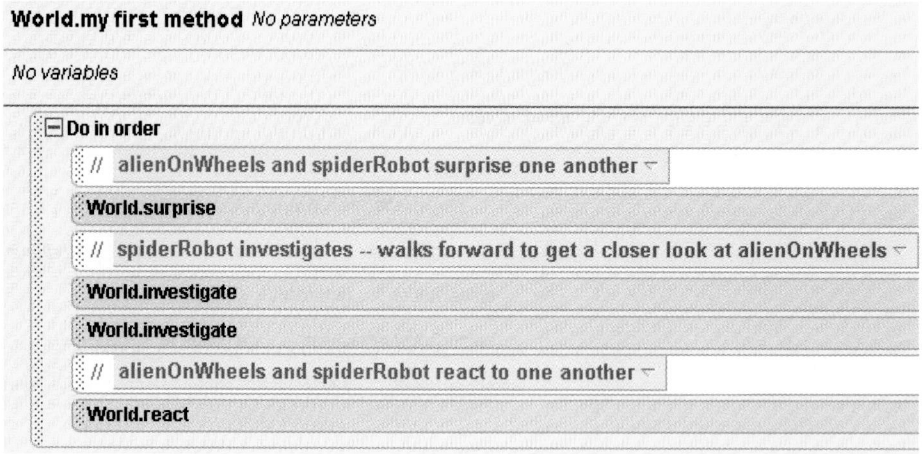

Figure 4-1-11. The *World.investigate* method is called twice

Deleting a method

Built-in methods and methods that are predefined for a model should not be deleted. In other words, delete a method only if you have written the method and want to discard it. Before deleting a method, delete all calls to the method and then close its edit window (right click on the method's edit panel and select "close"), if open. To delete a method, drag its name tile (from the methods list) to the trash bin, as illustrated in Figure 4-1-12.

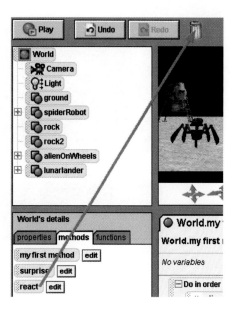

Figure 4-1-12. Deleting a method you have written

4-2 Parameters

It is clear from the examples in the preceding section that one program may be made up of several methods. Each method is its own small block of instructions, designed to perform a specific task when requested. We can appreciate that some communication might need to occur when a method is called. In this section, we look at parameters. Parameters are used to communicate with a method. We arrange to communicate values (for example, a number or a color) or names of objects from one method to another by using parameters in our methods.

Example

An example world will illustrate the creation and use of parameters. For a spring concert, our entertainment committee has hired a popular music group—the Beetle Band. Our job is to create an animation to advertise the concert. In the animation, each band member wants to show off his musical skills in a short solo performance.

Setting the stage: Figure 4-2-1 shows an initial scene. The world is simple to set up. To a new world, add a table as a stage (Furniture on CD or Web gallery), georgeBeetle, lennonBeetle, paulBeetle, and ringoBeetle (Animals). Give each band member a musical instrument: bass, saxophone, timbalesCowBell, and guitar (Musical Instruments).

Make the vehicle of each musical instrument be the band member who plays the instrument. For example, the vehicle of the bass guitar is georgeBeetle. Using the vehicle property is a convenient way to make the musical instrument move with the band member as the band member jumps up and down in his solo.

In the scene in Figure 4-2-1, we used a table to simulate a stage for the band and conserve memory. (Worlds that take up less memory load faster.) If you want a fancier scene, you could use the concert stage (Environments on CD or Web gallery) as shown in Figure 4-2-2.

Figure 4-2-1. Beetle Band on stage

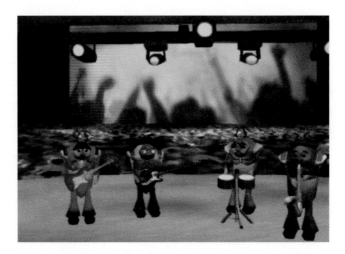

Figure 4-2-2. Beetle Band on a concert stage

Storyboard

The storyline for this animation is that each band member will perform a short solo—the band member will jump up and down at the same time as a sound plays. (If your computer does not have sound, you can have the band member *say* lyrics, rather than play a sound.) Let's create a storyboard for each band member's solo. Because we have four band members (georgeBeetle, ringoBeetle, paulBeetle, and lennonBeetle), four textual storyboards can be composed:

```
Do together
  Do in order
    georgeBeetle move up
    georgeBeetle move down
  play sound
```

```
Do together
  Do in order
    ringoBeetle move up
    ringoBeetle move down
  play sound
```

```
Do together
  Do in order
    paulBeetle move up
    paulBeetle move down
  play sound
```

```
Do together
  Do in order
    lennonBeetle move up
    lennonBeetle move down
  play sound
```

Now a method can be written for each storyboard. We begin with a method for the solo performed by georgeBeetle. Of course, the bass guitar will move with georgeBeetle when he moves up and down because the bass guitar's vehicle property is set to georgeBeetle. In a *Do together* block, a *play sound* instruction will be used to play a sound at the same time as georgeBeetle and the bass guitar instrument move up and down. Before a sound can be played, a sound file must be imported into Alice. (Alice will play either MP3 or WAV sound files.) Alice provides a few sounds for your use. Many non-copyrighted sound files are available on the internet. You can also use sound editing software to record your own sound files or you can purchase sound recordings on the internet (for educational projects, only).

In this world, a sound is associated with a musical instrument. For this reason, the sound will be imported for the instrument object. To illustrate how to import a sound file, let's import a bass guitar sound for the bass instrument. Click on the bass instrument in the Object tree and then on the **import sound** button in the bass object's property list. A file selection box appears. Navigate to a directory where you have stored your sound files and then select the sound file to be used, as shown in Figure 4-2-3. (Note that our sound files have been stored in a directory we created and named Sounds, but you may have them stored in some other directory. It may be necessary to navigate through several folders on your computer to find a sound file you wish to import.) Once the file has been selected, click on the **Import** button.

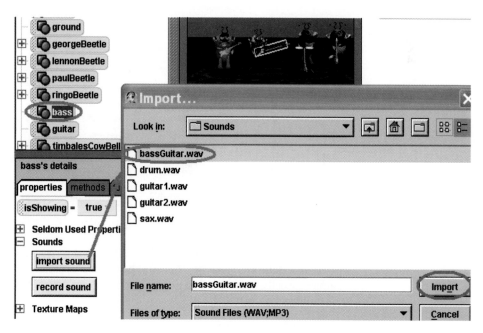

Figure 4-2-3. Importing a sound file for an object

The name of the sound file automatically appears in the list of properties for the bass object, as shown in Figure 4-2-4. The green arrow is a preview button and can be clicked to test the sound file.

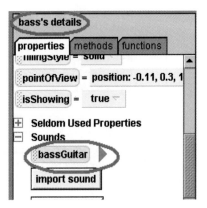

Figure 4-2-4. Imported sound file in the properties panel

For this world, we used this technique to import four sound files—one for each musical instrument (bass, sax, timbalesCowbell, and guitar) in the world. Now that the sound files have been imported, a method can be created for a solo performed by one of the members of the Beetle Band. The code for a solo by georgeBeetle is shown in Figure 4-2-5. The *play sound* instruction is created by dragging the play sound method tile into the editor and selecting the appropriate sound from a popup menu. The *play sound* instruction automatically includes the *duration* of the sound. The bassGuitar sound used in our example will play for a *duration* of 1.845 seconds. If you wish to change the duration of the sound, we recommend that you use a sound editor to modify the sound (rather than modify the duration in the Alice instruction).

Figure 4-2-5. Solo method for georgeBeetle

To complete the animation, four methods are needed—one for each band member's solo. It is quite clear that the four storyboards are strikingly similar and four methods will be almost exactly the same. The major differences are which band member will solo and which instrument will play a sound.

Parameters

This is where parameters come in. A parameter allows you to send information to a method when the method is called. You have been using parameters all along. Most primitive methods have parameters that allow you to send information to the method. For example, a *move* instruction has parameters that allow you to send in the direction, distance, and duration. In the *move* instruction shown below, the direction is up, the distance is .25 meters and the duration is 0.5 seconds. We say that the values are sent in as arguments to the parameters.

We can use parameters in our own methods. In the Beetle Band example, the four storyboards are so similar that we can collapse them into one storyboard by using a parameter to communicate to the method which band member will perform the solo. The storyboard with a parameter is:

```
solo

Parameter: bandMember
Do together
  Do in order
    bandMember move up
    bandMember move down
  play sound
```

The *bandMember* parameter name (an arbitrary name) is taking the place of the name of the specific object that will perform the solo. You can think of a parameter as acting like someone who stands in a cafeteria line for you until you arrive—sort of a placeholder. For example, when georgeBeetle is sent in as an argument, then *bandMember* represents georgeBeetle. But, when lennonBeetle is sent in as an argument, *bandMember* represents lennonBeetle. By creating a parameter, we can write just one method (instead of four methods) and use the parameter to communicate which band member will perform the solo.

An object parameter

A new world-level method, named *solo*, is created. The editor creates a new editor tab for the World.solo method, as seen in Figure 4-2-6. A **create new parameter** button automatically appears in the upper right corner of the editor. When the **create new parameter** button is clicked, a dialog box pops up as shown in Figure 4-2-7. The name of the parameter is entered and its *type* is selected. The *type* of a parameter can be a *Number*, *Boolean* ("true" or "false"), *Object*, or *Other* (for example, a color or sound). In this example, the name of the parameter is *bandMember* and its type is *Object*.

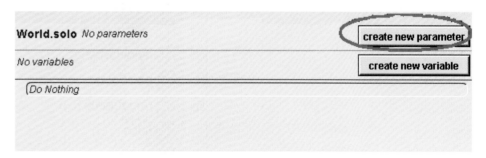

Figure 4-2-6. *World.solo* method pane

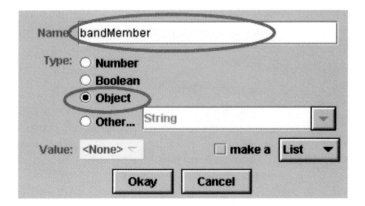

Figure 4-2-7. Enter the name and select a type for a parameter declaration

When completed, the parameter name is in the upper left of the method panel, as shown in Figure 4-2-8. Now, whenever the *World.solo* method is called, an object must be sent as an argument to the *bandMember* parameter.

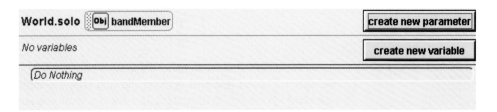

Figure 4-2-8. Resulting parameter

Now, we can translate the storyboard into program code. The first part of the storyboard is a *Do in order* block to make the *bandMember* jump (move up and then down). Intuitively, we look at the Object tree to find *bandMember* so that its *move* instruction can be dragged into the editor, but *bandMember* is not in the Object tree. (See Figure 4-2-9.) This makes sense because, as mentioned earlier, *bandMember* is not an actual object—it is acting as a placeholder for an object.

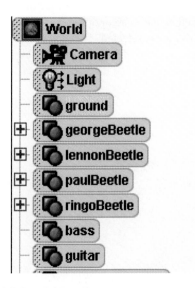

Figure 4-2-9. The *bandMember* parameter is not in the Object tree

Instead of dragging a *move* method into the editor, drag the parameter tile into the editor. For example, in Figure 4-2-10, the *bandMember* parameter tile is dragged into the editor and *move, up,* and 1/2 *meter* are selected from the popup menus.

Figure 4-2-10. Instruction for an arbitrary object

The resulting instruction looks like this:

Using the same procedure, another instruction is written to *move bandMember* down 0.5 meters. The duration for the *move up* and *move down* instructions is selected as 0.5 seconds. The resulting method is shown in Figure 4-2-11.

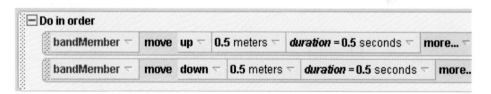

Figure 4-2-11. The *bandMember* jumps (moves up and down)

Test with arguments

This is a good time to save and test the code. To test the *World.solo* method, the *solo* method is called from *my first method*. When *solo* is dragged into *my first method*, a popup menu (Figure 4-2-12) allows the selection of an object that *bandMember* will represent for that call of the method. To be certain the *solo* method works for each Beetle Band musician, four statements are written, as seen in Figure 4-2-13. In this example, georgeBeetle, lennonBeetle, ringoBeetle, and paulBeetle are each used as an argument in a call to the *solo* method. For example, in the first call the *solo* method will be performed with *bandMember* representing georgeBeetle; in the second call *bandMember* will represent lennonBeetle.

Completing the animation

You may have noticed that the above code does not yet complete the animation. In each solo, the band member should not only move but also a musical instrument should play a sound. An instruction is needed in the *solo* method to play a sound. If your computer does not have a

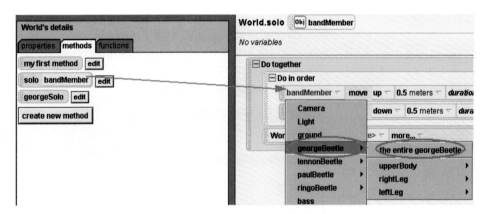

Figure 4-2-12. Selecting an argument for the *bandMember* parameter

Figure 4-2-13. Calling *World.solo* with different arguments

sound card or you do not have access to sound files, a *say* instruction (see below) can be used to display the lyrics of a song.

Multiple parameters

Each *bandMember* plays a different musical instrument, and each instrument should have a different sound. (In this example, we want a bass sound for georgeBeetle, saxophone for paulBeetle, drum for ringoBeetle, and guitar for lennonBeetle's performance.) Let's create two additional parameters: *instrument*, for the object playing the sound, and *music*, for the sound to be played. The type of the *instrument* parameter is Object (created in the same way as *bandMember*, above) and the type of the *music* parameter is Sound. Figure 4-2-14 illustrates creating a Sound parameter named *music*.

As with the *bandMember* parameter above, the *instrument* and *music* parameters are placeholders, and do not appear in the Object tree. When a parameter does not represent an object, the parameter tile often must be dragged into the editor to replace the tile in an existing instruction. In this example, the instrument tile is dragged in to the editor to create a play sound instruction, as illustrated in Figure 4-2-15. A popup menu allows the selection of *play sound* as the method and *music* as the sound.

The code shown in Figure 4-2-15 is complete. A *Do in order* block is used to have the *bandMember* move up and then down. And, a *Do together* block causes the sound to play at the same time as the *bandMember* moves up and down.

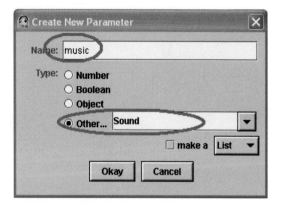

Figure 4-2-14. The *music* parameter *Type* is *Sound*

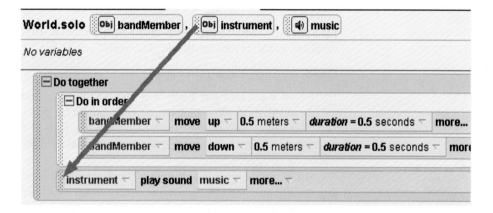

Figure 4-2-15. Dragging the *instrument* and *music* parameters in to create a *play sound* instruction

Calling the revised method

Calls to *World.solo* are revised in *my first method* to pass in three arguments (two objects and a sound), as in Figure 4-2-16.

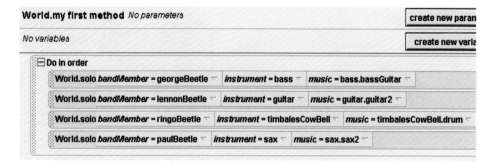

Figure 4-2-16. Completed *World.my first method*

As mentioned above, this animation can be completed without the use of sound. An alternate version of the *solo* method is shown in Figure 4-2-17. A string parameter, *songLyric*, is used instead of a sound parameter. (A string is just several text characters or words.)

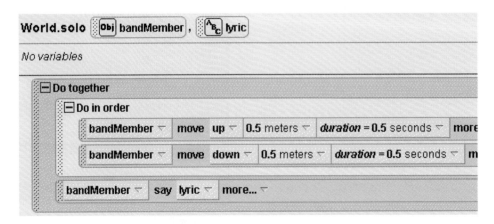

Figure 4-2-17. Lyric version of *solo*

The *songLyric* string is displayed using a *say* instruction. To call this method, an argument for *songLyric* could be something like "Oh, yeah!"

Other types of parameters

The Beetle Band example above was used to illustrate three types of parameters: objects, sound and strings. A parameter can also be a number, a Boolean value (*true* or *false*), a color (red, blue, green, etc.), or any of several other types. Each of these types of values contributes to a rich environment for programming. Number values play an important role in many programming languages.

In the *World.solo* method, a *bandMember* moved up and down an arbitrary amount, 0.5 meters. We could send in the amount for the move by adding a number parameter. The first step, of course, is to create a number parameter, as shown in Figure 4-2-18. We used the name *height* and selected Number as the type.

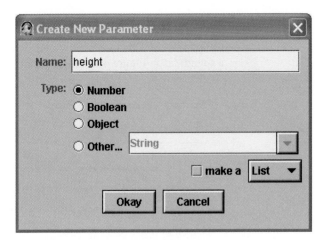

Figure 4-2-18. Creating a number parameter

The *height* parameter can then be dragged into the *move up* and *move down* instructions. Figure 4-2-19 shows a revised *solo* method where the *bandMember* moves up and down an amount specified by the *height* parameter.

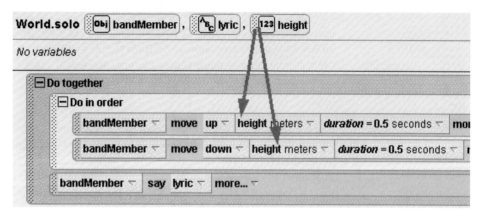

Figure 4-2-19. Using a number parameter

4-3 Class-level methods and inheritance

The galleries of 3D models in Alice give us a choice of diverse and well-designed classes of objects for populating and creating a scenic backdrop in a virtual world. When you add an instance of a 3D model to an Alice world, it already "knows" how to perform a set of methods—*move, turn, roll,* and *resize* (to name a few). The 3D model class already defines these methods. After writing several programs, it is natural to think about extending the actions an object "knows" how to perform.

In this section, you will learn how to write new methods that define new actions to be carried out by an object acting alone (rather than several objects acting together). We call these class-level methods. Class-level methods are rather special, because we can save an object along with its newly defined method(s) as a new kind of object. In Alice, the new kind of object is saved as a new 3D class model. Later instances of the new class still know how to perform all the actions defined in the original class but will also be able to perform all the actions in the newly defined methods. We say that the new class inherits all the properties and methods of the original class.

Example

Consider the iceSkater shown in the winter scene of Figure 4-3-1. (The IceSkater class is from the People collection, and the Lake class is from the Environments collection in the gallery.)

Figure 4-3-1. The iceSkater

We want the skater to perform typical figure-skating actions. She is dressed in a skating costume and is wearing ice skates, but this does not mean she knows how to skate. However, all Alice objects "know" how to perform simple methods such as *move, turn,* and *roll*. We can use a combination of these simple methods to "teach" the ice skater how to perform a more complex action. We begin with a method to make the skater perform a skating motion.

A Class-Level Method

Skating movements are complex actions that require several motion instructions involving various parts of the body. (Professional animators at Disney and Pixar may spend many, many hours observing the movement of various parts of the human body so as to create realistic animations.) To skate, a skater slides forward on the left leg and then slides forward on the right leg. Of course, the entire skater body is moving forward as the legs perform the sliding movements. The steps in a skating action are put together as a sequence of motions in a storyboard, as shown next.

```
skate

Do together
Move skater forward 2 meters
    Do in order
        slide on left leg
        slide on right leg
```

Notice that the storyboard breaks down the skating action into two pieces—slide on the left leg and slide on the right leg. The sliding motions can each be broken down into simpler methods. Breaking a complex action down into simpler actions is called refinement. Here we are using a design technique known as stepwise refinement. We first describe general actions, and then break each action down into smaller and smaller steps (successively refined) until the whole task is defined in simple actions. Each piece contributes a small part to the overall animation; the pieces together accomplish the entire task.

The following diagram illustrates the refinement of the *slideLeft* and *slideRight* actions. The actions needed to slide on the left leg are to lift the right leg and turn the upper body slightly forward. Then, lower the right leg and turn the upper body backward (to an upright position). Similar actions are carried out to slide on the right leg.

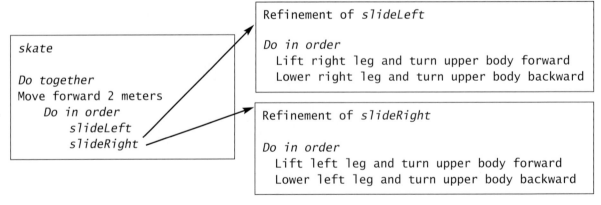

Nothing else needs to be refined. We are now ready to translate the design into program code. We could translate this design to instructions in just the one method, but it would be lengthy. Furthermore, you can quickly see that we have used stepwise refinement to break the skate task down into distinct pieces. So, we will demonstrate how to write several small methods and make them work together to accomplish a larger task.

Skate is a complex action that is designed specifically for the iceSkater and involves no other objects. Likewise, the *slideLeft* and *slideRight* actions are designed specifically for the iceSkater. The methods should be written as class-level methods because they involve only the ice skater. We begin with the *slideLeft* method. The iceSkater is selected in the Object tree and the **create new method** button is clicked in the details panel. We enter *slideLeft* as the name of the new method. (The result is shown in Figure 4-3-2.) Notice that the editor tab is labeled *iceSkater.slideLeft* (not *World.slideLeft*)—indicating that the method is a class-level method.

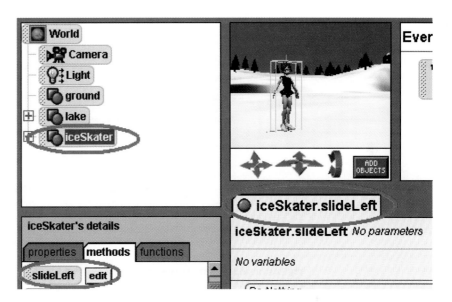

Figure 4-3-2. A *slideLeft* class-level method

To implement the *slideLeft* method, we enter instructions in the editor. The idea is to translate the design into actual program instructions. For example, to translate the design steps for sliding on the left leg, we use the following:

Design step	Instruction
Lift the right leg	*turn* the rightLeg forward
Turn upper body forward	*turn* the upperBody forward
(We inserted a short *wait* to allow time for forward movement.)	
Lower the right leg	*turn* the rightLeg backward
Turn the upper body backward	*turn* the upperBody backward

Figure 4-3-3 illustrates translating the textual storyboard into instructions for sliding on the left leg. The instructions for sliding forward on the right leg are similar. So, writing the *slideRight* method is rather easy. Figure 4-3-4 illustrates translating the textual storyboard into instructions to slide forward on the right leg.

With the *slideLeft* and *slideRight* methods written, we are now ready to write the *skate* method. The *skate* method is really quite simple: *slideLeft* and then *slideRight* at the same time as the entire skater is moving forward. The skate method moves the skater forward and calls the *slideLeft* method and then calls the *slideRight* method. Note that the calls to the *slideLeft* and *slideRight* methods are enclosed in a *Do in order* block, nested within a *Do together*. The *Do together* block is needed to ensure that the instruction that moves the skater forward is performed simultaneously with the left and right sliding motions.

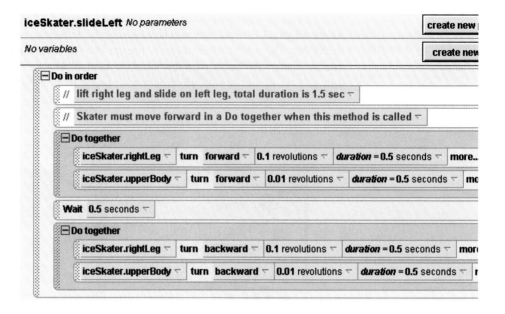

Figure 4-3-3. The *slideLeft* method

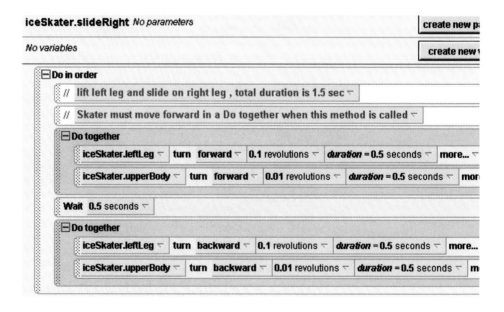

Figure 4-3-4. The *slideRight* method

The duration of the forward movement of the skater is the sum of the durations of the left and right slides. Paying attention to the durations of the instructions in a *Do together* block will help coordinate the motions to begin and end at the same time. In this case, we wanted to coordinate the *slideLeft* and *slideRight* motions with the forward motion of the entire body. When the *skate* method is called, the skater glides forward in a realistic motion. Figure 4-3-5 illustrates the *skate m*ethod.

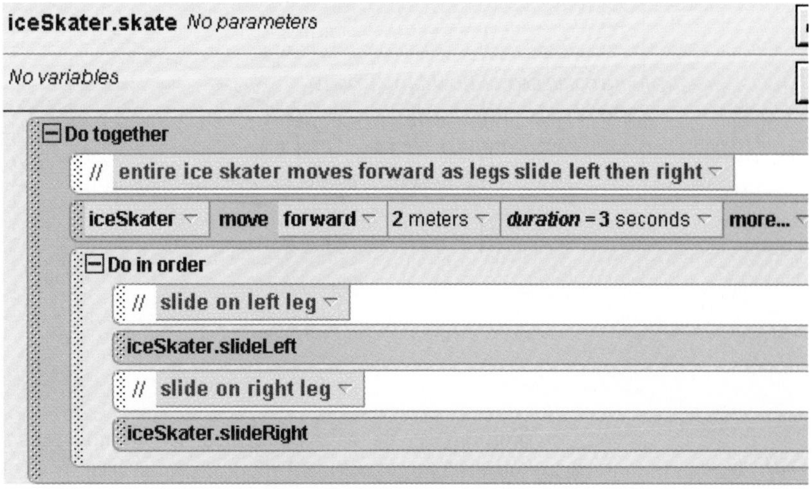

Figure 4-3-5. The *skate* method

A second example—using a parameter

The forward skate motion is truly impressive! Building on this success, let's write a second method to make the ice skater perform a spin. Once again, we will need to write several methods that work together to complete a complex action. In a spin, the ice skater should spin (turn around) several times.

A spin maneuver generally has three parts, the preparation for the spin, the spin itself, and the end of the spin (to finish the spin). In preparation for the spin, the skater's arms and legs change position to provide the strength needed to propel her body around. Then the skater spins around. After the spin, the arms and legs should be repositioned to where they were before the spin. A parameter, *howManyTimes,* is needed to specify the number of times the ice skater will spin around. The storyboard is shown next.

```
spin

Parameter: howManyTimes
Do in order
    prepare to spin
    spin the skater around howManyTimes
    finish the spin
```

We can use stepwise refinement to design the simple steps for each part of the spin. The "prepare to spin" step can be written as a method (*prepareToSpin*) where the skater's arms move up and one leg turns. The "finish spin" step can also be written as a method (*finishSpin*) to move the arms and legs back to their original positions, prior to the spin. The following diagram illustrates a refinement of the *spin* method.

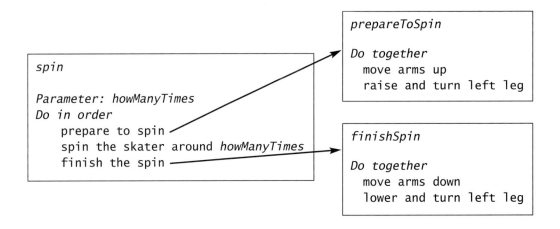

Nothing else needs to be refined. We are now ready to translate the design into program code. Once again, class-level methods should be used, because we are defining a complex motion specifically for the ice skater.

Figure 4-3-6 illustrates the *prepareToSpin* method, where the ice skater raises her left leg as she lifts her arms.

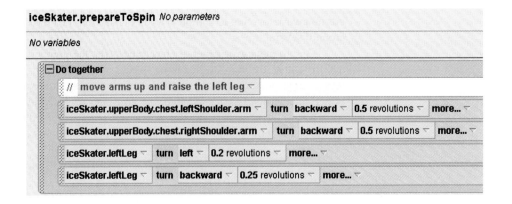

Figure 4-3-6. The *prepareToSpin* method to raise arms and one leg

Figure 4-3-7 presents the *finishSpin* method to reposition the skater's arms and leg to their original positions at the end of her spin.

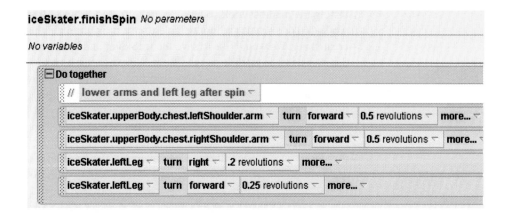

iceSkater.finishSpin *No parameters*

No variables

- Do together
  - // lower arms and left leg after spin
  - iceSkater.upperBody.chest.leftShoulder.arm | turn | forward | 0.5 revolutions | more...
  - iceSkater.upperBody.chest.rightShoulder.arm | turn | forward | 0.5 revolutions | more...
  - iceSkater.leftLeg | turn | right | .2 revolutions | more...
  - iceSkater.leftLeg | turn | forward | 0.25 revolutions | more...

Figure 4-3-7. The *finishSpin* method to lower arms and leg

Now that the *prepareToSpin* and *finishSpin* methods have been written, we can write the *spin* method, as seen in Figure 4-3-8. The *howManySpins* parameter is a number that specifies how many times the skater is to turn around (1 revolution is 1 complete spin around). The order in which the methods are called is important so as to adjust the skater's arms and legs in preparation for the spin and after the spin.

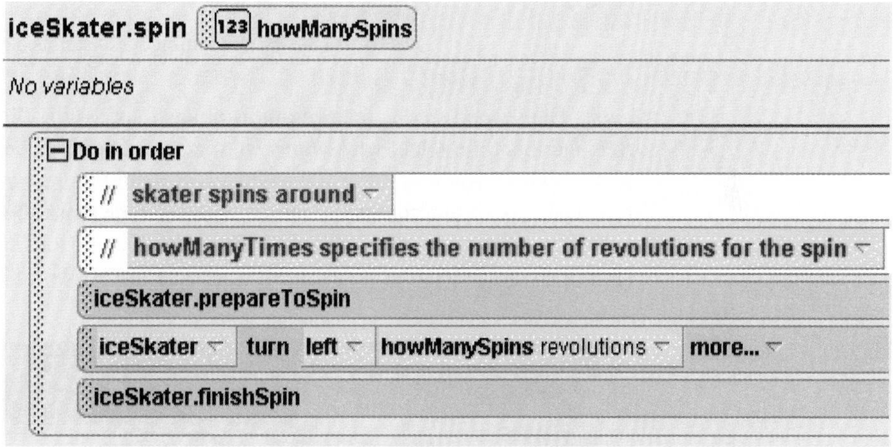

iceSkater.spin 123 howManySpins

No variables

- Do in order
  - // skater spins around
  - // howManyTimes specifies the number of revolutions for the spin
  - iceSkater.prepareToSpin
  - iceSkater | turn | left | howManySpins revolutions | more...
  - iceSkater.finishSpin

Figure 4-3-8. The *spin* method

The code for the two examples above (the *skate* and *spin* methods) is a bit longer than we have written in previous chapters. It is important that the code is easy to understand, because we have carefully broken down the overall task into smaller methods. The small methods all work together to complete the overall action. Also, the methods have been well documented, with comments that tell us what the method accomplishes. Good design and comments make our code easier to understand as well as easier to write and debug.

Creating a new class

The iceSkater now has two class-level methods, *skate* and *spin*. (She also has several smaller class-level methods that implement small pieces of the *skate* and *spin* methods.) Writing and testing the methods took some time and effort to achieve. It would be a shame to put all this work into one world and not be able to use it again in another animation program we might create later. We would like to save the iceSkater and her newly defined methods so we can use them in another world (we won't need to write these methods again for another animation program). To do this, the *iceSkater* must be saved out as a new 3D model (class).

Saving the iceSkater (with her newly defined methods) as a new class is a two-step process. The first step is to rename the iceSkater. This is an IMPORTANT STEP! We want Alice to save this new class with a different 3D filename than the original IceSkater class. To rename an object, right-click on the name of the object in the Object tree, select *rename* from the popup menu, and enter the new name in the box. In this example, we right-clicked on iceSkater in the Object tree and changed the name to cleverSkater, as shown in Figure 4-3-9.

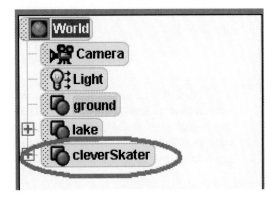

Figure 4-3-9. Renaming iceSkater as cleverSkater

The second step is to save out as a new class: right click on cleverSkater in the Object tree and this time select *save object*. In the Save Object popup box, navigate to the folder/directory where you wish to save the new class, as in Figure 4-3-10, and then click the Save button. The class is automatically named with the new name, beginning with a capital letter and a filename extension .a2c, which stands for "Alice version 2.0 Class" (just as the .a2w extension in a world filename stands for "Alice version 2.0 World").

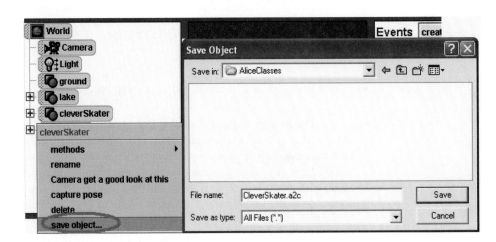

Figure 4-3-10. Save Object dialog box

Once a new class has been created, it can be used in a new world by selecting **Import** from the **File** menu, as illustrated in Figure 4-3-11. When an instance of the CleverSkater

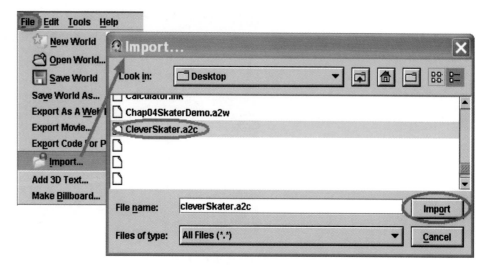

Figure 4-3-11. Importing a new object from a saved-out class

class is added to a world, she will be just like an instance of the IceSkater class, except that a cleverSkater object knows how to *skate* and *spin* in addition to all of the methods an iceSkater object can perform.

Inheritance—benefits

Creating a new class based on a previously defined class is called inheritance. Inheritance in most object-oriented languages is more complicated than in Alice. The basic idea is the same—adding functionality by defining new methods for a new kind of inherited class. Inheritance is considered one of the strengths of object-oriented programming because it allows you to write code once and reuse it in other programs.

Another benefit of creating new classes is the ability to share code with others in team projects. For example, if you are working on an Alice project as a team, each person can write class-level methods for an object in the world. Then, each team member can save out the new class. Objects of the new classes are added to a single team-constructed world for a shared project. This is a benefit we cannot overemphasize. In the "real world," computer professionals generally work on team projects. Cooperatively developed software is often the way professional animation teams at animation studios work.

Guidelines for Writing Class-Level Methods

Class-level methods are a powerful feature of Alice. Of course, with power there is also some danger. To avoid potential misuse of class-level methods, we offer some guidelines.

1. Do create many different class-level methods. They are extremely useful and helpful. Some classes in Alice already have a few class-level methods defined. For example, the Lion class has methods *startStance, walkForward, completeWalk, roar,* and *charge*. Figure 4-3-12 shows a thumbnail image for the Lion class (from the Web gallery), including its class-level methods and sounds.

2. Play a sound in a class-level method **ONLY IF** the sound has been imported for the object (instead of the world). If the sound has been imported for the object and the object is saved out as a new class, the sound is saved out with the object. Then the sound can be played anywhere in any world where an object of this class is added. On the other hand, if the sound is imported for the world, the sound is not saved out with the object and you cannot depend on the sound being available in other worlds.

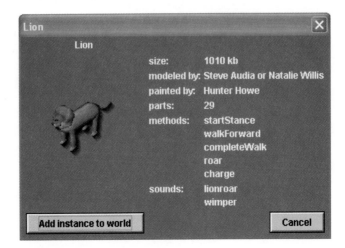

Figure 4-3-12. Class-level methods and sounds for the Lion class

3. Do not call world-level methods from within a class-level method. Figure 4-3-13 illustrates *cleverSkater.kaleidoscope*—a class-level method that calls a world-level method named *World.changeColors*. If the cleverSkater (with the *cleverSkater.kaleidoscope* method) is saved out as a new class and an instance of the CleverSkater class is then added to a later world where the *World.changeColors* method has not been defined, Alice will complain that the *World.changeColors* method cannot be found. Alice stops running your program and opens an Error dialog box with a description of the specific error in your program.

Figure 4-3-13. Bad example: calling a world-level method from a class-level method

4. Do not use instructions for other objects from within a class-level method. Class-level methods are clearly defined for a specific class. We expect to save out the object as a new class and reuse it in a later world. We cannot depend on other objects being present in other programs in other worlds. For example, a penguin (Animals) is added to the winter scene, as in Figure 4-3-14. We write a class-level method named *skateAround*, where the penguin object is

Figure 4-3-14. The skater will skate around the penguin

specifically named in two of the instructions (circled in Figure 4-3-15). If the cleverSkater with the *skateAround* method is saved out as a new class and then a cleverSkater object is added to a later world where no penguin exists, Alice will open an Error dialog box to tell you about a missing object. The error would be that the cleverSkater cannot skate around a penguin that does not exist in the world!

Note: Possible exceptions to guideline #4 are the world and camera objects, which are always present.

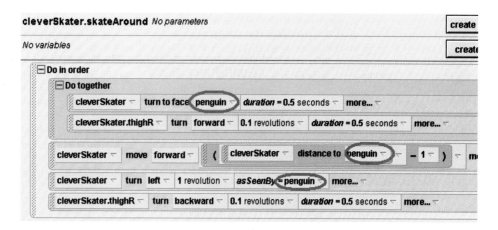

Figure 4-3-15. Bad example: instructions specifying another object in a class-level method

A class-level method with an object parameter

What if you would like to write a class-level method where another object is involved? The solution is to use an object parameter in the class-level method. Let's use the same example as above, where we want a cleverSkater to skate around another object. The *skateAround* method can be modified to use a parameter, arbitrarily named *whichObject*, as shown in Figure 4-3-16. The *whichObject* parameter is only a placeholder, not an actual object, so we do not have to worry about a particular object (like the penguin) having to be in another world. Alice will not

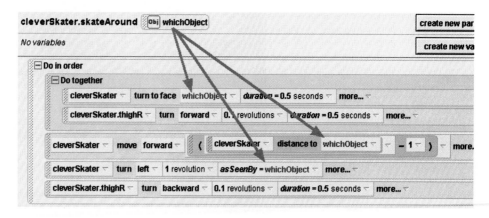

Figure 4-3-16. Using an object parameter in a class-level method

allow the *skateAround* method to be called without passing in an object to the *whichObject* parameter. So, we can be sure that some sort of object will be there to skate around.

Testing

Once you have created and saved out a new class, it should be tested in a new world. The initial scene was shown in Figure 4-3-14. A sample test program is presented in Figure 4-3-17. In this test, we have called the *skate, spin,* and *skateAround* methods to test each method.

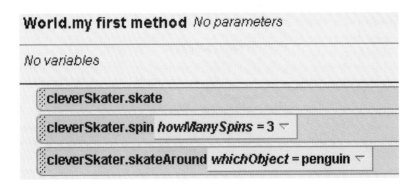

Figure 4-3-17. A sample program

Tips & Techniques 4
Visible and Invisible Objects

Properties of objects are sometimes used in games and simulations to achieve a special effect, such as making an object visible or invisible. In this section we look at techniques and examples of changing the visibility of objects.

The opacity property

The following example changes the opacity of a fish in an ocean world. (Opacity is how opaque something is: how hard it is to see through.) Figure T-4-1 shows an aquatic scene. This world is easily created by adding an oceanFloor (Ocean) and a lilfish (Ocean). (Optional items— seaweed and fireCoral were added from the OceanFloor folder in the CD or Web gallery.)

Figure T-4-1. An ocean floor scene with lilfish

The lilfish is swimming out to lunch, and her favorite seafood is seaweed. Instructions to point lilfish at the seaweed and then swim toward it are shown in Figure T-4-2. The *wiggletail* instruction is a method, shown in Figure T-4-2(b), that makes the fish wiggle its tail in a left-right motion.

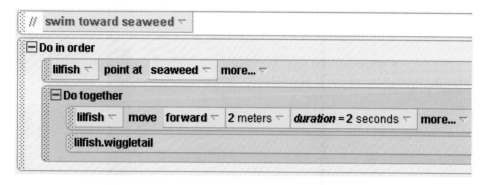

Figure T-4-2(a). Code to make lilfish swim toward the seaweed

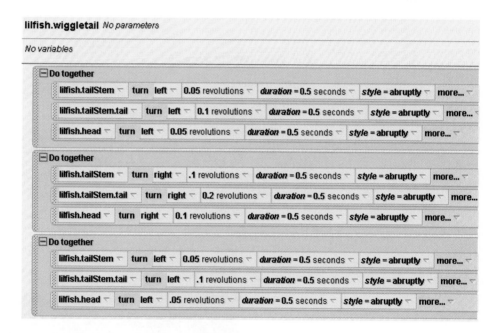

Figure T-4-2(b). The *wiggletail* method

As the fish moves toward the seaweed, she will also move away from the camera. So she should fade, because water blurs our vision of distant objects. We can make lilfish become less visible by changing the opacity property. As opacity is decreased, an object becomes less distinct (more difficult to see). To write an instruction to change the opacity, click on the lilfish's properties tab and drag the *opacity* tile into the editor. From the popup menu, select the *opacity* percentage, as shown in Figure T-4-3.

The resulting code is in Figure T-4-4.

When the world is run, lilfish will become less visible, as shown in Figure T-4-5. At 0% opacity, an object will totally disappear. This does not mean that the object has been deleted; it is still part of the world but is not visible on the screen.

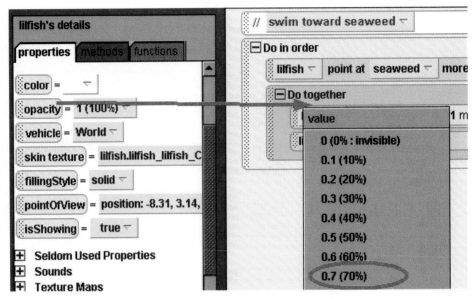

Figure T-4-3. Dragging the *opacity* tile into code editor

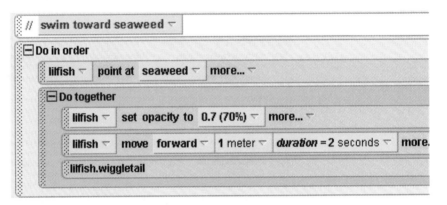

Figure T-4-4. Code now includes a *set opacity* instruction

Figure T-4-5. The lilfish becomes more difficult to see as *opacity* is decreased

The isShowing property

Each object has a property called *isShowing*. At the time an object is first added to a world, the object is made visible in the scene and *isShowing* is set to *true*. Changing the value of this property is especially useful in game like programs where you want to signal the end of a game. Figure T-4-6 illustrates the *isShowing* property as *true* for "You won!" Setting *isShowing* to *false* makes the "You won!" text invisible, as shown in Figure T-4-7. (For this world, we used the bottleThrow object from the Amusement Park folder in the CD or Web gallery.)

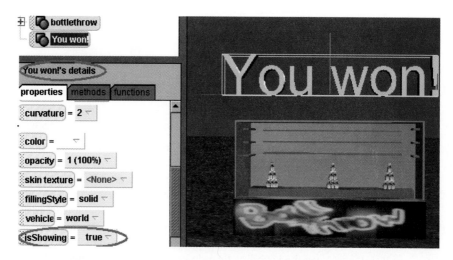

Figure T-4-6. The *isShowing* property is *true* and "You won!" is visible

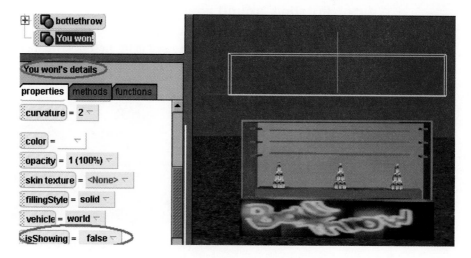

Figure T-4-7. The *isShowing* property is *false* and "You won!" is not visible

When its *isShowing* property is set to *false*, the object is not removed from the world; it is simply not displayed on the screen. The object can be made to "reappear" by setting its *isShowing* property back to *true*.

In this example, we want the text to appear when the player wins the game. To create an instruction that sets the *isShowing* property to *true*, drag the *isShowing* property tile into the world and select *true* from the popup menu. The result is shown in Figure T-4-8.

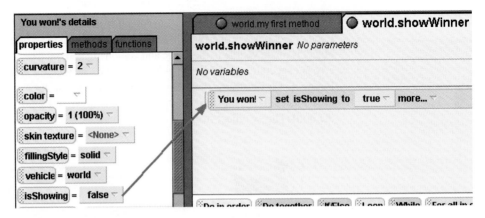

Figure T-4-8. An instruction to set *isShowing* to *true* at runtime

Relationship of *isShowing* and *opacity* properties

The *isShowing* and *opacity* properties track different (though related) states of an object. The *isShowing* property is strictly *true* or *false*—like a light switch that can be either on or off. *Opacity* is a sliding scale—like a dimmer switch that can adjust the brightness of a light. Though it is true that when *opacity* is 0%, the object is invisible, nonetheless when you make an object have an *opacity* of 0%, Alice does not automatically make *isShowing false*. Likewise, when you make *isShowing false*, Alice does not automatically make *opacity* 0%.

A good piece of advice is: "Be consistent." If you are using *isShowing* in your program to set the visibility, then do not use *opacity* to check whether the object is visible. Likewise, if you are using *opacity* to set the visibility, do not use *isShowing* to check whether the object is visible.

Rotating around an invisible object

An invisible object is a good way to set up a stationary reference point for actions by other objects. Consider the world illustrated in Figure T-4-9. We want the pterodactyl (Animals) to fly around the dragon (Medieval).

Figure T-4-9. A dragon and a pterodactyl

This is no problem. The pterodactyl will fly around the dragon if we use *asSeenBy = dragon* in a *turn right* instruction for the pterodactyl object. (The *asSeenBy* parameter was described in Tips & Techniques 2.)

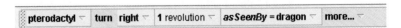

Suppose that we want the pterodactyl and the dragon to both fly around in a half-turn relative to each other (facing each other down—sort of a bluffing technique). This would mean that the dragon should end up at the pterodactyl's location (facing the pterodactyl's new location), and the pterodactyl should end up at the dragon's location (facing the dragon's new location). A first attempt might be as follows:

When this program is run, each animal ends up where it started, facing in the opposite direction! The problem is that once each animal has begun to move, its location changes, so that further moves relative to each other lead to unexpected results! What we need is an object that does not move, located somewhere between the dragon and the pterodactyl. Let's add a sphere object between the dragon and the pterodactyl and make it invisible by changing its *isShowing* property to *false*. Now we can write:

When this code is run, the dragon and pterodactyl exchange places, as seen in Figure T-4-10!

Figure T-4-10. The pterodactyl and dragon change places

Exercises and Projects

4-1 Exercises

Reminder: Be sure to add comments to your methods to document what each method does and what actions are carried out by sections of code within the method.

1. *Snowpeople Flip Hats*
   Write a new world-level method for the Snowpeople world (from Chapter 2, Exercise 3). The new method, named *flipHats*, will be called when the snowwoman turns her head to look at the snowman. In the *flipHats* method, the snowman uses his right arm to grab his hat and graciously tip his hat to the snowwoman and then returns his hat to his head. After the snowman flips his hat, the snowwoman flips her hat.

2. *Confused Kanga*

Scrounging for breakfast on the outback, Kanga (kangaroo from Animals) encounters a rather confusing sign (Roads and Signs folder). Kanga stares at the sign for a few seconds and tilts her head sideways to show that she is confused. Kanga then hops left and turns toward the sign and then hops right and turns toward the sign and then left and then right.

Create a simulation that implements this comical story. Write methods *hopLeft* (Kanga turns left a small amount and hops, and then turns to face the sign) and *hopRight* (Kanga turns right a small amount and hops, then turns to face the sign). With each hop, Kanga should make some progress toward the sign. In *World.my first method*, alternately call the *hopLeft* and *hopRight* methods (twice) to make Kanga take a zigzag path toward the sign.

3. *Gallop and Jump*

Kelly (People) has entered an equestrian show as an amateur jumper. She is somewhat nervous about the competition so she and the horse (Animals) are practicing a jump. Create an initial scene with a horse and rider facing a fence (Buildings), as shown below.

Write two world-level methods, one named *gallop* (horse and rider gallop forward one step) and another named *jump* (horse and rider jump the fence). In the gallop method, the horse's front legs should lift and then go down as the back legs lift and the horse moves forward. Then the back legs should go back down. The jump method should be similar, but the horse should move up far enough to clear the fence in mid-stride. Test each method to be sure it works as expected. You will need to adjust the distance amounts to make each look somewhat realistic.

Hint: If you make the horse a *vehicle* for Kelly (Tips & Techniques 2), you will only need to write an instruction to move the horse and Kelly will go along for the ride. When you think the gallop and jump methods are both working properly, write instructions in *World.my first method* that call the *gallop* method as many times as needed to move the horse and rider up close to the fence; then call the *jump* method. Use trial-and-error to find out how many times the *gallop* method must be called to make the animation work well.

4. *Helicopter Flight*
   Create a world with a helicopter (Vehicles on CD or Web gallery), airport (Buildings), and a control tower (Buildings). Create a *circleTower* method that makes the helicopter fly toward the control tower and then around it. In *my first method*, call the *circleTower* method twice and then make the helicopter land on the airport landing strip.

4-2 Exercises

5. *Beetle Band Duet*
   In Section 4-2, the Beetle Band example has a method named *solo*, where each member of the band jumps and plays a musical instrument. Recreate the Beetle Band example and write a method named *duet*, where the solo method is called to have two members of the band jump together and play their musical instruments. This exercise can be done with sound (as in Figure 4-2-15) or with lyrics (as in Figure 4-2-17). Parameters must be used to send in the name of the band member and the music to be played or the lyric to be said.

6. *Frog Escape*
   At the local lily pond (Environments on CD or Web gallery), the frogs (Animals) enjoy climbing out of the water now and then to warm up in the sun. Of course, they get a bit jumpy when a predator is sighted. On this fine day, a hungry snake (Animals) wanders into the scene. Create a world scene similar to the one below and animate the frogs jumping into the pond when the snake approaches. Write a method that turns the snake toward the frog and slides the snake forward. Then, have the frog turn to the pond and jump in. Your method should use a parameter to specify which frog is escaping.

7. *Magic Act*

A magician is performing a levitation illusion, in which objects seem to rise magically into the air. The magician (People) points a magic wand (Objects) at his assistant (Girl from People folder), and she gently rises into the air and then floats back down to her original position on the table (Furniture on CD or Web gallery). Then the magician performs the same trick with the rabbit (Animals). The rabbit, being a lighter object, floats up higher than the magician's assistant. Because the magician's assistant and rabbit are each to levitate in the same way, use a single method and use parameters to communicate which object is to float and the distance the object is to move upward (and back down).

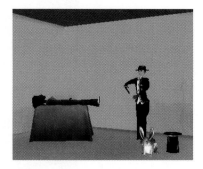

Hint: The magician's assistant is reclining on the surface of the table. A *move up* instruction will cause the assistant to move upward from her point of view, as shown below. Use the *asSeenBy* argument to make the magician's assistant move upward as seen by the ground.

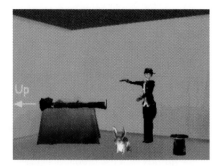

8. *Dragons*

Legend has it that dragons are distant relatives of chickens. We are not surprised, then, that a favorite pastime of dragons was a game of "chicken." The scene below shows a world with four dragons (Medieval) carefully placed in a diamond like pattern (similar to baseball players at the four bases). Create a simulation of a game of chicken where any two dragons face each other and fly upward to a slightly different height above the ground. Then the dragons fly toward each other, nearly missing one another. Each dragon should land in the position where the other dragon was located. That is, the two dragons trade places. Your simulation should use a method named *dragonFlight* that has four parameters—the two dragons that will face off in a game of chicken and the height for each dragon's flight.

4-3 Exercises

9. *Enhanced cleverSkater*
   Create an even better cleverSkater than the one presented in Section 4-3. In addition to the *skateForward, spin* and *skateAround* methods, create *skateBackward* and *jump* class-level methods. In *skateBackward*, the skater should perform similar actions to those in the *skateForward* method, but slide backward instead of forward. In a *jump* method, the skater should move forward, lift one leg, then move upward (in the air) and back down to land gracefully on the ice and lower her leg back to its starting position. Save out your enhanced skater as EnhancedCleverSkater.
   Test your newly defined class by starting a new world with a frozen lake. Add an enhancedCleverSkater to the world. Also, add a penguin and a duck.

   (a) Call each of the methods you have written.
   (b) Then call the *skateAround* method—to make the skater skate around the penguin and then the duck. (This will require two calls to the *skateAround* method.)

10. *Lock Combination*
    Create a world with a comboLock (Objects folder). Create four class-level methods—*leftOne, rightOne, leftRevolution,* and *rightRevolution*— that turn the dial 1 number left, 1 number right, 1 revolution left, and 1 revolution right, respectively. Then, create a class-level method named *open* that opens and another named *close* that closes the lock.

    Hints: One position on the dial is actually 1/40 of a revolution. Use the *endGently* style to make the motion more realistic.) Rename comboLock as TurningComboLock and save it as a new class.

11. *Funky Chicken Dance*

    Starting with a basic chicken, create a class-level method *walk* that will have the chicken perform a realistic stepping motion consisting of a left step followed by a right step. Create a second method to make the chicken perform a *funkyChicken* dance, where the chicken walks and twists its body in all different directions! Save the chicken as a new class named CoolChicken. Create a new world and add a coolChicken to the world. In *my first method*, call the *walk* and *funkyChicken* methods. Play a sound file or use a *say* instruction to accompany the funky chicken dance animation.

12. *Ninja Practice*

    Create a world with an evilNinja (People) and write class methods for traditional Ninja moves. For example, you can write *rightJab* and *leftJab* (where the Ninja jabs his hand upward with the appropriate hand), *kickLeft* and *kickRight* (where he kicks with the appropriate leg), and *leftSpin* and *rightSpin* (where he does a spin in the appropriate direction). Each method must contain more than one instruction. For example, in the *kickLeft* method, the left lower leg should turn and the foot twist at the same time as the entire leg kicks out to the left. Save the Ninja as a new class named TrainedNinja. Start a new world and add two trainedNinja objects. Create an animation where the two trainedNinja objects practice their moves, facing one another.

Projects

We are using the term project to describe advanced exercises that are more challenging than regular exercises. The projects in this chapter involve motion of human body parts. Professional animators spend many hours mastering the art of making these movements look realistic. Our focus is on mastering the art (and science) of writing methods in a program.

1. *Dance*

   Technical Note: To assist you in learning how to animate human body parts, this first project includes some explanations and coding suggestions. The goal of this animation is to have the couple perform a dance step in a traditional box (square) figure as used in the waltz and other dances. Create a scene with a sheriff (Old West) and a woman (People) inside a saloon (Old West), as illustrated below.

In the first step of a box figure, the sheriff takes a step forward, leading with his left leg and (at the same time) the woman takes a step backwards, leading with her right leg. This is not as simple as it sounds. One way to make an object with legs appear to take a "step" is to have the object raise one leg some small amount and then move forward as the leg moves back down. Then, the other leg performs a similar action. Thus, to make two objects appear to dance together requires coordinated leg lift, move and drop actions for both objects. The easiest way to do this is to write a method, perhaps named *forwardStep*. The *forwardStep* method will need two parameters: *howFar* (the distance forward), and *howLongToTake* (the time it takes). A possible storyboard is:

```
forwardStep

Parameters: howFar, howLongToTake
Do in order
        Do together
            sheriff's left leg moves up
            woman's right leg moves up
        Do together
            sheriff moves forward howFar
            sheriff's left leg moves down
            woman moves backward howFar
            woman's right leg moves down
```

To help you get started, an example of the code for the *forwardStep* method is shown below. The distances used in this code worked well for us in our example. You may need to experiment with the amount to move the legs up (and down), and with the size of step forward, backward, and sideways the couple is to take. The distances depend on the size of the models in your world.

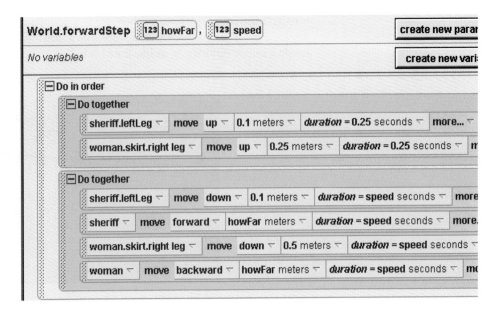

Other methods you will need are:

(a) *rightStep,* where the man and woman take a step sideways (his right, her left)
(b) *backStep,* where the man takes a step backward, leading with his left leg, and the woman takes a step forward, leading with her right leg
(c) *leftStep,* where the couple takes a step sideways (his left, her right)
(d) *spin,* which has the man spin the woman around

If *forwardStep, rightStep, backStep*, and *leftStep* are properly performed in sequence, the couple should move in a squarelike pattern on the dance floor. Create a method to call all the methods in order so the couple performs a box figure followed by a spin for a dance. Then, create a second method to animate a different dance figure—calling the dance steps in a different order.

2. *Hand Ball*
Create a world with a right hand (People) holding a toy ball (Sports). Have the fingers close to grasp the ball. Then, throw the ball into the air while opening the fingers of the hand. Finally, make the hand catch the ball as the hand re-closes its fingers.

Hint: Tips & Techniques 2 tells how to use the *vehicle* property to make the ball move as the hand moves.

3. *Ra Row Your Boat*
Create a world with a boat, a person sitting in the boat, an island, and a pier located 25 meters from the island. In the world shown below, Ra (Egypt) is sitting in a rowboat

(Vehicles). Create a method to make the Ra object row the boat 25 meters from the island to a pier (Beach). One suggested way to do this would be to create the methods: *rowLeft* and *rowRight* (to control the arms' motions), *controlTorsoAndHead* (to control back and head motions), and *startRow* and *stopRow* (to put Ra's body in and out of the rowing position).

4. *Cleanup Robot*
   The scene below shows a child's room with toys scattered around on the floor. The gorilla robot (SciFi) can be programmed pick up things in the room and put them behind the door in the closetRoom (Environments on CD or Web gallery). In the initial scene for this animation, the robot is standing in the middle of the room near several objects scattered around the floor (for example, a barbell, a pinata, and a teddy bear from the Objects folder).

   Write a program to teach the robot to pick up one object at a time and put it in the closet. Write three methods, named *pickup*, *putdown*, and *putInCloset*. The methods should have one parameter identifying the object to be picked up or put down. The *pickUp* method should make the robot pick up an object in its hand. The *putDown* method should have the robot put the object down. The *putInCloset* method should make the robot turn one-half revolution and move to the door. The door opens and the robot puts down the object. When these methods have been written, then write instructions in *my First Method* to make the robot pick up an object and put it down in the closet.

5. *Skater Competition*
   Add five enhancedCleverSkater objects to a world with a lake (Environments) scene. See Exercise 9 for a description of the EnhancedCleverSkater. Also, add three people to act as judges of a skating competition. Write a method for each skater that has her perform a skating routine (each skater should perform some combination of *skate, spin, jump* and other methods). Each skater (one at a time) will perform her skating routine; then have the three judges say a score. Scores range from 1 to 9. Then the skater that has just performed will move out of the way and the next skater will perform.

6. *Walking and Jogging Hare*

Add an instance of the Hare (Animals) to a new world. Write a class-level method to make the hare *walk* forward and a second method to make the hare *jog*. (A jog is similar to a walk, but the hare moves faster and the entire body moves up and down with each step.) Save the enhanced hare as a new class named AthleticHare.

Now, start a new world with a grassy scene. Add an instance of the AthleticHare to the world. Add a goalpost (Sports) and highway objects to the scene to create a track around the goalpost. Write a world-level method that calls the *walk* method three times (to get the hare started down the track); then call the *jog* method and turn the hare to have him jog around the goalpost.

7. *Your Own Creation (Open-ended)*

Choose an animal or a person from one of the galleries. The object selected must have at least two legs, arms, and/or wings that can move, turn, and roll. Write three class-level methods that substantially add functionality to what the objects of the class know how to do. Use Save Object to create a new class with a different name. Add an instance of your new class to a new world. Then write an animation program to demonstrate the new methods.

Summary

In this chapter we looked at how to write our own methods and how to use parameters to send information to a method when it is called. An advantage of using methods is that the programmer can think about a collection of instructions as all one action—abstraction. Also, methods make it easier to debug our code.

Two different kinds of methods can be written: world-level methods that involve two or more objects interacting in some way, and class-level methods that define a complex action carried out by a single object acting alone.

Parameters are used to communicate values from one method to another. In a method, a parameter acts as a placeholder for a value of a particular type. The values sent in to a method are known as arguments. When an argument is sent in to a method, the parameter represents that argument in the instructions in the method. Examples presented in this chapter included object, sound, string, and number parameters. Parameters allow you to write one method but use it several times with different objects, sounds, numbers, and other types of values.

In a way, class-level methods can be thought of as extending an object's behavior. Once new class-level methods are defined, a new class can be saved out. The new class has a different name and has all the new methods (and also the old methods) as available actions. It inherits the properties and actions of the original class but defines more things than the original class. A major benefit is that you can use objects of the new class over and over again in new worlds. This allows you to take advantage of the methods you have written without having to write them again.

Some guidelines were provided for writing class-level methods: only sounds imported for the class should be played in a class-level method; world-level methods should not be called; and instructions involving other objects should not be used. Following these guidelines will ensure that objects of your newly defined classes can safely be used in other worlds.

Stepwise refinement is a design technique where a complex task is broken down into small pieces and then each piece is broken down further—until the entire task is completely defined by simple actions. The simple actions all work together to carry out the complex task.

Important concepts in this chapter

- To run (or execute) a method, the method must be called.
- Parameters are used for communication with a method.
- In a call to a method, a value sent in to a method parameter is an argument.
- A parameter must be declared to represent a value of a particular type. Types of values for parameters include object, Boolean ("true" or "false"), number, sound, color, string, and others.
- A new class can be created by defining class-level methods and then saving out the class with a new name.
- Inheritance is an object-oriented concept where a new class is defined based on an existing class.
- Class-level methods can be written that accept object parameters. This allows you to write a class-level method and pass in another object. Then, the object performing the class-level method can interact with the parameterized object.

Chapter 5

Interaction: Events and Event Handling

Alice laughed, "There's no use trying," she said, "one can't believe impossible things." "I daresay you haven't had much practice," said the Queen. "When I was your age, I always did it for half-an-hour a day. Why, sometimes I've believed as many as six impossible things before breakfast."

The real world around us is interactive. A conversation, as between Alice and the Queen above, is a "give and take" form of interaction. As we interact with objects in our world, we often give directions to them. For example, we change the channel on a television set by sending a signal from a remote control. We press a button on a game controller to make a character in a video game jump out of the way of danger.

We have concentrated on writing programs that were not interactive—we watched the objects perform actions in a movie-style animation. It's time we looked at how to create interactive programs in Alice—where the objects in the scenes respond to mouse clicks and key presses. In this chapter we will see how programs can be made interactive.

Much of computer programming (and the movie-style animations seen earlier) is computer-centric. That is, the computer program basically runs as the programmer has intended it. The programmer sets the order of actions and controls the program flow. However, many computer programs today are user-centric. In other words, it is the computer user (rather than the programmer) who determines the order of actions. The user clicks the mouse or presses a key on the keyboard to send a signal to Alice about what to do next. The mouse click or key press is an event. An event is something that happens. In response to an event, an action (or a sequence of many actions) is carried out. We say the event triggers a response.

Section 5-1 focuses on the mechanics of how the user creates an event and how the program responds to the event. Naturally, all of this takes a bit of planning and arrangement. We need to tell Alice to listen for a particular kind of event and then what to do when the event happens. This means we need to write methods that describe the actions objects should take in response to an event.

Section 5-2 describes how to pass parameters to event handling methods. In some programming languages, arranging events and writing event handling methods is a rather complex kind of programming. We hope you will find that learning to use events and event handling methods is easy in Alice.

5-1 Interactive programming

Control of flow

Writing an interactive program has one major difference from writing a non-interactive one (like the movies we wrote in the previous chapter). The difference is in how the sequence of actions is controlled. In a non-interactive program, the sequence of actions is pre-determined by the programmer. The programmer designs a complete storyboard and then writes the program code for the animated actions. Once the program is constructed and tested, then every time the program runs, the same sequence of actions will occur. In an interactive program the sequence of actions is determined at runtime, when:

- The user clicks the mouse or presses a key on the keyboard.
- Objects in the scene move (randomly or guided by the user) to create some condition, such as a collision.

Events

Each time the user clicks the mouse or presses a key, an event is generated that triggers a response. Objects in the scene may move to positions that trigger a response. Each time the program runs, different user interactions or different object actions may occur and the overall animation sequence may be different from some previous execution of the program. For example, in a video game that simulates a car race, where the player is "driving" a race car, the sequence of scenes is determined by whether the player is skillful in steering the car to stay on the road through twists, turns, and hazards that suddenly appear in the scene.

Event handling methods

How do events affect what you do as an animation programmer? You must think about all possible events and make plans for what should happen—responses to the events. Animation methods are then written to carry out responses. Finally, the event must be linked to the responding method. The method is now said to be an event handling method.

When an event occurs and an event handling method is called, the location of objects in the scene may or may not be the same as the last time. This is because the user's actions may change the scene and the location of objects between calls to the event handling method.

Keyboard-control example

We begin with an acrobatic air-show flight simulator. The initial scene, as illustrated in Figure 5-1-1, consists of the biplane (Vehicles) in midair and some objects on the ground (house, barn, and so forth from the Buildings and Farm folders). A guidance system will allow

Figure 5-1-1. Initial scene

the user to be the pilot. The biplane has controls that allow the pilot to maneuver the plane forward, left, and right. We want to program the biplane to perform a popular show stunt—a barrel turn. In the exercises at the end of this Chapter, other stunts can be added.

Input

The whole idea of a flight simulator is to allow the user to interact with the biplane. The user provides input that sends a signal to animate a particular motion, perhaps by pressing a set of keys on the keyboard. For example, arrow keys can be used, each corresponding to a given direction of movement. Of course, input can also be obtained from mouse clicks, the movement of a trackball, or the use of a game stick controller. In this text, we will rely on the keyboard and mouse to provide user input for interaction with the animations.

In our flight simulator, the arrow keys and spacebar will be used to provide input from the user. If the user presses the up arrow key, the biplane will move forward. If the user presses the left or right arrow keys, the biplane will turn left or right. For the acrobatic barrel turn, we will use the spacebar. The selection of these keys is arbitrary—other keys could easily be used.

Design—storyboards

We are ready to design the flight simulator program—the set of instructions that tell Alice how to perform the animations. Each time the user presses an arrow key or the spacebar, an event is generated. The animation program consists of methods to respond to these events. To simplify the discussion, let's concentrate on two possible events: the spacebar press for the barrel turn and the up arrow key to move the biplane forward. Two storyboards are needed, as shown below. Note that sound is optional and can be omitted.

```
Event: Spacebar press

Response:
  Do together
    roll biplane a full revolution
    play biplane engine sound
```

```
Event: Up arrow key press

Response:
  Do together
    move biplane forward
    play biplane engine sound
```

Methods to respond to the events

The only object affected by key-press events is the biplane, so the methods can be class-level methods for the biplane. Two methods will be written, *flyForward* and *barrel*. The *flyForward* method will handle an up arrow key-press event by moving the biplane forward as illustrated in Figure 5-1-2. The barrel method will handle a spacebar-press event by rolling the biplane

Figure 5-1-2. The *flyForward* method

one complete revolution, illustrated in Figure 5-1-3. In the methods shown here, a sound is played simultaneously with the movement. The duration of the biplane movement is set to be approximately the same as the length of the sound (in seconds). As noted previously, sound is a nice feature but can be omitted. If sound is used, the sound should be imported for the biplane. (Importing a sound file was introduced in Chapter 4, Section 2.)

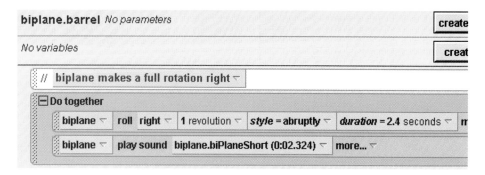

Figure 5-1-3. The *barrel* method

Link events to methods

Each method must be linked to the event that will be used to trigger the method as a response. The Events editor is where links are created. The Events editor is shown in Figure 5-1-4. As you know, Alice creates a link between *When the world starts* (an event) and *World.my first method*, as shown in Figure 5-1-4.

Figure 5-1-4. Event editor

In the flight simulator, two events (the up arrow key press and the spacebar key press) need to be linked to their corresponding method (*flyForward* and *barrel*). First, create an event by clicking the **create new event** button and then selecting the event from the popup menu. In Figure 5-1-5, the *When a key is typed* event is selected.

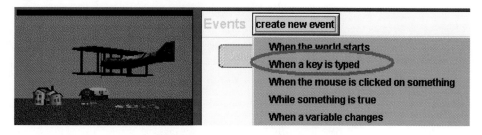

Figure 5-1-5. Creating a key-press event

In Figure 5-1-6, an event for *any key* pressed has been added to the Events editor. The "*any key*" and "*Nothing*" tiles are placeholders that need to be replaced. To tell Alice that we want to use the up arrow key, clicking on the *any key* tile and select *Up* from the popup menu.

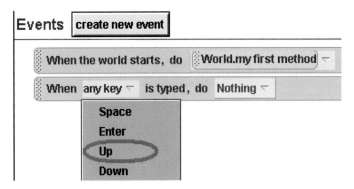

Figure 5-1-6. Specifying the up arrow key

Now that Alice has been notified that an up arrow key event may occur, we need to tell Alice what to do when the event happens. As shown in Figure 5-1-7, click on the *Nothing* tile and then select *biplane* and *flyForward* from the popup menu.

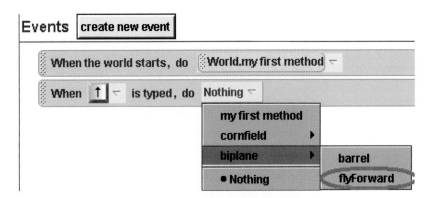

Figure 5-1-7. Link event-handling method to an event

The process is repeated to link the spacebar to the barrel method. Figure 5-1-8 shows the Events editor with both links completed.

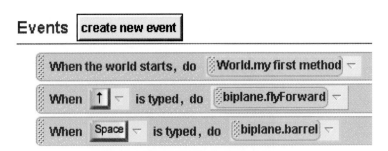

Figure 5-1-8. Links completed

Testing

Now the world should be tested. To test the flight simulator, just save the world and press the **Play** button. Nothing happens until the up arrow is pressed, which causes the biplane to call its *flyForward* method.

Events and methods could be created for the left and right arrow keys, and other acrobatic stunts could be written. (See exercise 1.) However, it is important to test event handling methods as they are developed. Write a method and test it, write a method and test it, until the program is completed. This is a recommended program development strategy called incremental development. Its advantage is in making it easier to debug your program. When something isn't working, it can be fixed before it causes problems elsewhere.

Note: An interactive world such as a flight simulator requires that the user know what keys to press to make the simulation work properly. A startup method could be written in *World.my first method* to display 3D text or a billboard for a quick explanation of the guidance system. After a few seconds, the 3D text (or billboard) can be made to disappear (by setting its *isShowing* property to *false*), and then the simulation can begin. 3D text and billboards were described in Tips & Techniques 2.

Events are world-level

In this example, the events were associated with the world. In Alice, we say that all events are world-level. Think about it this way: at all times, the Alice world is "listening" for an event to happen. When it happens, a method is called to respond to the event. With each new world, you can add events (as needed) in that world.

5-2 Parameters and event handling methods

As you have seen in Chapter 4, parameters are powerful tools. They allow us to customize methods to work with different objects and different numeric values. They are useful in building either world-level or class-level methods. In this section we will look at how to use parameters with events and event handling methods in interactive programs.

Once again, examples will provide a context for presenting the concepts of interactive programming. The first example illustrates how to use parameters in event handling methods. The second example illustrates how to allow the user to click on an object and then pass that object to an event handling method. Mouse-click selection is an important technique used in game programs and simulations.

A simple example

A firetruck (Vehicles) has been called to an emergency in a burning building (Buildings). A person and a fire object has been placed on each floor. The truck will need to extend its ladder so that each person can climb down to safety. The initial scene is illustrated in Figure 5-2-1.

Figure 5-2-1. Burning-building initial scene

Design—storyboard

To design an interactive program storyboard, we must give some thought to what events will occur and what event handling methods are needed. Let's allow the user to select the person to which the ladder should be extended. A textual storyboard is shown below.

```
Event: Click on guy1

Responding Method:
  Save guy on the first floor
```

```
Event: Click on girl2

Responding Method:
  Save girl on the second floor
```

```
Event: Click on girl3

Responding Method:
  Save girl on the third floor
```

Three events, one event handling method

Three events are possible, and three event handling methods could be written (one to respond to each event). Notice, however, that all three responses in the storyboards are exactly the same—save the person by extending the ladder and having the person slide down the ladder. Writing three event handling methods is unnecessary. A better solution is to write just one and send in the information needed to perform the action.

To simulate a rescue, the ladder must be aimed toward the floor and then extended to the window where the person is located. Then the person can slide down the ladder to the firetruck. Finally, the ladder should retract to prepare for saving another person. We will write one event handling method, named *savePerson*. A decision we have to make is whether to write the *savePerson* method as a world-level or as a class-level method. It makes sense to construct a class-level method for the firetruck because it is the object performing all the actions. On the other hand, other objects (guy1, girl2, and girl3) are the targets of the actions. We decided to create the *savePerson* method as a class-level method for the firetruck, passing in a target object to a parameter, named *whichPerson*. (This technique was previously described in Chapter 4, Section 3.) Using a class-level method will allow us to save out the firetruck with its *savePerson* method for reuse in other worlds.

In addition to the *whichPerson* parameter, two other parameters are needed: which floor the person is on (so the ladder can be made to point toward the right floor) and how far the ladder will need to be extended. The *whichFloor* and *whichPerson* parameters are of type *Object*. The third parameter, *howFar*, is a distance (for extending the ladder) and will be a *Number*. A possible storyboard for the *savePerson* method is:

```
savePerson

parameters: whichFloor, whichPerson, howFar
Do in order
  point ladder at whichFloor
  extend the ladder howFar meters
  whichPerson slides down the ladder to the firetruck
  pull the ladder back howFar meters
```

The code is presented in Figure 5-2-2. The swivel at the base of the ladder is pointed at *whichFloor* (the floor where the person is located). Then the ladder is extended *(smallLadder move forward) howFar* meters to reach the floor. The person slides down the ladder *(whichPerson move to)* to the firetruck. The ladder retracts backward the same distance *(howFar)* it was previously extended.

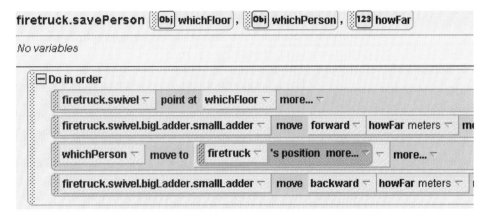

Figure 5-2-2. The code for the *savePerson* method

Link events to event handling method

Three events are possible, so three events are created in the Events editor, one for each person that can be selected by a mouse click, as shown in Figure 5-2-3. For each event, the same event handling method is called *(firetruck.savePerson)*. The arguments sent to the parameters depend on which person was selected. For example, if randomGirl3 was clicked (on the third floor), *whichFloor* is sent *burningBuilding.thirdFloor*, *whichPerson* is sent randomGirl3, and *howFar* is sent 3 meters (the distance of the ladder from the third floor). (In setting up our world, we positioned the burning building and the firetruck so the distance of the ladder from the third floor is 3 meters, the second floor is 2 meters, and the first floor is 1 meter.)

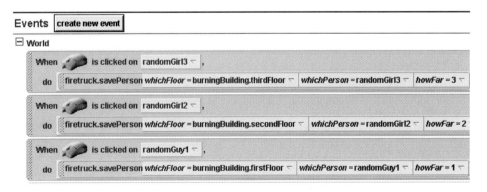

Figure 5-2-3. Three events: one for each object that can be clicked

Testing

When parameters are used in event-driven programming, it is especially important to run the animation several times, each time creating different events to be sure that each possible parameter value works as expected. A well-known guideline for testing numeric parameters is to try a small value, a large value, and perhaps even a negative value—just to be sure the program works with a range of parameter values. In this example no negative value is used, but we could put one in just to see what would happen. We recommend you try out these tests as you are reading this section, if you have a computer nearby.

A more complex example

In an event-driven program, the response to an event may involve multiple actions. Writing an event handling method to carry out the response can become a bit messy. One way to deal with a complex response is to use stepwise refinement to break down the event handling method into smaller pieces. We will use an example to illustrate how to use stepwise refinement to manage a multi-action response to an event.

This animation is a simulation of an ancient Greek tragedy. (The ancient Greeks were fond of tragic dramas.) In Greek mythology, Zeus was an all-powerful god. If Zeus was angered, a thunderbolt would be shot out of the heavens and strike anyone who got in the way. The initial scene is constructed with Zeus (People) overlooking a temple scene (Environments) from his position on a cloud, a thunderbolt object, and some Greek philosophers named Euripides, Plato, Socrates, and Homer. The initial temple scene is illustrated in Figure 5-2-4. The thunderbolt object has been hidden within a cloud (the one immediately in front of Zeus). Also, a smoke object (a special effect) has been positioned 5 meters below the ground. (The smoke is not visible in the initial scene.)

Figure 5-2-4. A Greek tragedy initial scene

Design—storyboard

To make this animation interactive, we will let the user choose the object that will be the next victim of Zeus's anger. When the user clicks on an object, the object will be passed to the event handling method. What actions need to occur in response to the mouse-click event? First, Zeus will turn to face the selected object and the thunderbolt will be made visible. Then, the thunderbolt will flash down to strike the object. Smoke will be used as a special effect to make the object appear to meet a sad fate. Then, the lightning bolt must be repositioned to prepare for another lightning strike. (In interactive worlds, the user can click on more than one object.)

Clearly, the event handling method will involve many different actions. To organize an event handling method (named *shootBolt*), let's begin with a storyboard that summarizes the overall actions. A parameter (arbitrarily named *who*) is needed to send in the object that was clicked.

```
Event: An object is mouse-clicked

Event handler: shootBolt

Parameter: who–the object that was clicked

Do in order
    prepare to strike the object that was clicked
    thunder plays and lightning strikes the object that was clicked
    lightning is repositioned for the next strike
```

In this storyboard, the first two steps in the *Do in order* block are actually composed of many actions. If we were to translate these into code in a single method, it would be many, many lines of code. A long method (consisting of many lines of code) is often difficult to read and debug. Let's use stepwise refinement to break the design down into smaller pieces. We could write a method, *prepareToShoot,* for the first step and a second method, *lightningAndThunder,* for the second step. In the third step, repositioning the lightning bolt for another strike can be performed as a single *move to* instruction. The revised storyboard would look like this:

```
Event: An object is mouse-clicked

Event handler: shootBolt

Parameter: who–the object that was clicked

Do in order
    call prepareToShoot method–send who as the target
    call lightningAndThunder method–send who as the target
    lightning move to cloud's position
```

Now the *shootBolt* method will be easy to write because all it does is call two other methods and then reposition the lightning bolt behind the cloud. A method that does very little other than organizing the calls to other methods is known as a driver. The driver organizes and calls the methods. The called methods do almost all the work. An important role played by the *shootBolt* method is to pass along (to the called methods) the object that was clicked (*who*). Each of the called methods will use the object that was clicked as the target of its own actions.

For now, let's assume that the *prepareToShoot* and *lightningAndThunder* methods have been written (we will write them later). Then, we can write the *shootBolt* method, as in Figure 5-2-5.

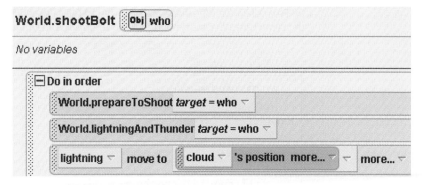

Figure 5-2-5. The *shootBolt* event handling method calls other methods

Now that you have the overall idea of how an event handling method can act as a driver to call other methods, let's write the methods that are called. First, the *prepareToShoot* method prepares Zeus and the lightning bolt for shooting at the object that was clicked. A simple storyboard is:

---

prepareToShoot

Parameter: *target*
Do together
   turn Zeus to face the target
   make the lightning bolt visible

A *turn to face* instruction will make Zeus look at the target. In setting up the world, the lightning bolt was made invisible by setting its opacity to 0 (0%). To make the lightning bolt visible (so we can see it flash across the scene), we write an instruction to set its opacity to 1 (100%). The code for the *prepareToShoot* method is shown in Figure 5-2-6.

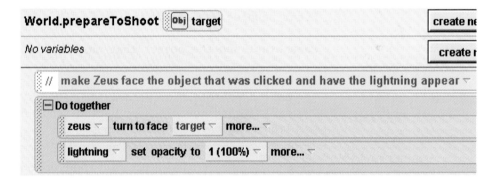

Figure 5-2-6. The *prepareToShoot* method

In the second method, *lightningAndThunder,* a sound (thunder) plays at the same time as lightning strikes the targeted philosopher. Of course, the lightning strike should have some special effects (smoke, color change, philosopher jumps). The special effects involve many actions. Once again, we will use stepwise refinement to break our code down into smaller pieces. A *Do together* block will be used to play the sound and call a *specialEffects* method at the same time. The storyboard for the *lightningAndThunder* method is:

---

lightningAndThunder

Parameter: *target*

Do together
   play sound
   call *specialEffects* method–send *target* as the victim

Now that we have a design, the next step is to translate it into program code. Let's pretend that the *specialEffects* method is already written. Then, the *lightningAndThunder* method could be written, as shown in Figure 5-2-7. Playing a sound at the same time as other actions requires that the amount of time the sound plays must be synchronized with the amount of time needed for the special effects. In this program, we found it worked best if we inserted a *Wait* instruction with the *play sound* instruction (in a *Do in order*) to create a short delay. The call to the *specialEffects* method passes along *target* as the victim of the lightning strike.

World.lightningAndThunder `Obj` **target**

No variables

```
// play a sound of thunder at the same time as special effects ▽

Do together
    Do in order
        Wait  0.5 seconds ▽

        World ▽  play sound  World.thunder (0:03.345) ▽  more... ▽

    World.specialEffects victim = target ▽
```

Figure 5-2-7. Code for the *lightningAndThunder* method

Finally, it is time to write the *specialEffects* method. First the lightning should strike, and then smoke should appear around the targeted object (*victim*). The victim should show the effects of a lightning strike—change color and jump up and down. A storyboard for *special Effects* is:

```
specialEffects

Parameter: victim

Do in order
  Do together
      lightning bolt move to victim
      smoke move to victim
  Do together
      set smoke to visible
      set lightning to invisible
      call smoke cycle–built-in method
      set victim's color to black
      move target up and down
  Do together
      set smoke's opacity to 1
      smoke move down 5 meters
```

Using an object parameter with *move to*

We are now ready to translate the storyboard for *specialEffects* into program code. The only troublesome instructions are "lightning bolt move to victim" and "smoke move to victim." A *move to* instruction needs to know a position (location in the world) to which an object will be moved. This is no problem when *move to* is targeted at the position of another object and that object is listed in the Object tree (and thereby in the popup menu for the *move to* instruction). For example, moving the lightning from the *cloud* to *homer* is easy to do. Just drag the *lightning move to* tile into the editor and select *homer's* position as the targeted victim from the popup menu, as in Figure 5-2-8.

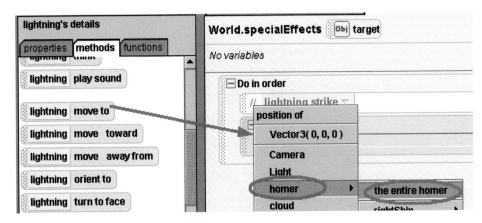

Figure 5-2-8. Selecting homer's position for a *move to* instruction

What about a selected parameter's position in the popup menu for a *move to* instruction? The parameter (*victim*) does not appear in the popup menu of available positions. This is because *victim* is just a placeholder (is not a real object) and does not appear in the Object tree in the world. It is not reasonable to expect that Alice would put a non-existing object in a menu of available positions for the *move to* instruction.

Not to worry—a two-step process can be used to put the *victim* parameter in a *move to* instruction:

1. From the popup menu of available positions, select a position (we chose homer arbitrarily, but any object is okay to select). The result should look something like this:

2. Drag the *victim* parameter tile into the editor and drop it onto the position tile. The result is:

An instruction to move the smoke to the position of the victim is created in a similar manner. We realize that this is a bit of a subterfuge technique. It is, though, a reasonable way to handle the fact that an object parameter (in this example, *victim*) is a nonexistent object and cannot appear in the popup menu as a targeted victim for the *move to* instruction.

After the lightning strikes, we need to make the lightning bolt invisible and the smoke visible. This is accomplished using *set opacity* instructions. Figure 5-2-9 shows the complete implementation of the *specialEffects* method.

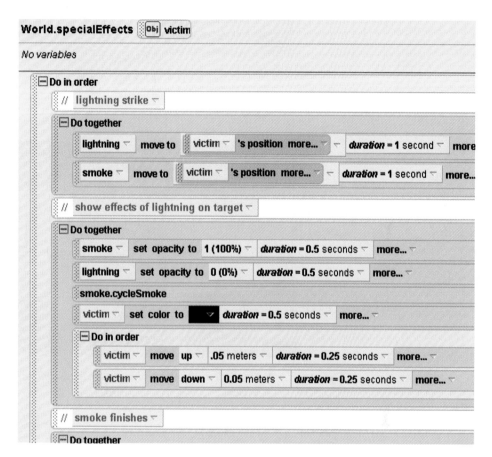

Figure 5-2-9. The *specialEffects* method

In the *specialEffects* method, we took advantage of a built-in method for smoke (*cycleSmoke*) to create a smoke animation. To animate the effects of the lightning strike, the target color is set to black and made to move up and down.

Link the event to the event handling method

All that is left to do is link the mouse-click event to the *shootBolt* event handling method. In the Events editor, select *when the mouse is clicked on something*. Then drag the *shootBolt* method tile into the link. Of course, *shootBolt* expects to be passed an argument to identify the object that was clicked. Select *expressions* and then *object under mouse cursor*, as shown in Figure 5-2-10.

Testing the program

The Zeus world is now complete. Naturally, we should test the program by running it and having Zeus shoot thunderbolts. When we tested this program, we clicked on each of the philosophers, to make sure the thunderbolt properly hit the target. But when we clicked on the clouds, the thunderbolt struck the clouds, turning them black. And when we clicked on the scene itself, the whole scene was turned black! And, clicking on Zeus causes Alice to complain. (Zeus can't zap himself with lightning!) This is not the behavior we wanted or expected. Another problem with the animation is that the user can click on an object that has already been zapped with lightning. A solution to these problems will be presented in the next chapter.

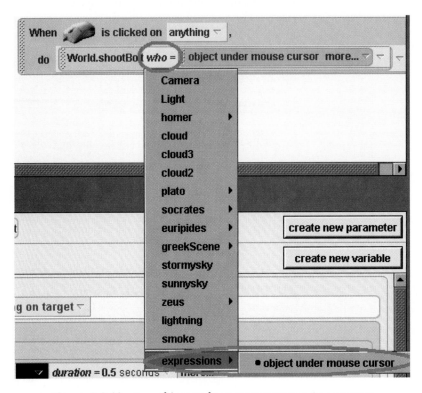

Figure 5-2-10. Pass *object under mouse cursor* as the parameter

Tips & Techniques 5
Events

 A Quick Reference to Events

Figure T-5-1. Possible events in Alice

- *When the world starts.* This event happens once, when the Play button is first pressed and the Alice world begins to run.

- *When a key is typed.* This allows for a method to be called in response to the user pressing one of the keys on the keyboard.

- *When the mouse is clicked on something.* Each time the mouse is clicked on an object in the world, a method is called to handle the event.

- *While something is true.* This is a sophisticated event that will be presented after repetition has been introduced in Chapter 7.

- *When a variable changes.* Variables will not be introduced until Chapter 10. This event allows for calling a method every time a specified variable changes value.

- *Let the mouse move objects.* This event automatically calls an internal Alice method that moves the object in a drag-and-drop manner.

- *Let the arrow keys move <subject>.* This allows the user to move a specified object by pressing the arrow keys. The up arrow moves the object forward, down arrow backward, the right and left arrows move the object right and left.

- *Let the mouse move the camera.* This allows the user to "steer" the camera with the mouse during an animation. Note that it is possible to point the camera away from the animation. If this happens, you will no longer see what is going on.

- *Let the mouse orient the camera.* Like the preceding event, this one must be used with caution, as you can easily orient the camera to point into space and then miss the rest of the animation that is running.

Exercises and Projects

5-1 Exercises

1. *Flight Simulator Completion*

    (a) Create the world for the biplane acrobatic air-show example as presented in this section. Implement the *flyForward* and *barrel* event handling methods and link them to the corresponding events. Make the move and roll actions have an abrupt style to reduce the pause in the animation between key presses. If your computer has sound, use a biplane sound to make the animation more realistic.

    (b) When you have the *flyForward* and *barrel* methods working, add *flyLeft* and *flyRight* event handling methods for the left and right arrow keys to steer the biplane left or right.

    (c) Add a *forwardLoop* stunt that works when the user presses the Enter key.

2. *Flight Simulator—Alternate Version*
    The arrow key-press events work when the user releases the key. Of course, this means that multiple key-press/release events are needed to keep the biplane moving. In this exercise, you can experiment with a different kind of event. Create a second version of the biplane world (use **File → SaveAs** to save the world with a different name). In the second version of the world, remove the events that link the arrow keys to the *flyForward*, *flyLeft* and *flyRight* event handling methods. In the Events editor, create a new event by selecting *let the arrow keys move <subject>*, as shown below.

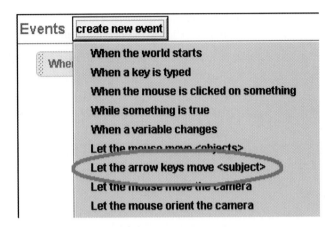

Then, link the biplane, as shown below. Run the flight simulator again to see the effect.

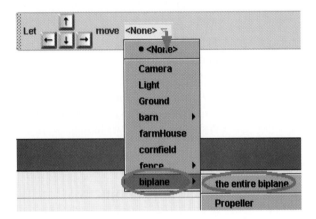

3. *Robot Remote Control*

The world for this exercise is similar to the FirstEncounter world in Chapters 2 through 4. In this world, however, we want to allow the user to control the robot using some sort of remote control. One possibility is to use the TwoButton switch (Controls) to simulate a robot control system. When the user clicks the green button on the switch, the robot should move forward, with two of its legs providing a walking motion. When the user clicks the red button on the switch, the robot should move backward, with two different legs walking in the opposite direction. Use the world-level function *ask the user for a number* to allow the user to determine how many meters the robot moves forward or backward.

4. *Typing Tutor*

Learning to type rapidly (without looking at the keyboard) is a skill requiring much practice. In this exercise, you are to create a typing tutor that encourages the beginning typist to type a specific set of letters. Use 3D text letters (3D Text folder) to create a word in the world, (for example, you could create the word ALICE with the letters A, L, I, C, and E) and create a method for each letter that spins the letter two times. When the user types a letter key on the keyboard that matches the letter on the screen, the letter on the screen should perform its spin method. Also include an additional method, *spinWord*, which spins all the letters when the user presses the spacebar.

Hint: Use *asSeenBy* to spin the word.

5. *Rotational Motion*

A popular topic in Physics is the study of rotational motion. Create a world with at least four objects (such as a compass, mailbox, mantleClock and tire.) Create a realistic rotation method for each object that has the object rotate 1 full revolution and then perform some other action. For example, if one of your objects is a compass, make the compass needle spin around quickly in one direction and then spin around again in the opposite direction. Add events that will call the rotational motion method for an object when the object is clicked. (If the world has four objects, four events will be needed.)

6. *Mad Scientist Magic*

Who says that a mad scientist has no magic skills? Create a world using a mad scientist (People) behind a table (Furniture). Place three objects on the tabletop—for example a blender and mug (Kitchen). The point of the exercise is that when the mouse clicks any one of the objects on the tabletop, the mad scientist will turn to face that object, raise his arm (like he is casting a spell of some sort), and have the object spin or turn in any way you wish. The mug has some kind of liquid in it. Make the liquid disappear (by setting its *isShowing* property to *false*) when the mad scientist performs his "spell" on it.

7. *Ninja Motion*

   A ninja (EvilNinja in People folder) is trying out for a karate movie, and he needs a little practice. Create a world with a ninja object in a dojo. The motions the ninja needs to practice are: jump, duck, chop, and kick. If you have not already done so, (see Exercise 12 in Chapter 4), write motion methods for the ninja that include the following:

   kickRight, kickLeft: allows the ninja to kick his right/left leg, including all appropriate movements (e.g., foot turning, etc.)

   rightJab, leftJab: allows the ninja to do a jabbing motion with his right/left arms

   Create events and event handling methods that provide the user with controls to make the ninja jump, duck, jab and kick.

8. *The Cheshire Cat*

   Consider the Cheshire cat (Animals) from the *Alice in Wonderland* books. Sometimes, the cat would disappear, leaving only his grin. At other times, the cat would reappear. Create such a world, where the cat (except for its smile) disappears when the red button of the switch (Controls) is clicked, then reappears when the green button is clicked. (The tree is found in the Nature folder.)

5-2 Exercises

9. *Zeus Modification*

   Recreate the Zeus world presented in Section 5-2. In this world, a philosopher that has been zapped by lightning and is scorched to show he has met a tragic ending. The philosopher is still in the scene, however, and the user can zap him again. Revise the program to make the zapped philosopher fall down below the ground, where he can't be mouse-clicked again.

10. *Furniture Arrangement*

    Create a world where the user will rearrange the furniture in a room. (A variety of furniture items can be found in the Furniture folder on the CD and Web galleries.) An example of a room arrangement is shown below. (We used a rectangle Shape to represent the floor of the room.) To allow the user to move the furniture around, create a *Let the mouse move objects* event.

11. *Carousel Go-round*

    Create an amusement park scene with a carousel. (Amusement Park) In this animation, the carousel is to have at least four animals. (You can use the animals that come with the carousel or add your own.) Add a two-way switch (Controls) to the initial scene. Create two event handling methods—one to make the carousel rotate clockwise and one to make it rotate counterclockwise. When the green button is clicked, the carousel should rotate clockwise, and a click on the red button should make the carousel rotate counterclockwise. Optional: Import a sound file and have it play as the carousel goes around.

12. *Snow Festival*

    Your team has created a snowman as the centerpiece of an entry in the Winter Snow Festival competition. To attract attraction to your display, you have set up colored spotlights that will turn the color of the snowman any one of four different colors. Create an initial world with four spotlights (spheres from the Shapes folder, of four different colors) and a snowman, as shown below. Write only one method to change the color of the snowman. When the user clicks on a spotlight pass the color of the spotlight to the method and make the snowman change to be that color.

13. *Flowerbox*

It's spring and you are anxiously waiting for flowers to grow. You decide to give them a little help. Create an initial scene of a flowerbox (Box from Shapes, change color to red) with five flowers (of your choosing) in it. (Use instructions in the initial scene to move the flowers down out of sight.)

Write one method to grow a flower in the box (move the flower up into view). The flower that grows in the box depends on which key the user presses on the keyboard. For example, if the user presses "S" key, the sunflower will grow but if the user presses the "D" key, the daisy will grow. To grow the flowers, create a *"When <key> is typed"* event for each key selected to represent a specific flower. Link the key-press event to the *growFlower* event handling method, using the particular flower represented by that key as its parameter. When all the flowers are grown, the flowerbox will look something like the following:

14. *Penguin Slide*

A favorite activity of penguins in the local zoo is to slide down an icy slope into a pool of water in the pond. Create a world with a lake scene (Environments) and three penguins (Animals) on the slope, as shown below. Make the program event-driven. Allow the user to click on the next penguin to slide down the slope into the pool of water. Each penguin slides on its belly and spins around as it slides. Each penguin should spin some number of times. When the penguin reaches the pond, move the penguin down 5 meters so it disappears below the water. Write only one event handling method. When the penguin is mouse-clicked, pass the penguin object that was clicked and the number of times the penguin is to spin around as it slides down the slope.

Optional: Add a water-splash sound as the penguin hits the water.

15. *Hockey*

    Jack (Jock from High School/Students and Teachers folder on the CD or Web gallery) is planning to try out for the school hockey team this fall. As a successful athlete, Jack knows that "practice is the name of the game." Jack has set up a hockey net (Sports) on the lake and is going to practice his aim with the hockey stick (Sports) to improve his chances of making the team.

    This animation could be the first phase of developing an interactive ice-hockey game. To design an interactive program storyboard, some thought must be given to what events will occur and what event handling methods are needed. Let's allow the user to select the power factor behind Jack's swing of the hockey stick. The power factor will determine how fast Jack swings the stick and how far the hockey puck travels when hit by the stick. The power factor will be selected by a mouse-click on one of the power buttons (GumDrops from Kitchen/Food folder) in the lower right of the scene. The yellow button will select low, green will select average, and red will select a high power factor.

16. *Slappy*

    Slappy, an adventuresome squirrel (Animals on CD or Web gallery), has just gotten her own squirrel-sized snowmobile (Vehicles on CD or Web gallery). Create a program to animate Slappy's first ride on the snowmobile. The user controls the forward and reverse motion of the snowmobile, using a two switch box (Controls). When the user clicks the green button on the switch, the snowmobile and Slappy move forward and Slappy screams something like "wahoo!" When the user clicks the red button on the switch, the snowmobile and Slappy move in reverse and Slappy looks at the camera and says something like "!oohaw."

Projects

1. *Skater World*

   The goal of this world is to simulate a person doing various skating movements on a skate board. Create a world with a skater girl (People) on a skateboard (SkatePark). Add one or two objects she can jump over. We used a rail ramp from the SkatePark folder on the CD or Web gallery. A sample scene is shown below.

The skater should have both *jump* and *spin* methods. Allow the user to press the up/down arrow keys to move the camera and skater forward/backward and the left/right arrow keys to make the skater lean left/right while the camera goes left/right. At the end of each motion, the skater should lean back to her original position. The "**j**" key can be used to make the skater jump and the "**s**" key to make her spin.

Hints:
(a) If you are having problems with the skater girl moving where you want her to move, trying using *asSeenBy* camera or *asSeenBy* skateboard.
(b) One way to make the camera follow the action is to position it behind the skater and make the skater its vehicle.

2. *Skydiving Guidance System*

Alice Liddell (People) has taken up a new hobby: skydiving. She is on a helicopter (Vehicle), wearing a parachute (Objects). She is to jump to the carrier (Vehicle), which is a little way in front of her. In the world shown below, we added a half cylinder (Shapes) inverted and connected to the helicopter to be used as a jump platform. A torus (Shapes) was used to create a harness for Alice Liddell. (Although this isn't absolutely necessary, it is helpful due to Alice Liddell's small waist compared to the parachute's cords.)

The idea of this animation is to provide a skydiving guidance system to allow the user to guide the movement of Alice Liddell as she jumps from the platform of the helicopter and glides down to the carrier. When the user thinks Alice Liddell has hit the top of the carrier, the user can press the Enter key to have Alice Liddell drop her chute.

Guidance system methods (as smooth and lifelike as possible):

jump: jump from the helicopter's platform

glideForward, glideBack, glideRight, glideLeft: glide in the appropriate direction

swingLegs: legs swing a bit when gliding or jumping

> *dropChute*: get rid of parachute (to simplify things, just have the chute rotate as if it were falling and make it disappear)

Keyboard controls:

> Space bar—jump off the platform
> Up/Down/right/left arrow—glide forward/back/right/left
> Enter key—parachute drops

Remember that Alice Liddell should first jump off the platform prior to gliding and should not drop her chute until she hits the carrier.

3. *Turtle Motion Control*

In this project, you are to create a turtle motion controller to help the turtle (Animals) perform exercises for his upcoming race with the rabbit. Create a world that contains only a turtle and then create motion control methods for the turtle:

> ***headBob:*** allows the turtle's head to bob a little
> ***tailWag:*** allows the turtle's tail to wag
> ***oneStep:*** allows the turtle to move forward one step; his legs should move while he is taking that one step
> ***walkForward:*** combines the above three methods, to make a realistic step; all movements should take the same amount of time and occur at the same time
> ***turnAround:*** turns the turtle 180 degrees; he should be walking while turning
> ***turnLeft, turnRight:*** turns the turtle left/right, walking while he is turning
> ***hide:*** allows the turtle to hide in his shell (you may assume that the turtle is currently outside of his shell); remember not to leave the shell hanging in midair
> ***reappear:*** allows the turtle to reappear from his shell (you may assume that the turtle is currently hidden)
> ***talk:*** has the turtle look at the camera and say "hello" (or something different, if you wish) to the user

Create keyboard controls:

> When the up arrow key is pressed, the turtle is to walk forward.
> When the down arrow key is pressed, the turtle is to turn around.
> When the left arrow key is pressed, the turtle is to turn left.
> When the right arrow key is pressed, the turtle is to turn right.
> When the letter "H" is pressed, the turtle is to hide in his shell.
> When the letter "R" is pressed, the turtle is to reappear from his shell.
> When the letter "T" is pressed, the turtle is to talk to the user.

Test the turtle motion control system by running your world and trying all the interactions at least once. Be sure to hide the turtle only when he is already out of his shell and have him reappear only when he is hiding.

Summary

The focus of this chapter was the creation of interactive (event-driven) worlds. Creating worlds with events will allow you to build significantly more interesting worlds such as game-like animations and simulations. In many object-oriented programming languages, event-driven programming requires knowledge of advanced topics. The Events editor allows you to create events and link them to event handling methods. The event handling method has the responsibility of taking action each time the event occurs. The Events editor handles many of the messy details of event-driven programming.

Important concepts in this chapter

- An event is something that happens.
- An event is created by user input (keyboard press, mouse click, joystick movement).
- An event is linked to an event handling method.
- Each time an event occurs, its corresponding event handling method is called. This is what is meant by event-driven programming.
- The event handling method contains instructions to carry out a response to the event.
- A parameter can be passed to an event handling method when an event occurs.
- Parameters allow us to write one method that can handle several related events.
- Incremental development means that you write and test a small piece of your program, then write and test the next small piece, and so forth, until the entire program is completed. Incremental development is another technique that makes it easier to debug your programs.

Part III
Using Functions and Control Statements

Chapter **6**

Functions and *If/Else*

*"I know what you're thinking about," said
Tweedledum: "but it isn't so, nohow."
"Contrariwise," continued Tweedledee, "if it
was so, it might be; and if it were so, it would
be: but as it isn't, it ain't. That's logic."*

This chapter presents functions and conditional execution control statements (two key concepts in programming), as used with methods. Functions allow you to check certain conditions within a world while an animation is running. While Alice provides some built-in functions that are useful in methods, in this chapter we will look at examples of programs where we want to use a function that does not already exist in Alice. In such a situation, you can write your own function.

A function is similar to a method in that it is a collection of instructions and (like a method) is called. The purpose of a method is to perform an animation, but that of a function is to return a value. What difference does this make? Well, an animation performed by a method moves, turns, or performs some other action with objects in the world. We call this changing the state of the world. In a function, however, objects do not move, turn, or perform some other action. So, functions leave the state of the world unchanged. Mathematicians say these are pure functions.

An exciting thing about writing your own function is you can then use it (along with built-in functions) to check out a current condition in the world and make a decision about whether (or not) a method is called. In Alice, we use an *If/Else* statement as a conditional execution control statement that uses a condition for making a decision.

Section 6-1 introduces the use of functions in methods and explains how to write your own function as a method that returns a value. We need functions as a way of getting information about objects as the program is running (at runtime).

In Section 6-2, we use conditional execution (*If/Else* statement) to make decisions about whether (or not) to call a method. We will write our own Boolean function (which returns *true* or *false*) to be used as part of the execution control mechanism. In your programs, you will use decisions to make animations execute in different ways depending on a condition, such as whether an object is visible or where an object is located. In an interactive world, we can use *If/Else* to decide what is done in an event handling method.

6-1 Functions

In writing program code, we often need some information about the objects in the world and the World itself. The most commonly used properties (such as *color* and *opacity*) are listed in a properties list for the object. To get information about other properties (for example, *height*

147

or *width*) we use a function to ask a question. The value returned by a function can be a number, an object, a Boolean (*true* or *false*), or some other type.

A function may receive values sent in as arguments (input), perform some computation on the values, and return (send back) a value as output. In some cases no input is needed, but often values are sent in. The diagram in Figure 6-1-1 outlines the overall mechanism. One way of thinking about a function is that it is something like an ATM machine. You enter your bankcard and password as input and click on the button indicating you would like to see your balance (another input). The ATM machine looks up your account information and then tells you what your current balance is (as output).

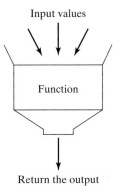

Input values

Function

Return the output

Figure 6-1-1. Overview of how a function works

Abstraction

As with class-level and world-level methods, one important benefit of a function is that it allows us to think about the overall process rather than all the nitty-gritty little details. When we use an ATM, for example, we think about getting the balance in our account—not about all the operations that are going on inside the machine. In the same way, we can call a function in our program to perform all the small actions, while we just think about what answer we are going to get. Like methods, functions are an example of abstraction—collecting lots of small steps into one meaningful idea to allow us to think on a higher plane.

Using a built-in function in a method

Alice provides built-in functions that can be used to provide information for instructions in a method. As an example, consider the world shown in Figure 6-1-2. In setting up this world, we put the toyball (Sports) on the ground next to the net (Sports) and then move it 1 meter away from the net (so that we know the ball is exactly 1 meter from the net).

Figure 6-1-2. A world containing a toyball and a tennisNet

We want to bounce the ball over the tennis net. Do not be deceived. This is not as easy as it sounds because we cannot easily tell just by looking at the ball what its orientation is. In other words, we don't know "which way is up" in terms of the ball's sense of direction. The ball should move up and forward and then down and forward:

Actually, we are thinking about the ball's up and down motion relative to the ground, so we need to align the ball's sense of direction with the ground. Orientation is done by using an *orient to* method, as shown in Figure 6-1-3.

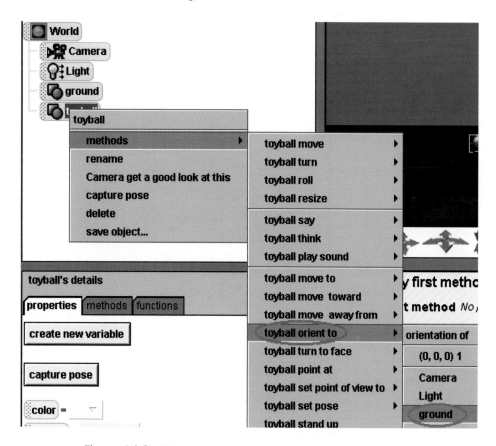

Figure 6-1-3. Using an *orient to* method to orient the ball with the ground

Having properly set up the initial scene, we can write a method to bounce the ball over the net. Since two objects are involved in this action, we will write a world-level method named *ballOverNet*.

A storyboard would look like this:

```
ballOverNet

Do in order
  toyball turn to face the net
  Do together
    toyball move up
    toyball move forward
  Do together
    toyball move down
    toyball move forward
```

We know how far to move the ball forward because we set up the world with the ball exactly 1 meter from the net. We do not know how far up to move the ball to clear the net. We can use a built-in function for the tennisNet to determine its height and then use that as the distance the ball moves up (and then back down). We don't have to think about what Alice is doing to figure out the height of the tennis net, we can just call the function and get the height. This is a 2-step process, 1) Drag the toyballs's, *move* tile into the editor and select 1 as a default distance. 2) Drag the tennis Net's *height* function tile on top of the 1. Figure 6-1-4 illustrates dragging the tennisNet's *height* function onto the *move up* and *move down* instructions.

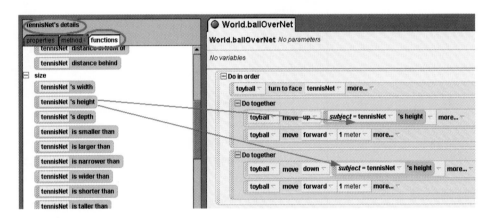

Figure 6-1-4. Dragging the built-in *height* function into a method

The need to write your own function

Sometimes when you want to call a function, none of the built-in functions will work for what you want to do. This is where you need to write your own function. It is helpful to illustrate with a simple example. Let's simulate rolling the ball forward. Once again, this is more challenging than it looks. Think about how the ball can be made to roll along the ground. The ball should appear to roll along the ground, not just glide along it. (A gliding motion is fine for an ice skater, but a ball should roll.) An obvious instruction would be to write a simple *turn* instruction.

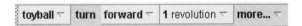

Surprise—the turn instruction simply rotates the ball in place! (It spins the ball around, but the ball does not move along the ground.) To actually roll, the ball must turn and also move in the same direction. A storyboard for a method to simulate a rolling action (*realisticRoll*) would be:

```
realisticRoll

Do together
  move ball forward 1 meter
  turn ball forward 1 revolution
```

With this in mind, we can write a class-level method named *realisticRoll*, Figure 6-1-5.

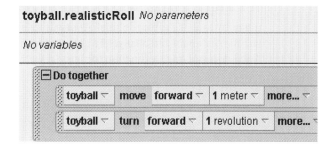

Figure 6-1-5. Move and turn instructions in a *Do together*

Our testing of this code, however, is disappointing. The effect of moving and turning the ball at the same time is that the ball ends up at the same place it started. (The turning action prevents the ball from moving forward.)

Why is this? Well, the ball is moving relative to itself, not relative to the ground. A solution to this problem is to use *asSeenBy = ground* in the *move* statement. The code in Figure 6-1-6 moves and turns the ball forward 1 meter, simulating a real-life ball rolling on the ground.

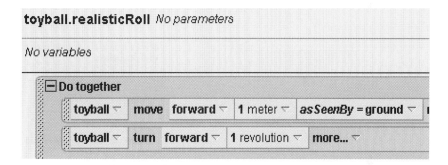

Figure 6-1-6. The toyball rolls along the ground

We guessed that 1 revolution would look realistic. But when it is run, it is not quite right. We must now think about how many revolutions the ball needs to turn in covering a given distance in a forward direction. This presents a challenge because the number of times the ball needs to turn is proportional to the ball's diameter. To cover the same forward distance, a small ball turns more times than a larger ball. In Figure 6-1-7, the larger ball covers the same distance in one revolution as the smaller ball covers in four revolutions.

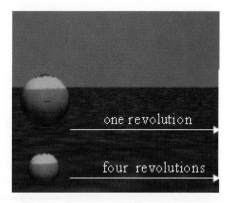

Figure 6-1-7. Distance covered by a revolution is proportional to diameter

Of course, the number of revolutions needed for the ball to roll, say, 10 meters could be found by trial and error. But then, every time the ball changed size you would have to figure it out all over again and change the code. A better way is to compute the number of revolutions. Alice does not have a function for this, so we will write our own.

Writing a new function

Since we are concerned only with the ball rolling, and no other objects are involved, we can write a class-level function. (A class-level function allows you save out the ball as a new class and reuse the function in future worlds.) To write your own class-level function, select the object in the Object tree (for a world-level function you would select the World). In the functions tab, click on the **create new function** button, as in Figure 6-1-8.

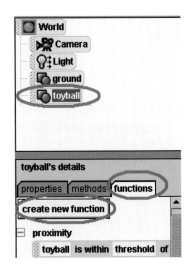

Figure 6-1-8. Creating a new function

A popup New Function box (Figure 6-1-9) allows you enter the name of the new function and select its type. Your new function is categorized by the type of information it returns. The types of functions include Number, Boolean, Object, and Other (such as String, Color, and Sound). In this section, we will write functions that return Number values. Examples and exercises later in the chapter use functions that return other types of values.

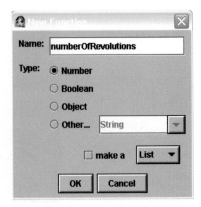

Figure 6-1-9. Enter a name and select a return type

A click on the OK button creates an editor panel where you can write the code for the function, as shown in Figure 6-1-10.

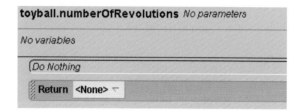

Figure 6-1-10. Editor panel for writing your own function

The Return statement

Every function must have a *Return* statement. The reason is that all functions return some information. When you first create a function, Alice automatically adds a *Return* statement at the end, reminding you that your function must return some information. You cannot remove the *Return* statement.

In our example, we want to ask the function: "How many revolutions does the ball have to make to move a given distance along the ground?" The number of revolutions depends on the distance traveled by the outside (circumference) of the ball in a single revolution, so we use the formula:

$$\text{number of revolutions} = \text{distance}/(\text{diameter} * \pi)$$

To use this formula, we need three pieces of information: the distance the ball is to roll, the diameter of the ball, and something named π. To provide this information,

- A parameter will be used to send in the distance the ball is to roll.
- The built-in function *toyball's width* will be called to get the diameter.
- The symbol π (also known as pi) is a constant value (it does not change). Pi represents the ratio of the circumference of a circle to its diameter. We will use 3.14 as the constant value of pi.

The code shown in Figure 6-1-11 implements the function. The number of rotations is computed by dividing the distance the ball is to move (the *distance* parameter) by the product of the ball's diameter (*toyBall's width,* a built-in function) and pi (described above). The *Return* statement tells Alice to send back the computed answer.

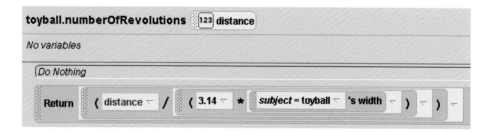

Figure 6-1-11. The *toyBall.numberOfRevolutions* function

The order of evaluation of the values in the function must be carefully arranged. Alice uses nested tiles and parentheses to emphasize the order in which the values are evaluated. The innermost expression is computed first. In this example, *3.14* is multiplied by the *toyBall's width,* and then that value is divided into the *distance.*

Calling the function

Now that the toyBall has a function named *numberOfRevolutions*, the function can be used to revise our *realisticRoll* method, as shown in Figure 6-1-12. An arbitrary distance of 10 meters is used for the move forward instruction. The same value, 10 meters, is also used as the distance parameter for the *toyBall.numberOfRevolutions* function.

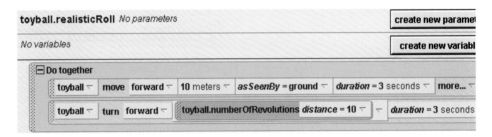

Figure 6-1-12. Calling the *numberOfRevolutions* function

Although 10 meters was used as a test value in the example above, we should really be testing our program by using low distance values (for example, −2 and 0) and also with high distance values (for example, 20). Using a range of values will reassure you that your program code works on many different values. One way to do this is to parameterize the *realisticRoll* method so it can be called with different test values, as illustrated in Figure 6-1-13.

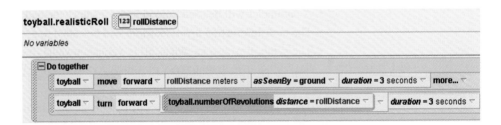

Figure 6-1-13. A parameter for *rollDistance* allows testing with different distance values

6-2 Execution control with *If/Else* and Boolean functions

We expect that you have written several methods as part of programs for exercises and projects in previous chapters. In some programs, you may want to control when a method gets called. You can do so with a program statement called a control structure. In methods, *Do in order* is used to make certain instructions run sequentially and *Do together* to make a collection of instructions run all at the same time. To control whether a block of instructions is executed or a method is called, an *If/Else* statement is used. In this section, we look at the use of *If/Else* statements in Boolean functions and makeing decisions about calling methods.

As stated previously, an *If/Else* is a statement that makes a decision based on the value of a condition as a program is running. (For simplicity, we often refer to it as an *If* statement.) Figure 6-2-1 illustrates the processing of an *If* statement. The statement checks to see whether

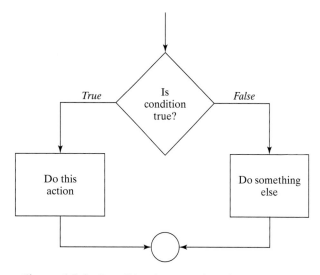

Figure 6-2-1. Describing the processing of an *If* statement

a condition is *true*. If it is, a set of program instructions are run. If the condition is *false*, a separate set of program instructions are run.

Using an *If* statement in a Boolean function

Execution control structures are a big part of game-type and simulation programs. The current conditions guide the actions of the objects in a game. In a basketball game a method is called to increase a team's score only if the ball goes through the net. In a driver-training simulation, a method is called to move the car forward only if the car is still on the road.

As an example of using an *If* statement for conditional execution, consider the world shown in Figure 6-2-2. A biplane (Vehicle) and a helicopter (Vehicle) are flying in the same fly-space at approximately the same altitude near the airport (Buildings). One function of radar and software in the control tower (Buildings) is to check for possible collisions when two vehicles are in the same fly-space. If they are too close to one another, the flight controller can radio the pilots to change their flight paths.

Figure 6-2-2. Fly-space collision danger

First, let's write a function to check whether the biplane and helicopter are in danger of collision. The type of value the function will return is Boolean—*true* if the vertical distance between the two aircraft is less than some minimum distance, otherwise *false*. Three parameters will be needed: the two aircraft objects (aircraftOne and aircraftTwo) and a minimum vertical distance (*minimumDistance*). A storyboard for *isTooClose* is:

```
isTooClose

Parameters: aircraftOne, aircraftTwo, minimumDistance

If the vertical distance between aircraftOne and aircraftTwo is less than
    minimumDistance
       return true
Else
    return false
```

To translate the storyboard to program code, we create a new world-level function named *isTooClose*. The function should return *true* or *false*, so Boolean is selected as the type, as shown in Figure 6-2-3.

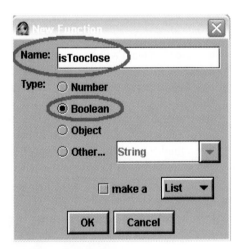

Figure 6-2-3. Creating a Boolean function

In the editor for the function, create the three parameters aircraftOne, aircraftTwo, and *minimumDistance*. Then, drag an *If/Else* tile into the editor, as in Figure 6-2-4. The condition selected from the popup menu for the *If* statement is *true*.

Although *true* was selected as the condition from the popup menu, it is acting as a placeholder. In this example the condition of the *If* statement should be "the vertical distance is less than the *minimumDistance*." To compare the vertical distance between the two aircraft to a minimum distance, we will use a built-in world-level function, the "<" (less than) operation. The "<" is one of six relational operators used in the World's build-in *math* functions, as shown in Figure 6-2-5.

A relational operator computes a *true* or *false* value based on the relationship between the two values. For example, "==" is "is equal to" and "!=" is "is not equal to."

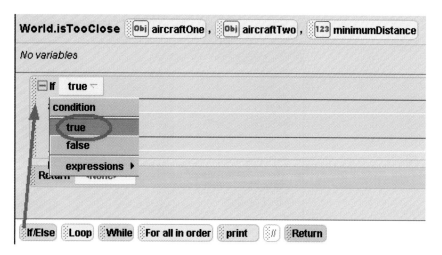

Figure 6-2-4. Dragging an *If* statement into a function and selecting *true* condition

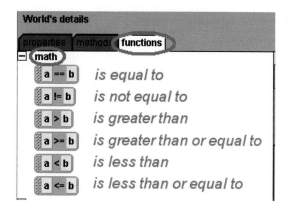

Figure 6-2-5. Relational operations in the built-in World functions

In this example, we want to check whether the distance between the two aircraft is less than a minimum distance. If this condition is true, the air traffic controller will tell the pilots to move the aircraft apart.

To create a conditional expression for the *If* statement, we drag a *less than* function $(a < b)$ from the World's functions into the editor and drop it on top of *true*, as in Figure 6-2-3. From the popup menu, we select 1 (for *a*) and *minimumDistance* (for *b*). (The vertical distance between the two aircraft is not an option in this popup menu as a choice for *a*, so we arbitrarily selected 1 as a placeholder. We will show you how to replace the 1 with the actual vertical distance in the next paragraph.)

We want to replace the placeholder (1) with the vertical distance between the two aircraft. Since we don't know whether the helicopter is above the biplane or the biplane is above the helicopter, we use an *absolute value* function. The absolute value of 4 is 4 and the absolute value of −4 is also 4. In other words, absolute value ignores a negative sign. To use absolute value, drag the absolute value function on top of the 1, as shown in Figure 6-2-7.

Now, we want to replace the value 1 with a *distance above* function to determine the distance of aircraftOne above aircraftTwo. Of course, aircraftOne is a parameter, not an actual object. So, we select the biplane from the Object tree to serve as a specific object to create the

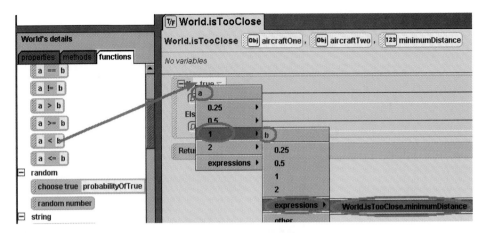

Figure 6-2-6. Creating a *less than* condition for an *If* statement

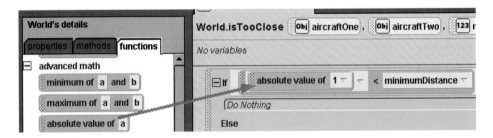

Figure 6-2-7. Drag the *absolute value* function on top of the 1

distance above function. Then we drag aircraftOne in to replace the biplane, as in Figure 6-2-8. (This is the same technique introduced in the Zeus world in Chapter 5, Section 2.)

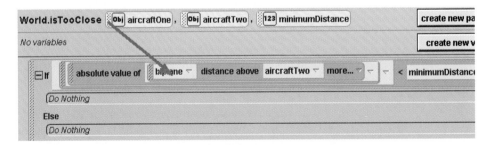

Figure 6-2-8. Creating an expression to compute the vertical distance

The vertical distance can now be compared to *minimumDistance*. Return statements are dragged into the *If* and *Else* parts of the *If* statement. If the vertical distance is less than *minimumDistance*, return *true*; otherwise return *false*. Figure 6-2-9 shows the completed *If* statement in the *isTooClose* function.

Once again, note that the nesting of tiles in a conditional expression creates an order of evaluation. First Alice computes the *distance above*, and then *absolute value* is applied to the result. For example, suppose aircraftOne is 500 meters above the ground and aircraftTwo is

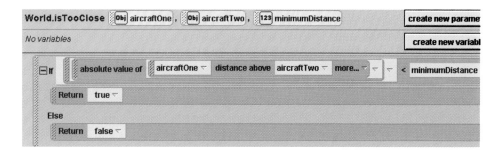

Figure 6-2-9. The *isTooClose* function

520 meters above the ground. Then, the distance of aircraftOne above aircraftTwo is −20 meters (500 − 520). The absolute value of −20 is 20, so the vertical distance between the two aircraft is 20 meters.

Using an *If* statement to control calling a method

Another common use of an *If* statement is to control whether a method is called. To show how this works, let's continue with the same example. The scenario for this world indicated that if the aircraft were too close, the flight controller should radio the pilots to change their flight path to avoid a collision. The storyboard could look like this:

```
If isTooClose
     avoidCollision
Else
     <Do nothing>
```

The *isTooClose* function is called to check whether the biplane (aircraftOne) and the helicopter (aircraftTwo) are too close to each other. If the function returns *true*, a method named *avoidCollision* is called. Otherwise, nothing is done (the method is not called). Let's pretend that the *avoidCollision* method is already written. Then, the previous storyboard can be implemented as shown in Figure 6-2-10 (10 is an arbitrary minimum distance).

Figure 6-2-10. Controlling a call to a method

In the *avoidCollision* method, the aircraft that is above the other should move up and the lower aircraft should move down. Since we don't know which aircraft is above the other, we can use an *If* statement to check their relative heights and move each one up or down, as needed. The storyboard for the *avoidCollision* method is:

```
avoidCollision

Parameters: aircraftOne, aircraftTwo

If aircraftOne is above aircraftTwo
  Do together
    aircraftOne move up
    aircraftTwo move down
Else
  Do together
    aircraftOne move down
    aircraftTwo move up
```

The translation of this storyboard to program code is shown in Figure 6-2-11. The condition for the *If* statement calls a built-in function, *is above*, to determine which aircraft is above the other. The instructions executed depend on the value returned. If aircraftOne is above aircraftTwo, aircraftOne will move up and aircraftTwo will move down. Otherwise, the *Else* part kicks in so aircraftOne will move down and aircraftTwo will move up. Either way, the aircraft move away from one another.

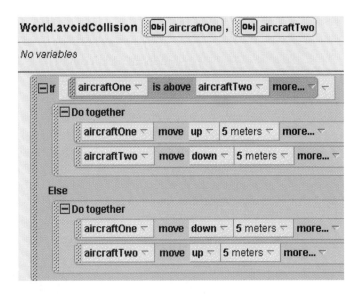

Figure 6-2-11. The *avoidCollision* method

An important part of any *If* statement is the condition. In these examples, the condition involved calls to functions (both built-in functions and our own function). One example (see Figure 6-2-11) used a Boolean expression with a relational operator. Regardless of how the condition is written, it must evaluate to *true* or *false*. The value of the condition determines whether the *If* part or the *Else* part of the *If* statement is executed.

An expression with multiple conditions

In Chapter 5, we created a Zeus interactive world where a user can choose the next target of the god's anger by clicking on a philosopher. Zeus shoots his thunderbolt at the selected philosopher, and special effects are used to show the results. (For convenience, the code for the *shootBolt* method is reproduced in Figure 6-2-12.)

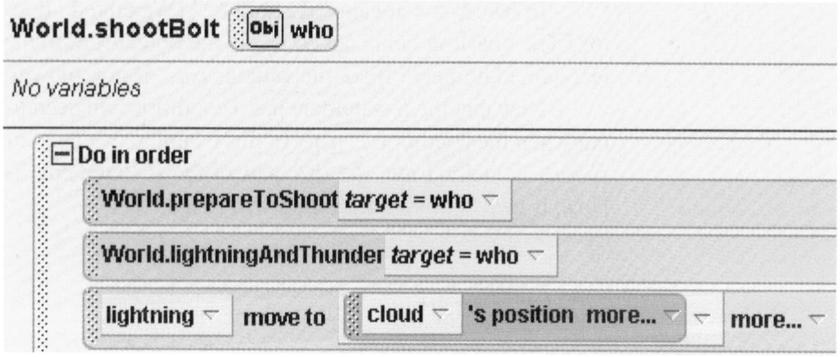

World.shootBolt Obj who

No variables

─ Do in order

    World.prepareToShoot *target* = who ▽

    World.lightningAndThunder *target* = who ▽

    lightning ▽   move to   cloud ▽ 's position more... ▽ ▽ more... ▽

Figure 6-2-12. The *shootBolt* method (from Zeus world in Section 5-2)

We had intended that Zeus shoot the thunderbolt only at a philosopher. Unfortunately, we found that if the user clicks on any other object that happens to be in the world, Zeus zaps that object as well. We want to control the lightning so that the bolt is shot at an object only if *who* is one of the philosophers.

We have four philosophers in this world, so we will need to check whether the object clicked was one of them. This is an example where a conditional expression contains multiple conditions. To show how to use multiple conditions, we begin with a single condition to check for just one philosopher—then expand it to four philosophers.

First, drag an *If* statement into the top line of the *shootBolt* method. Next, create a condition to test whether the object clicked was homer. To create the condition *If who* == homer, drag the *who* tile on top of the *true* tile in the *If* statement. Then select *who* == homer from the popup menu, as shown in Figure 6-2-13.

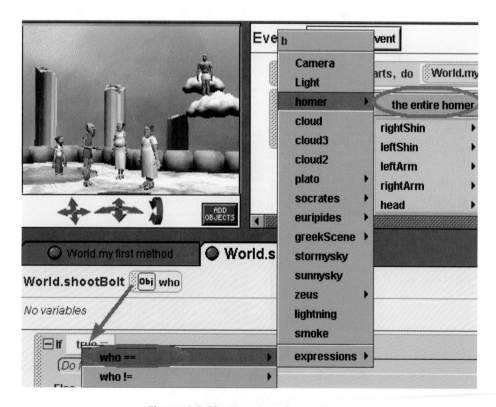

Figure 6-2-13. Selecting *who* == *homer*

In Alice, == means "is equal to." (We talked about "==" above as a relational operator.) The question being asked is: "Is the object sent to the *who* parameter the same as the object named homer?" If so, the value is *true*. If not, the value is *false*.

Now that the *If* statement has a condition, we need to supply the instructions to be carried out when the condition is *true*. In this example, we need only drag the *Do in order* block of the *shootBolt* method into the *true* part of the *If* statement. The result is shown in Figure 6-2-14. Now, if *who* is homer, lightning will strike.

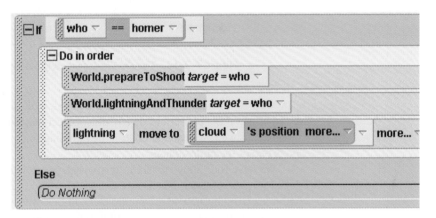

Figure 6-2-14. If *who* == homer, lightning will strike

Now it is time to expand the *If* statement's condition to allow any of the four philosophers. A logical operator "or" is needed (one of three logic operators found in the World functions list, shown in Figure 6-2-15). The *or* operation means "either this or that or possibly both." While this makes sense, the way we actually use "or" in daily life is somewhat different. When you say, "I am going to the movies or I am staying home," you mean that either you are going to the movies or you are staying home, but not both. However, the Alice expression *either a or b, or both* means that either the first statement is true, or the second statement is true, or they are both true! (The other two logic operators are discussed at the end of this section.)

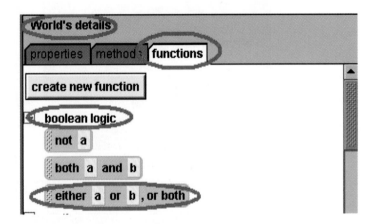

Figure 6-2-15. Functions that use logic operators

To use the *or* operator, drag the *either a or b or both* tile over the condition tile in the *If* statement. In this example, the *or* operator must be dragged into the condition tile three times to account for all four philosophers. The code below illustrates the modified *If* statement. (The statement is broken into two lines to make it fit on the width of this page—but is all on one line in Alice.)

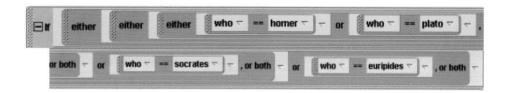

Figure 6-2-16 shows the revision of the *shootBolt* method. (Not all of the multiple conditions can be seen, because the code runs off the edge of the window.) Now, clicking on any one of the four philosophers results in Zeus shooting a thunderbolt at that philosopher, but clicking on something else in the world causes no action.

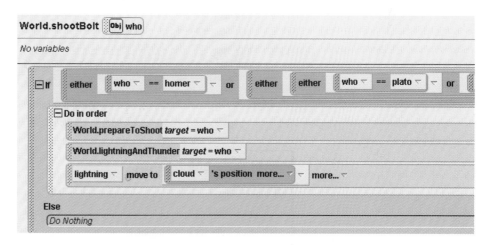

Figure 6-2-16. The *If* statement condition in the *shootBolt* method

A function using nested *If* statements

The condition in the *shootBolt* method above is somewhat complicated and difficult to read. The reason is that four different philosopher objects must be checked using three *or* operators—all in one conditional expression.

An alternative is to write a function with multiple *If* statements. Each *If* statement will check a single condition. Of course, if we find one that works, we do not need to check any further. To make this happen, we nest the *If* statements one inside another, as shown in Figure 6-2-17. The nested *If* statements check one philosopher at a time. If one of the *If* statements is *true*, the function returns *true*; otherwise it returns *false*. This example makes clear an important fact about *Return* statements in a function. As soon as a *Return* statement is executed (as a result of an *If* statement being true), a *true* value is returned and the function is all over. Any remaining statements in the function are skipped. If none of the *If* statement conditions are true, the final *Return false* is executed.

What do we gain by writing a function such as *isPhilosopher*? For one thing, the code in the function is a lot easier to understand. Also, a call to the *isPhilosopher* function can now be used as the condition for the *If* statement in the *shootBolt* method, as shown in Figure 6-2-18.

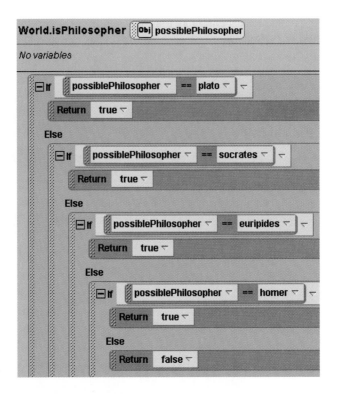

Figure 6-2-17. A function with multiple *If* statements

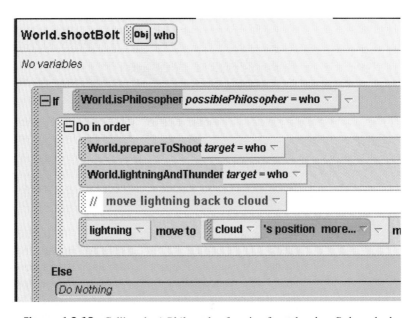

Figure 6-2-18. Calling the *isPhilosopher* function from the *shootBolt* method

Using a parameter in a condition

One last problem (that we know of) still exists in our Zeus world! Clicking on a philosopher who has already been shot by a thunderbolt results in Zeus shooting another thunderbolt at the "already-zapped" philosopher. (That seems like a waste of energy.) How can we prevent this from happening? One solution is to use another *If* statement to make sure Zeus only zaps a philosopher who isn't already frizzled.

How can we tell if a philosopher has already been zapped? In this example, we turned a zapped philosopher a black color (to dramatize the effect of a lightning strike). The color property can be used to determine whether the object has already been struck by lightning. Once again, we have the problem of a using a parameter as an object. (We saw this problem before in Chapter 5 when we wanted to use a *move to* instruction with the parameter *who*.) We will use the same technique of dragging in an arbitrary object and then replacing the object tile with *who*.

Here are the steps:

1. Drag an *If* statement into the method. In this example, drag it into the line immediately under the first *If* statement.

2. Select one of the philosophers from the Object tree (we arbitrarily chose plato). Drag its color property onto the condition tile and select the != operator and the color black. The result should look like this:

3. Drag the *who* parameter on top of plato to allow the color of any philosopher object to be checked. Now the statement should look like the one in Figure 6-2-19.

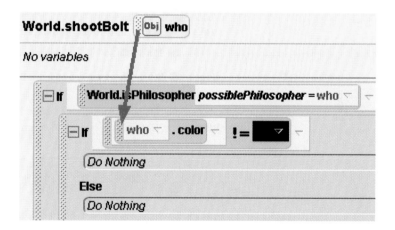

Figure 6-2-19. Replacing plato with the parameter *who*

Code is now added to the *If* and *Else* parts of the *If* statements. The completed code is illustrated in Figure 6-2-20.

The effect of the nested *If* statements is that both *If* statement conditions must be met before the *Do in order* block will be run. If the object clicked is a philosopher and the selected philosopher has not yet been struck by lightning, Zeus shoots his thunderbolt at the philosopher. On the other hand, if the user clicks on an object other than one of the four philosophers, Zeus says, "*I only shoot at philosophers!*" Finally, if the user clicks on a philosopher who has already been hit by a thunderbolt, Zeus now says, "*That philosopher is already zapped!!!*"

Other logic operators

In the Zeus program above, we used an *or* logic operator to create a condition that contained multiple parts. The *or* operator is one of three logic operators available in Alice. Another is the

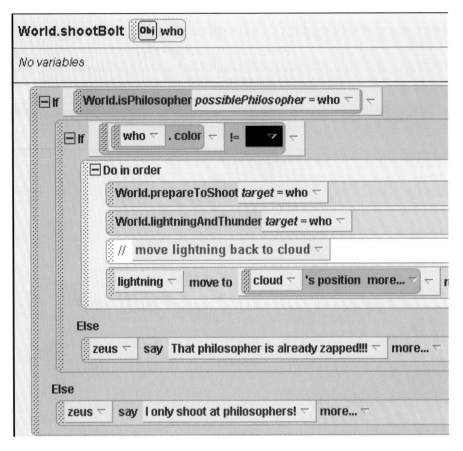

Figure 6-2-20. The complete code for the revised *shootBolt* method

not logical operator. The *not* operator behaves quite logically—if the value is *true*, *not true* is *false*; if the value is *false*, *not false* is *true*. The example

evaluates to *true* only when *who* is not homer. In other words, clicking anywhere on the screen (on one of the other philosophers, on a cloud, etc.) would cause this expression to evaluate to *true*. If the object clicked is homer, the expression evaluates to *false*.

A third logical operator is *and*. The *and* logical operator requires both Boolean expressions to be true in order to evaluate to *true*. The example

evaluates to *true* only if *who* is homer and his color has been set to blue.

It is important to be very careful with expressions containing two or more logical operators. The following expression evaluates to *true* only if *who* is homer and homer's color is black or blue.

This is because the nested tiles represent the expression:

*both (who == homer) and (either who.color == blue or who.color
== black, or both)*

Below is an expression that looks almost the same but is very different. It evaluates to
true if *who* is black. It will also evaluate to *true* if *who* is homer and his color is blue.

The reason this expression is different is that the logical tiles are nested differently, so
the order of evaluation is different. These nested tiles represent the expression:

*either (both (who == homer) and (who.color == blue)) or (who.color
== black) or both*

These examples point out that the level of nesting in logical expressions can be tricky.
In general, we recommend not including more than one logical operator in a Boolean expression. If more are needed, we recommend using nested *If* statements. It isn't that we think nested *If* statements are better than combinations of logical operators. Instead, we just realize it
can be quite difficult to understand exactly the order of evaluation when a Boolean expression
has several nested logical operators.

Tips & Techniques 6
Random Numbers and Random Motion

Random numbers

Random numbers play a big role in certain kinds of computing applications. For example,
random numbers are used in creating secure encryptions for transmission of information on
the internet. An encrypting utility uses random numbers to create a code for scrambling the
information stored in a file. Then the scrambled information is transmitted across the net.
When the information arrives at the target location it must be decrypted (unscrambled). To
decrypt the information, you need to know the code that was used. Various kinds of scientific
simulations also make use of random numbers. For example, random numbers are used to create "what-if" situations in weather simulation programs.

To illustrate the use of random numbers in Alice, let's create an animation where an object's motion is random. A random number is created by selecting the world-level function
random number, shown in Figure T-6-1.

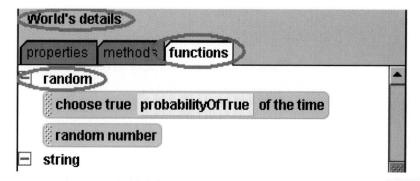

Figure T-6-1. World's *random number* functions

As an example, consider the world scene in Figure T-6-2. An Eskimo (People) and a penguin (Animals) are playing together, sliding around on the ice in a winter world.

Figure T-6-2. Pet penguin sliding on the ice

Suppose you want to write code to make the penguin slide forward a random distance. This easily is accomplished by first creating a *move* instruction and then dragging the *random number* function tile into the distance parameter. The result is shown here:

The *random number* function returns a fractional value between 0 and 1. When the above instruction is executed, the penguin will slide forward some fractional amount between 0 and 1. Although you know the range of values (somewhere between 0 and 1) you don't know the exact number. Also, each time the program is executed the distance is likely to be different. This unpredictability is what makes it random.

Selecting a range for random number

The default range of values for *random number* is 0 to 1. Suppose you want a random number between 1 and 5, instead of between 0 and 1. To specify the range of numbers for the random number function, click *more* in the *random number* tile (purple) and select the *minimum* value. Then, do the same to select a *maximum* value. The instruction with a range of 1 to 5 is shown here:

Now, each time the program is executed, the penguin will slide forward 3.8 meters or 2.3 meters or some other random amount between 1 and 4.999. We suggest that you test this out by creating and running the world. Press the **Restart** button several times to observe the sliding motion.

Integers (whole numbers)

Sometimes you may want a random number that has no digits to the right of the decimal point. For example, instead of numbers such as 3.8, or 2.3 you may want whole numbers such as 2 or 3 or 4. Numbers that are whole numbers (have no digits to the right of the decimal point) are known as integer values. To use the *random number* function to obtain random integer values, click *more* in the *random number* tile (purple) and select *integerOnly* and *true* in the pull-down menu, as shown in Figure T-6-3. In this example, the generated random number will be 1, 2, 3, or 4.

Figure T-6-3. Selecting *integerOnly* for the *random number* function

Random motion

If the *random number* function is combined with the *move* instruction, a form of random motion is created where objects move to a random location. Random motion is essential in many different kinds of games and simulations. As an example, consider the world in Figure T-6-4. The goldfish (Animals) is to swim in a random-like movement. We want to restrict the movement to a nearby position. Otherwise, successive moves would make the goldfish jump around here and there on the screen—not at all like a goldfish swimming.

Figure T-6-4.   The goldfish in a water world, for a random motion animation

Because Alice objects live in a three-dimensional world, you can write a *move* instruction that moves the goldfish in any of six possible directions (*forward, backward, left, right, up,* and *down*). Combining the *random number* function with six *move* instructions might be a bit clumsy. Let's try to make our work easier by taking advantage of negative numbers. If a negative number is used as the distance in a *move* instruction, the object is to move in the opposite direction. For example, the instruction shown next is to *move* the goldfish *left* −1 meters. When executed, this instruction will actually move the goldfish *right* 1 meter.

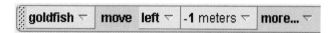

If we use both positive and negative distance values, only three *move* instructions are needed. We will use *up, left,* and *forward* directions. With this idea in mind, let's write a storyboard for a *randomMotion* method:

```
randomMotion

Parameters: min, max
Do together
  fish move up a random distance between min and max
  fish move left a random distance between min and max
  fish move forward a random distance between 0 and max
```

The *goldfish.randomMotion* storyboard contains a *Do together* block and three *move* instructions. In each move instruction, the random number function is called to generate a random distance. The parameters (*min* and *max*) are used to select the range of minimum and maximum values for the *random number* distance. In this example, we are going to use a *min* of −0.2 and a *max* of 0.2. So the *random number* function will return a value in the range of −0.2 to 0.2 for the move up and move left instructions. Note that *min* for the *move forward* instruction is 0. This is because goldfish do not swim backwards.

Now we can translate the storyboard into program code. The code for the *randomMotion* method is shown in Figure T-6-5. Think about how this method works. In each *move* instruction, the *random number* function is called to get a random distance. Let's say the *random number* function returns a negative distance for the *move up* instruction; the goldfish will actually move *down*. A negative distance for the *move left* instruction will move the goldfish *right*. The distance for the *move forward* instruction will always be positive, so the goldfish will always move forward.

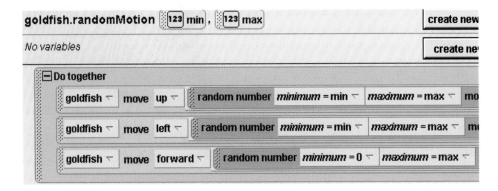

Figure T-6-5. The *randomMotion* method

The *Do together* block executes the *move up, move right,* and *move forward* all at the same time. As a result the goldfish will move to some random location within a cube of space defined by the minimum and maximum random number distances.

Once the *randomMotion* instruction has been written, it should be tested. To call the *randomMotion* method, *min* and *max* arguments must be passed to the method, as shown below. In this example, the *min* (−0.2) and *max* (0.2) arguments will restrict the movement of the goldfish to a random location near the current location.

Exercises and Projects

6-1 Exercises

1. *Adding Acrobats to the Rolling Ball*
   Begin by creating the rolling ball world as presented in Section 6-1. Add two objects/acrobats of your own choosing. (we used the Pharaoh and Anabas from the Egypt folder). Position them on top of the ball (Sports), one on top of the other. In the world shown below, we resized the ball to twice its size. Write a program for a circus act, where the acrobats move with the ball, staying on top of it, as the ball rolls. The acrobats should put their arms up half way, to help them balance as they move along with the rolling ball.

   Hint: Use the scene editor quad view to be certain the acrobats are standing directly on top of one another and are centered on the ball. Also, use pull-down menu methods to be sure that the acrobats and the ball all have the same orientation. (See Tips & Techniques 2 on how to use the *orient to* instruction to ensure that objects are synchronized for movement together.)

2. *Rotating Tires on a Car or Truck*
   Create a new world with a car or truck (Vehicles). Write a program to make the four wheels of the car turn forward as the car moves forward. The code should be very similar to the code used to make a ball roll forward (see the *realisticRoll* method in Section 6-1).

3. *Bee Scout*
   It has been a hot, dry summer and a hive of bees is in desperate need of a new supply of pollen. One bee (Animals/Bugs) has ventured far from the hive to scout for new pollen sources. A natural place to look is near ponds in the area. Set up the initial scene with a circle (Shapes) flat on the ground and colored blue to look like a pond. Add plants,

trees, and other natural scenery including some flowers (Nature). Be sure the bee is located somewhere around the edge of the pond, as shown in the screen shot here.

Write a program to animate the bee scouting the edge of a pond for flowers that are in bloom. The bee is to fly around the perimeter of the pond (circle). Write a method to move the bee scout around the perimeter of the pond in which the circumference of the circle is used to guide the motion. (Yes, *asSeenBy* could be used—but that is not the point of this exercise.) The formula for computing the circumference of a circle is $\pi \times$ the diameter of the circle. π is 3.14 and the diameter is the object's width. Write a function that computes and returns the circumference of the circle. Then have the bee fly around the perimeter of the pond by moving forward the amount of meters returned by the circumference function while turning left one revolution.

4. *Pyramid Climb*

On spring break, a student is visiting the land of the Pharaohs. The student (for example, randomGuy 1 from the People folder on the CD or Web gallery) decides to climb one of the pyramids (Egypt), starting at the bottom and moving straight up the side. Set up an initial scene consisting of a person and a pyramid, as shown in the screen shot below. Write a method to animate the *climb* so that the person's feet are always on the side of the pyramid.

Begin by pointing the person at the pyramid and walking him/her up to edge. Then, turn the person about 1/8 of a revolution so as to lean into the climb. (Play with this leaning movement until you get a reasonable angle for the person to climb the pyramid.) After reaching the top, the person should stand up straight.

To determine how far the person must move to complete the climb, the *climb* method must call a function. The function computes the side length of the pyramid. The formula for computing the distance up the side of the pyramid is based on the Pythagorean theorem $(a^2 + b^2 = c^2)$. The value of c will provide a rough estimate of how far the person should move (in a diagonal direction) up the side of the pyramid. The formula is:

$$\text{length of the pyramid's side} = \sqrt{((\text{pyramid's height})^2 + (\text{pyramid's width}/2)^2)}$$

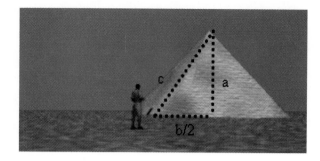

5. *Baking Lessons*

In this exercise, a woman (People) is learning how to make rolled cookies. Before she can cut out the cookies, she needs to roll the dough with her rolling pin (Kitchen). Create a function that determines how much the rolling pin is to roll as she slides it along the table, flattening the dough. Use the function in a world that animates rolling pin rolling across the table (Furniture on CD or Web gallery).

6-2 Exercises

6. *Modifications to the Zeus World*

(a) Modify the Zeus world to make each philosopher say something different when clicked.

- Euripides says, "Come on guys, I want to take a bath."
- Plato says, "I call it Play Doe" and then extends his right hand to show the other philosophers his Play Doe.
  - Homer says, "By my calculations, pretzels are the optimum solid food."
- Socrates says, "Like sands in the hour glass, so are the days of our lives."

Use an *If* statement to determine which philosopher was clicked.

(b) Modify the Zeus world so that if homer gets clicked and zapped by the thunderbolt, he falls over, says "d'oh", and then stands back up again (instead of turning color). Allow repeated clicking on homer, which should result in his repeated falling down and getting back up.

7. *Practice Turns*

Create a skater world, as illustrated below. Import an enhancedCleverSkater object, as designed and created in Chapter 4, Exercise 9. (If you have not created the Enhanced-CleverSkater class, an iceSkater can be used from the gallery, but you will have to write your own methods to make her skate forward and skate around an object.)

For this world, write a program to make the skater practice her turns on the ice. First, place the skater 1 meter from the second cone, facing forward. She then skates forward toward

the first cone (a sliding step). When she gets close, she should skate halfway around the cone and end up facing the other way to skate back toward the other cone. Next, have the skater skate toward the other cone and when close enough make a turn around it. In this way, the skater should complete a path around the two cones.

Hint: To find out whether the skater has gotten close enough to do a half-circle turn around the cone, you can use the *is within threshold of object* function for the enhancedCleverSkater. (The phrase *is within threshold of object* evaluates to *true* if the second object is within the specified distance of the first object.) Another possibility is to use the *distance to* function and the relational operator $a < b$ (available as a world-level function) to build the logical expression "Is the skater's distance to the cone less than 2 meters?"

8. *Figure-Eight*
   This exercise is an extension of Exercise 7. Modify the world to have the skater complete a figure-eight around the cones.

9. *Ice Danger*
   For this exercise, you can begin with a world completed in either Exercise 7 or 8—or create a new skater world from scratch. Add a hole in the ice (a blue circle).

Make the world interactive to allow the user to use the mouse to move the hole around on the icy surface. (See Tips & Techniques 5 for using the *let mouse move objects* event.) Now, as the skater is moving across the surface of the ice, the user can move the hole into the skater's path. Modify your method that skates the skater forward to use an *If* statement that checks whether the skater is skating over the hole. If she is on top of the hole, she will drop through it. If you have sound on your computer, you may want to add a splash sound.

10. *Flying Between Two Trees*

    Create a world with a lichenZenspider (Fantasy/Fairies) between two trees (Nature). Animate the lichenZenspider flying back and forth between the two trees. Make the world interactive so that lichenZenspider flies forward a short distance each time the user presses the enter key. LichenZenspider should move forward until she reaches a tree, then turn around to fly back toward the other tree. When she gets to the second tree, she should turn around to fly back toward the first tree. Be sure to avoid lichen-Zenspider's colliding with a tree.

11. *Spanish Vocabulary*

    A common exercise in teaching someone a new language is to show the person familiar objects and ask for the word for that object. In this exercise, you are to write a simple vocabulary builder to help someone learn the Spanish word for cat. The scene below shows a cat sitting on the grass and three Spanish words (3D text) displayed in front of the cat. The user is expected to click on the correct Spanish word for cat. A click on any other object will not work. Write a function (*isGato*) that returns *true* if the word (a 3D text object) selected is "gato," and *false* otherwise. The function will use one parameter (*objectClicked*) to send in the 3D text word clicked by the user. If the user clicks on "gato," the cat will say "Si, si!" Otherwise, the cat should turn its head left and right (indicating that the choice was incorrect).

12. *Switch*

    Create a world using a Switch object (in the Controls folder of the gallery). Write a method called *flipSwitch* that handles the "when the Switch is clicked" event. It the switch is clicked, its handle will flip from up to down or down to up. Also, write a Boolean function *isHandleUp* which returns *true* if the handle is up and *false* if it is down. (*flipSwitch* will call *isHandleUp* to decide whether to turn the handle forward $\frac{1}{2}$ revolution or backwards one-half revolution.)

Hint: To write *isHandleUp*, some reference point is needed to test the handle's position. One way to do this is to put a small invisible circle (Shapes folder) on the center of the switch plate. When the handle is up, the handle is above the circle. When the handle is turned down, the handle is below the circle. (See Tips & Techniques 4 for details on moving an object relative to an invisible object.) Do be careful to place the circle immediately below the handles center of gravity, as illustrated below.

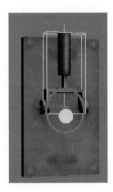

13. *Lightbulb*

    Create a world with a lightbulb (Lights) and a method *turnOnOff* that turns the lightbulb on/off depending on whether it is already on/off. When the lightbulb is on, its emissive color property has a value of yellow. When the lightbulb is off, its emissive color is black. Write a Boolean function *isLightOn* that returns *true* if the light bulb is on and *false* if it is off. When clicked, the lightbulb should turn on/off.

14. *Frighten Away the Dragon*

    Create an initial scene of a troll and a dragon (Medieval) as shown below. The troll is trying to frighten away the dragon from his favorite hunting grounds. The troll is to rant and rave while moving toward the dragon if the two are more than 5 meters apart. The troll should move toward the dragon every time the space bar is pressed. Use your own function to find out when the troll gets too close to the dragon. When the troll is less than 5 meters away from the dragon, have the dragon fly away.

15. *Zombie World*

     Create a world with a zombie (Spooky) and an open grave (a black square on the ground). In a scene from a scary movie, the zombie walks forward toward the grave and falls in. In this animation, every time the user presses the space bar, the zombie should walk forward. A Boolean function named *isAboveGrave* returns *true* if the zombie is within one-half meter of the grave. When the function returns *true*, make the zombie fall in.

16. *Does the Shoe Fit?*

     A common use of animation is to prepare educational software for young children. This animation is taken from a classic children's story. The prince (People) is trying to find the woman whose foot fits the glass slipper. He has come to Cinderella's home, and Cinderella and the two stepsisters (People) are waiting to try on the shoe, as shown in an initial scene below. This world will be interactive in that the user will click on one of the women in the scene. Write a function that returns *true* if the object clicked is Cinderella and *false* otherwise. If the shoe fits (it only fits Cinderella), the prince should move toward Cinderella and ask her to marry him. The glass slipper then appears on Cinderella's foot. If one of the stepsisters is clicked, the shoe will not fit, and the prince should indicate that she is not the one for him.

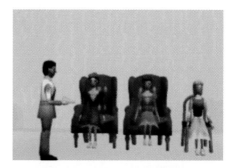

     Hint: To make this program easier to write, use two glass slippers: one the prince is holding and one on Cinderella's foot. Make the glass slipper on Cinderella's foot invisible. When the prince proposes marriage, make the shoe in the prince's hand invisible and the one on Cinderella's foot visible.

     Note: Do NOT use a "?" in the filename when saving a world.

6-2 Projects

1. *Gatekeeper*

    Build a world with four different objects of your choice (people, shapes, vehicles, etc.). We used objects from the Egypt folder. Position them in a lineup. The objects are facing the player and are spaced equally from one another.

In this game, one of the objects is a gatekeeper, holding a secret password to allow the user to open a hidden door into the pyramid. To find the secret password, the user must rearrange the objects in the lineup until the gatekeeper is on the far right. (If the objects in the lineup are counted from left to right, 1–2–3–4, the gatekeeper must be moved into position 4.) When an object is clicked, it switches position with the object farthest from it, 1 and 4 will switch with each other if either one is clicked, 3 will switch with 1 if clicked, and 2 will switch with 4 if clicked). Make one of the objects (in position 1, 2, or 3) the gatekeeper. You must use a Boolean function that returns *true* when the objects have been rearranged so the gatekeeper is on the far right of the lineup and *false* if it is not. When the gatekeeper is in position, display a 3D text object containing the password.

2. *Binary Code Game*

Build a world with three switches (Controls) and a lightbulb (Lights), as seen below. Set the *emissive color* property of the lightbulb to *black* (turned-off).

In this game, the positions of the levers on the switches represent a binary code. When a lever is up, it represents 1 (electric current in the switch is high) and when down, 0 (electric current in the switch is low). In the above world, all three levers are up, so the binary code is 111. The correct binary code is chosen at the beginning of the game. (You can enter a given code, and then have a friend try to guess it, or you can use the world-level *random number* function, as described in Tips & Techniques 6.) The idea is to have the user try to guess the correct binary code that will light up the light bulb (its emissive color will be yellow). To guess the binary code, the user will click on the levers to change their position. Each time the user clicks on a lever, it moves in the opposite direction—up (if currently down) or down (if currently up). When all three switches are in the correct position for the binary code, the bulb will turn on.

Each switch should respond to a mouse-click on the switch. If the handle is down, flip it up. If the handle is up, flip it down. To track the current position of a handle, an invisible circle can be placed on the switch and used as a point of reference. When the handle is above the circle, turn it down. When the handle is below the circle, turn it up. See Exercise 12 for more detail.

Your program must include a Boolean function that determines whether the Boolean code is correct.

Hint: You can use the color of the circles (even though they are invisible) as a flag that indicates the correct position of the lever.

3. *Driving Test*
   Create a world that simulates a driving test. The world should have a car (Vehicles), 5 cones (Shapes), and a gate (Spooky). Set up your world as shown in the image below. Also, create two 3D text-phrase objects: "You Pass" and "Try Again". Set the *isShowing* property of each text-phrase to *false*, so that they are not visible in the initial scene.

In this driver test, the user will use arrow-key presses to move the car forward, left, or right to swerve around each of the five cones. If the car hits one of the cones, the driver fails the test, the car stops moving and the "Try Again" text object is made visible. If the user manages to steer the car past all 5 cones, the car should drive through the gate and the "You Pass" text object become visible. Write a function named *isTooClose* that checks the car's distance to a cone. If the car is within 2 meters of the cone, the function returns *true*. It returns *false* otherwise. Also, write a function named *isTestPassed*, which evaluates whether the user has passed the test (i.e., whether the car has been driven past the gate).

Hint: Work under the assumption that the user will not cheat (i.e., pass all the cones and head straight through the gate). Due to the differences in the width and depth of the car, do not be concerned if part of the front or back of the car hits a cone.

4. *Phishy Move*
   Phishy fish (Animals) has just signed up at swim school to learn the latest motion, the *sineWave*. Your task is to write a method to teach her the *sineWave* motion. The initial scene with a fish and water is seen here.

Note: This world is provided on the CD that accompanies this book. We recommend that you use the prepared world, as setting up the scene is time consuming. If you are an adventuresome soul, here are the instructions for setting up the world on your own: Use popup methods to move the fish to the world origin (0,0,and 0) and then turn the fish right one-quarter revolution. Because Phishy is partially submerged, set the opacity of the water to 30% so the fish can be seen in the water. Now, use camera controls to reposition the camera (this takes a bit of patience as the camera must be moved horizontally 180 degrees from its default position). Then, adjust the vertical angle to give a side view of the fish in the water, as seen above. The fish should be located at the far left and the water should occupy the lower half of the world view, as seen in the screen shot above.

Alice has a *sine* function that can be used to teach Phishy the *sineWave* motion. (The sine function is often used to determine the relationship between the lengths of the sides of a right triangle. For the purposes of this animation, that relationship is not really important.) If the sine function is computed over all angles in a full circle, the sine value starts at 0, goes up to 1, back through 0 to −1 and returns to 0:

Angle	Sine of the angle
0	0
45	0.707
90	1
135	0.707
180	0
225	−0.707
270	−1
315	−0.707
360	0

This function is continuous, so if sine values are plotted some multiple of times, we will see the curve repeated over and over:

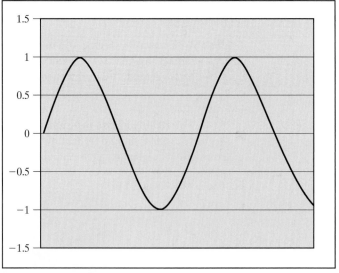

Sine wave

For the *sineWave* motion, Phishy is to move in the sine wave pattern. In the world provided on the CD, Phishy has been positioned at the origin of the world. In a 2D system, we would say she is at point (0,0). To simulate the sine wave pattern, she needs to move up to height that is 1 meter above the water, then down to a depth of 1 meter below the surface of the water (-1 meter), back up to 1 meter above the water, and so on, at the same time as she moves to the right in the water. The Alice sine function expects to receive an angle expressed in radians (rather than degrees). Write a function, named *degreesToRadians*, which will convert the angle in degrees to the angle in radians. To convert from degrees to radians, multiply the angle degrees by π and divide by 180. The *degreesToRadians* function should return the angle in radians.

Now, write a method to have Phishy move in the sine wave pattern. Remember that in the world provided on the CD, Phishy has already been positioned at the origin of the world. So, Phishy is already at the position for 0 degrees.

Hint: One way to create the sine wave pattern is to use *move to* instruction (Tips & Techniques 2). A *move to* instruction should move Phishy to a position that is (*right, up*, 0), where *right* is the radian value and *up* is the *sin(radian value)*. After adding a *move to* instruction, the built-in world level function *(right, up, forward)* can be dropped onto the target of the *move to*, allowing individual specification of each coordinate. Use *move to* instructions for angles: 45, 90, 135, 180, 225, 270, 315, and 360. For a smoother animation, make each *move to* instruction have *style = abruptly*. Using *style = abruptly* seems counter intuitive to making an animation run more smoothly. The reason is that animation instructions begin slowly (gently) and end slowly (gently) by default. If we wish to have 2 instructions appear to behave as a single instruction, we do not want each instruction to slow down as the instruction starts/ends. Hence we use the abrupt option.

5. *Cosine Wave*

   Teach Phishy how to move in a cosine wave pattern, instead of the sine wave pattern described in the preceding project.

Summary

Examples in this chapter presented ways to use functions and *If* statements in methods. In Alice, an *If* statement allows for conditional execution of a section of code (based on the value of a Boolean condition, *true* or *false*). The Boolean condition is used to determine whether the *If* part or the *Else* part of the statement will be executed at runtime. Thus, an *If* statement allows us to control the flow of execution of a section of our program code.

Built-in functions do not always meet the particular needs of a program. In this chapter, we looked at how to write your own functions that return different types of values. The benefit of writing your own functions is that you can think about the task on a higher plane—a form of abstraction. Functions that compute and return a number value make program code much less cluttered and easier to read, because the computation is hidden in a function. Such functions will be useful in many situations. For example, we might want to write a function to return the number of visible objects on the screen in an arcade-style game. The function would be called to keep track of how many objects the user has eliminated (made invisible). When only a few objects are left, we might decide to speed up the game.

Parameters can be used to allow a function to be used with different objects. As with class-level methods, you can write a class-level function and save it out with the object. This allows the function to be reused in another program.

Important concepts in this chapter

- An *If* statement is a block of program code that allows for the conditional execution of that code.
- An *If* statement contains a Boolean condition used to determine whether the segment of code will execute.

- If the Boolean condition evaluates to *true*, the *If* part of the statement is executed. If the expression evaluates to *false*, the *Else* part is executed.
- Boolean conditions may call built-in functions that return a *true* or *false* value.
- Logical operators (*and, or, not*) can be used to combine simple Boolean expressions into more complex expressions.
- Relational operators ($<, >, >=, <=, ==, !=$) can be used to compare values in a Boolean expression.
- Functions can be written to return a Boolean value and used in *If* statements.
- Functions can also be written to compute and return other types of values.

CHAPTER **7**

Repetition: Definite and Indefinite Loops

"Are we nearly there?" Alice managed to pant out at last. "Nearly there!" the Queen repeated. "Why, we passed it ten minutes ago! Faster!"

In example programs, we have used *If* statements to make a choice about whether to execute a section of program code. In this way, *If* statements can be used to control program execution. This is why an *If* statement may be thought of as a control statement. In this chapter, we look at control statements where instructions and methods are repeated.

In Section 7-1, examples are presented where a *Loop* statement is used to execute a block of instructions again and again. The *Loop* statement can be used when we know exactly how many times a block of instructions should be repeated (that is, a definite number of times). We use the word count to describe the number of times a loop repeats. For this reason, a *Loop* statement is referred to as a counted loop.

In Section 7-2, the *While* statement is introduced for repeating a block of instructions where we do not know exactly how many times it should be repeated (an indefinite number of times). A *While* statement corresponds naturally to the way we say and think about certain actions in our everyday conversation. For example, we might say, "While I am driving, I will continue to keep my hands on the wheel and my eyes on the road," or perhaps something like, "While I am a member of the baseball team, I will practice batting." The *While* statement is intuitive—a way to think about actions that repeat while some condition remains true.

7-1 Loops

As our worlds become more sophisticated, the code tends to become longer. One reason is that some animation instructions and methods must be repeated to make the same action occur over and over. Perhaps you have already written programs where you needed to write a call to a method several times. In this section, we look at using a *Loop* statement to call a method repeatedly.

Using a loop for repeating a call to a method

Let's begin with a very simple world, shown in Figure 7-1-1. A bunny (Animals) has snuck into his neighbor's garden (Nature) and has spotted some nice broccoli shoots. We resized several tree (Nature) objects to a very small size to create the broccoli-like objects. The task is to write a program to animate the bunny hopping over to munch a few bites of broccoli.

Let's assume we have already written a method for the bunny named *hop*. The *hop* method enables the bunny to hop forward by moving his legs up and down at the same time as he moves forward. A possible implementation of the *hop* method appears in Figure 7-1-2. (The sound instruction is optional.)

Figure 7-1-1. A bunny in the garden

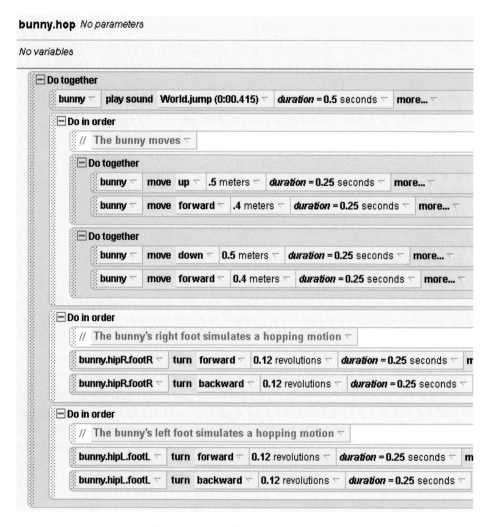

Figure 7-1-2. The *bunny.hop* method

The bunny in our example world is eight hops away from the broccoli. One possible way to animate eight bunny hops is given in Figure 7-1-3. In this program, a *Do in order* block is placed in the *World.my first method*. Then, a *turn to face* instruction is used to make the bunny turn to look at the broccoli. Finally, the call to the *bunny.hop* method is dragged into the editor eight times.

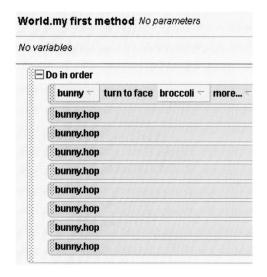

Figure 7-1-3. Eight hops

Of course, the code in Figure 7-1-3 will perform the task of making the bunny hop over to the broccoli. It was tedious, though, to drag eight *bunny.hop* instructions into the program. We want to look at a way to make our job easier by using a *Loop* statement. To create a *Loop* statement, drag the *Loop* tile into the editor. The popup menu offers a choice for the count (the number of times the loop will execute), as shown in Figure 7-1-4. In this example, the number 8 is entered as the count. Note that a loop can execute only a whole number of times.

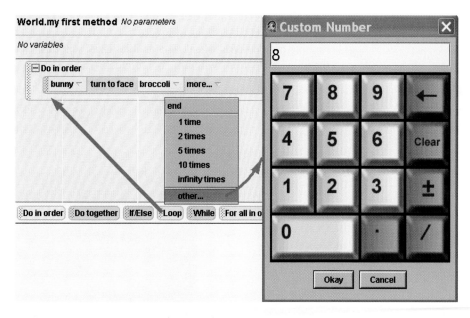

Figure 7-1-4. Selecting a count

Next, a call to the *bunny.hop* method is placed inside the *Loop* statement, as shown in Figure 7-1-5. When the program is run, the bunny will turn to face the broccoli and then hop eight times. That is, the loop will call the *bunny.hop* method eight times. The benefit of using a *Loop* is immediately obvious—the *Loop* is quick and easy to write. Although eight calls to the *bunny.hop* method is not a big deal, there are program situations where methods have to be repeated 20, 30, or even 100 times. It would be much easier to use a single *Loop* statement if the bunny had to hop 100 times!

In this simple example, we placed a single call to a method (*bunny.hop*) in the *Loop* statement. We could have dragged several instructions and method calls into the block, and all would have been repeated. A *Do in order* or *Do together* block can be nested inside the loop to control how the instructions are repeated; otherwise Alice will assume the instructions are to be done in order.

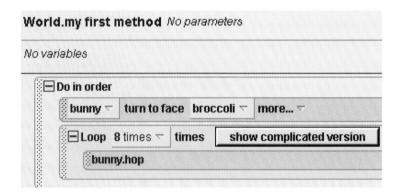

Figure 7-1-5. Using the *Loop* statement to call a method repeatedly

Nested loops

Each of the examples above used only one *Loop* statement. Of course it is possible to have several *Loop* statements in the same program. In fact, a *Loop* statement can be nested inside another *Loop* statement. In this section, we take a look at a world where this is an appropriate way to write the program code.

Consider an initial scene with a two-wheeled Ferris wheel (Amusement Park folder on the CD or Web gallery), as in Figure 7-1-6. An animation is to be written that simulates the running of this Ferris wheel. The double wheel will turn clockwise (roll right) while each of the individual wheels will turn counterclockwise (roll left).

Figure 7-1-6. A Ferris wheel

Figure 7-1-7 is code for a *Loop* to roll the Ferris wheel ten times. The *style = abruptly* parameter has been used to smooth out the rotating of the entire double wheel over each repetition. (We chose the *abrupt* style because the default style, *gently*, slows down the animation instruction as it begins and ends. Because we are repeating the instruction within a loop, we want to avoid having the wheel go through a repeated slowdown, speedup, slowdown, speedup ... kind of action.)

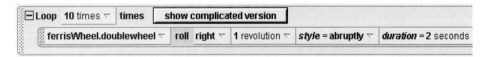

Figure 7-1-7. Rotating the double wheel 10 times

With the motion of the entire Ferris wheel accomplished, instructions can now be written to rotate each of the inner wheels counterclockwise (roll left) while the outer double wheel is rotating clockwise (roll right). The code to rotate the inner wheels is presented in Figure 7-1-8.

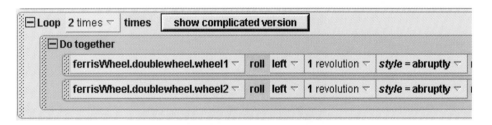

Figure 7-1-8. Rotating the inner wheels two times

Now the rotations can be combined. To increase the excitement of the ride, we will have the inner wheels rotate more frequently, perhaps twice as often as the outer wheel. So, each time the double wheel rotates one revolution clockwise, the inner wheels should rotate twice counterclockwise. Figure 7-1-9 shows the modified code.

In previous programs you have seen that actions in a *Do together* block need to be synchronized in duration. In this example the inner wheels need to rotate twice while the outer wheel rotates once. So, the duration of rotation for the outer wheel (*doublewheel*) is made to be twice the duration of rotation of the inner wheels (*doublewheel.wheel1* and *doublewheel.wheel2*).

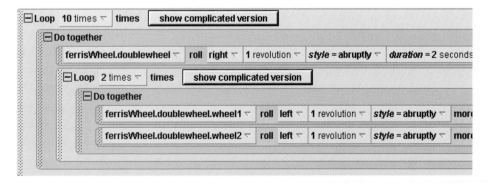

Figure 7-1-9. The complete code for the Ferris wheel

Each time the outer loop runs once, the inner loop runs twice. This means that the double wheel takes 2 seconds to complete its rotation, and the inner wheels require 1 second (the default duration) to complete their rotations, but rotate twice. In all, the inner wheels rotate 20 times counterclockwise as the outer wheel rotates 10 times clockwise.

Optical Illusion: Instructions within a *Do together* block can sometimes cancel each other out (in terms of the animated action we can observe). For example, in the First Encounter world described in Chapter 2, Section 2, turning the backLeftLegUpperJoint backward and forward at the same time made the animation look as though the leg was not turning at all. In the Ferris wheel example above, since the outer loop is set to execute only 1 time and the inner loop 2 times, the inner wheel will look as though it rotates only once.

Using a function call to compute the count

In the examples presented here, the number of times a block of code was to loop was a specific number, 2, 8, or 10. But the count can also be a function that returns a number. For example, the code in Figure 7-1-10 uses a function to determine the count for a loop. If the guy were 6 meters from the girl, the *Loop* would make the guy walk 6 times (assuming that the guy covers exactly 1 meter in his *walk* method). What would happen if the guy were 5.7 meters from the girl? The loop only executes a whole number of times. So the guy would walk only 5 times.

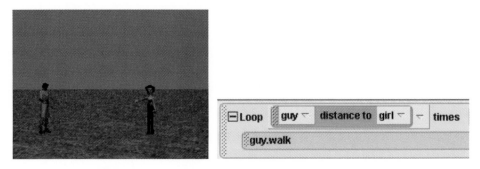

Figure 7-1-10. Using a function to determine a loop count

A tremendous advantage of using a function as the number of times to loop is that objects can be repositioned in the initial scene, and it will not be necessary to modify the code to specify the count. The function will automatically compute the distance between the guy and the girl and the loop will repeat only as many times as needed.

Infinite loop

One option in the popup menu for selecting a *Loop* count is *infinity*. (See Figure 7-1-11.) If *infinity* is selected, the loop will continue on and on until the program stops.

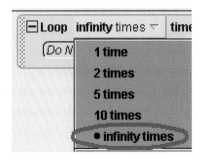

Figure 7-1-11. Selecting *infinity* as the count

Ordinarily, we advise that you avoid infinite loops. However, in animation programs an infinite loop is sometimes useful. Consider an amusement park animation where a carousel is one of the objects in the scene, as in Figure 7-1-12. To make the carousel go around in the background, call the carousel's built-in method *carouselAnimation* in an infinite loop, as shown in Figure 7-1-13.

Figure 7-1-12. Carousel in infinite motion

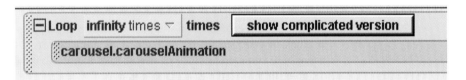

Figure 7-1-13. Loop *infinity* times

7-2 *While*—a conditional loop

The *Loop* statement requires that the programmer specify the number of times the loop is to be repeated. This could be a number, such as 10, or a function such as *boy.distance to girl*. The number of times a loop should repeat might not be known in advance. This is often the case in games and simulations, where objects move randomly. In this section, a form of looping known as the *While* statement will be introduced to handle situations where the programmer does not know (at the time the program is written) how many times the loop should be repeated.

The *While* statement is a conditional loop . One way to think about a *While* statement is:

While some condition is true perform instruction(s)

The instruction performed inside the while statement can be a single action or several actions enclosed in a *Do in order* or *Do together* block. The condition used in a *While* statement is a Boolean condition (the same type of condition used in *If* statements). The Boolean condition acts like a gatekeeper at a popular dance club. If the condition is true, entry is gained to the *While* statement and the instructions within the *While* statement are executed, otherwise the instructions are skipped. Unlike the *If* statement, however, the *While* statement is a loop. The diagram in Figure 7-2-1 illustrates how the *While* statement works as a loop.

If the condition is *true,* the instructions are performed; then the condition gets checked again. If the condition is still *true*, the instructions within the loop are repeated. If the condition has become *false*, the loop ends and Alice goes on to execute the next statement in the program. A *While* statement is useful for situations where we do not know how many times the loop should be repeated. All we need to know is the condition that determines whether the loop will be repeated.

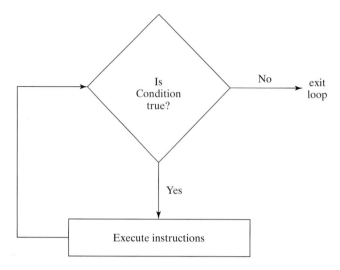

Figure 7-2-1. The *While* statement works as a loop

Chase scene

Let's look at an example of a situation where we do not know (ahead of time) how many times a block of code should be repeated. This animation is a "chase scene" simulation. Chase scenes are common in video games and animation films where one object is trying to catch another. In this example, a shark is hungry for dinner. The shark is going to chase after and catch a fleeing goldfish (Animals). OK, so this is not a gracious animation—but sharks have to eat, too! Figure 7-2-2 shows a very simple initial world.

Figure 7-2-2. Chase scene

Problem

Our task is to animate the shark chasing the goldfish, as it tries to get close enough (say, within 0.5 meters) to gobble the goldfish down for dinner. Naturally, as the shark chases it, the goldfish is not standing still. Instead, it is trying to escape by moving to a random position. Of course, we want the fish to look like it is swimming (not jumping all around on the screen), so we will move it to a random position that is close to the current position.

Storyboard solution

The basic idea is that if the goldfish is more than 0.5 meters away from the shark, the shark is going to point at the goldfish and swim toward it. Meanwhile, the goldfish is moving away to a random position nearby. If the goldfish is still more than 0.5 meters away, the shark will change course and swim toward it and the goldfish will try to swim away. Eventually, when the shark finally gets within 0.5 meter of the goldfish, the chase is over and the shark can catch and eat the goldfish.

Let's plan a method for the chase animation using the *While* statement. Think about it like this:

"While the shark is more than 0.5 meters away from the goldfish, move the shark toward the goldfish and, at the same time, move the goldfish to a random position nearby"

The condition in our *While* statement will be "the goldfish is more than 0.5 meter away from the shark." If this condition is true, the chase is on. A storyboard is shown here.

```
chase

Do in order
While the goldfish is more than 0.5 meters away from the shark
        Do in order
                shark point at the goldfish
                Do together
                        shark swim (toward the goldfish)
                        goldfish flee (away from the shark)
shark eat (the goldfish)
```

The condition must be *true* to allow entry into the loop. After running the instructions within the *While* statement, the condition will be evaluated again, and if the condition is still *true*, the instructions within the *While* statement will run again. This process continues until the condition finally evaluates to *false*.

In the storyboard, the *shark swim, goldfish flee*, and *shark eat* steps will each require several instructions. These actions will be written as methods.

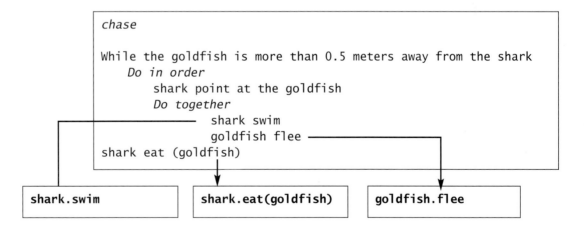

For now, let's pretend that these methods have already been written (we can write them next). A *chase* method to implement the overall storyboard is illustrated in Figure 7-2-3.

Now, let's look at how to write the *shark.swim, goldfish.flee,* and *shark.eat* methods that are called from the *chase* method. We can use stepwise refinement to complete the storyboard, as shown next. Please note that a *duration* of zero causes the instruction to occur instantaneously, without a gradual animation of the action.

The *shark.swim* method moves the shark forward and the turns the torso of the shark right and left to simulate a swimming motion through water. Figure 7-2-4 illustrates *shark.swim.*

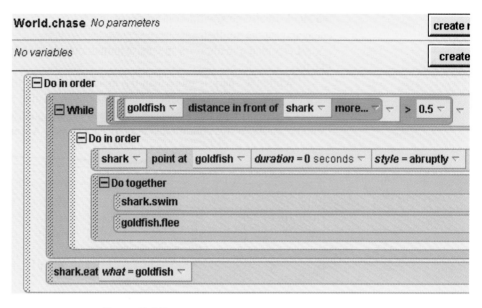

Figure 7-2-3. The *chase* method using a *While* statement

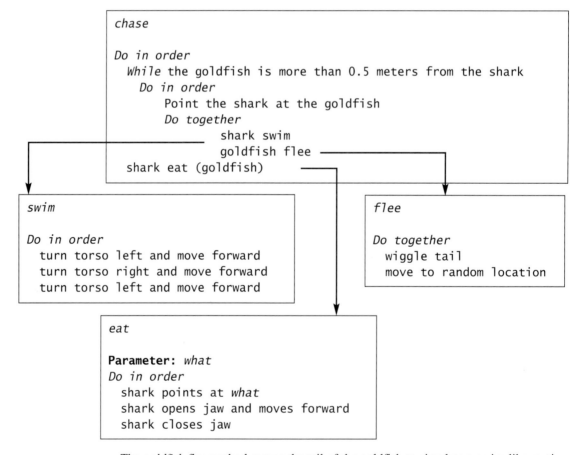

The *goldfish.flee* method moves the tail of the goldfish to simulate a swim-like motion and calls the *randomMotion* method (previously defined in Tips & Techniques 6) to move the fish to a nearby random location. The *goldfish.flee* method is shown in Figure 7-2-5.

After the While statement ends, the *shark.eat* method is executed, as is illustrated in Figure 7-2-6. The method uses a parameter to specify *what* object in the scene is on the menu.

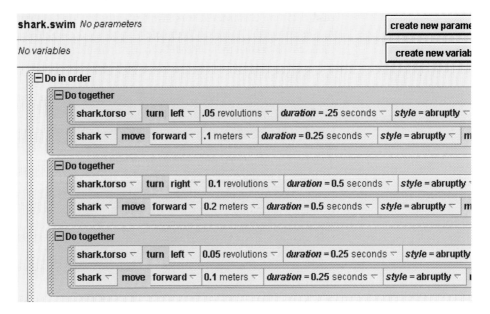

Figure 7-2-4. The *shark.swim* method gives realistic shark movement

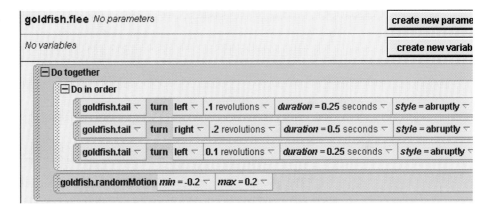

Figure 7-2-5. The *goldfish.flee* method—fish swims to a random location

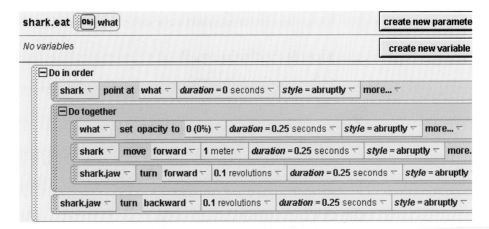

Figure 7-2-6. The *shark.eat* method

In this example, *shark.eat* was invoked with the goldfish object as the parameter. The shark moves forward 1 meter to completely swallow the goldfish. The opacity of the goldfish is faded to 0% so that the goldfish becomes invisible (disappearing into the shark's mouth).

Infinite *While*

As a general rule, a *While* statement should contain instructions that change conditions in the world so the *While* statement will eventually end. Otherwise, the loop would continue to execute in a never-ending cycle—an infinite loop. (An infinite loop is often a program error that makes the program seem to be "spinning its wheels.") In the shark chase example above, we avoided an infinite loop by carefully planning the distance the shark and the goldfish move with each execution of the loop. Although the goldfish is moving randomly, we set the maximum value to 0.2 meters in any one direction (forward, up/down, right/left). A bit of 3D geometry is needed to show that the total distance the goldfish travels must be less than .35 meters, as illustrated in Figure 7-2-7.

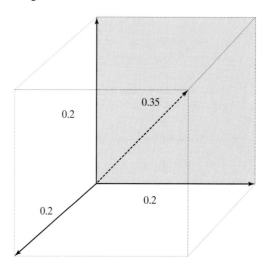

Figure 7-2-7. Maximum distance the goldfish can travel in one move

The goldfish, then, never moves more than 0.35 meters away from the shark, and the shark always moves 0.4 meters closer to the goldfish. The shark's distance advantage guarantees that the shark is eventually going to catch up to the goldfish and the loop will end.

We highly recommend that you carefully check the condition for a *While* statement to be sure the loop will eventually end. On the other hand, there are some kinds of programs where an infinite loop is desirable. This is particularly true in games and simulation animations, where an action should occur until the program shuts down.

Tips & Techniques 7

Events and Repetition

 #### The BDE (Begin-During-End) event

In a *While* statement, as described in Chapter 7, Section 2, actions occur while some condition remains true. Sometimes, we would like to make an action occur when the condition becomes *false* and the loop ends. For example, consider the world in Figure T-7-1, where a helicopter (Vehicles) has arrived to rescue the white rabbit (Animals). The helicopter is circling over the island (Environments). We want the rabbit to look at the helicopter and turn his head to keep an eye on it as long as the helicopter is in front of him. Of course, the helicopter is circling the island and will eventually fly out of sight of the rabbit. When the rabbit can no longer see the helicopter, we want him to look at the camera.

Figure T-7-1. The rabbit rescue scene

This animation has two repeated actions: a helicopter circling an island and a rabbit moving his head to watch the helicopter as it circles. Also, an action should occur as soon as the helicopter can no longer be seen by the rabbit: the rabbit looks back at the camera. The problem is how to make actions repeat (within a loop) but also make an action occur each time the loop ends. We have seen this situation before in working with interactive worlds and events. Perhaps we can create a solution to our problem by using events. In fact, Alice has a built-in *While* statement event for linking events to repeated actions. The event, highlighted in Figure T-7-2, is *While something is true*.

Figure T-7-2. Selecting *While something is true* in the events editor

Selecting the *While something is true* event from the pull-down menu causes a *While* event block to be added to the Events editor, as shown in Figure T-7-3. The event block automatically contains a Begin-During-End (BDE) block that allows you to specify what happens when the loop begins, during the execution of the loop, and when the loop ends.

To create a BDE behavior, we need to specify up to four pieces of information (any or all may be left as *Nothing*):

> **A conditional expression/function (evaluates to *true* or *false*)**—The *While* statement condition is *<None>* by default, but you must replace it with a Boolean expression or function.

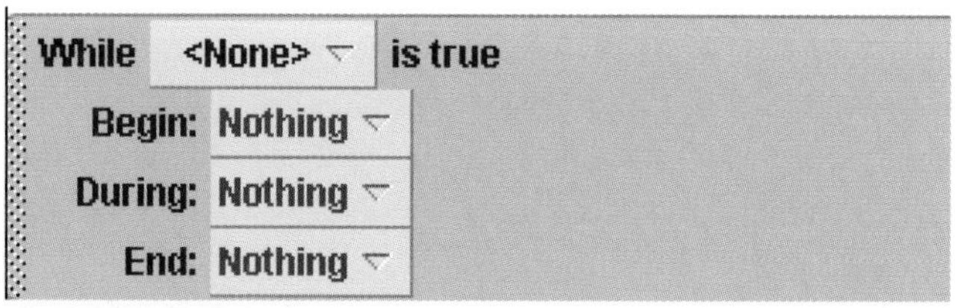

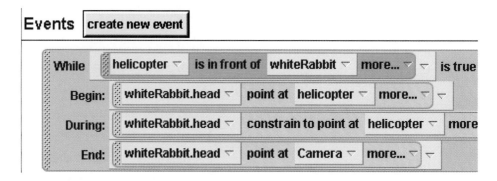

Figure T-7-3. *While* event with *Begin-During-End* (BDE)

Begin—An animation instruction or method that is to be done once, at the time the condition becomes true.

During—An animation instruction or method that is to be done repeatedly, as long as the condition remains true. Note that as soon as the condition becomes false, the animation instruction or method ceases running, even if it is in the middle of an instruction!

End—An animation instruction or method that is to be done once, at the time the condition becomes false.

In the above example, the helicopter is flying around the island. We would like to have the white rabbit's head look at (*point at*) the helicopter as soon as the helicopter is in front of the rabbit (Begin). Then, as long as the helicopter is still in front of the rabbit (During), we want the rabbit's head to continue to look at the helicopter. As soon as the helicopter is no longer in front of the rabbit (End), the rabbit should look back at the camera. The code in Figure T-7-4 accomplishes this task:

Figure T-7-4. *While statement in an event link*

The *constrain to point at* instruction is a built-in method that adjusts the position of an object to point at some other object. In this example, *constrain to point at* is used to make the rabbit's head continuously point at the helicopter as long as the *While* statement condition (helicopter is in front of whiteRabbit) is *true*.

Exercises and Projects

7-1 Exercises

1. *Caught in the Act*
   This exercise is to complete the bunny example in Section 7-1. You will recall that the bunny has snuck into his neighbor's garden and is hopping over to take a bite of the tempting broccoli shoots. Code was presented to make the bunny hop eight times (in a

loop) over to the broccoli. Just as the bunny reaches the broccoli, Papa rabbit (Hare from Animals folder) appears at the garden gateway and taps his foot in dismay. The bunny hops a quick retreat out of the garden. Write a program to implement the bunny in the garden animation. Your code should use a loop not only to make the bunny hop over to the broccoli (see the initial scene in Figure 7-1-1) but also to hop out of the garden.

2. *Square Bunny Hop*

This exercise explores the use of nested loops. Papa rabbit has been teaching the bunny some basic geometry. The lesson this morning is on the square shape. To demonstrate that the bunny understands the idea, the bunny is to hop in a square. Create a world with the bunny and the hop method, as described in Section 7-1. Use a loop to make the bunny hop three times. When the loop ends, have the bunny turn left one-quarter revolution. Then add another loop to repeat the above actions, as shown in the storyboard here.

```
Loop 4 times
        Loop 3 times
                bunny.hop
        turn left ¼ revolution
```

3. *Saloon Sign*

An old saloon (Old West) is being converted into a tourist attraction. Use 3D text to create a neon sign to hang on the front of the balcony. Then use a loop to make the sign blink 10 times. (Tips & Techniques 1 provides instructions on using 3D text. Tips & Techniques 4 shows how to make an object visible or invisible.)

4. *Lock Combination*

Exercise 10 in Chapter 4 was to create a new class of combination lock with four class-level methods—*leftOne, rightOne, leftRevolution*, and *rightRevolution*—that turn the dial 1 number left, 1 number right, 1 revolution left, and 1 revolution right, respectively. Also, the lock has a method named *open* that opens it, and another named *close* that closes it. The purpose of this exercise is to reuse the methods created in the previous exercise. Revise the previous world. Use a loop instruction to turn the dial left 25. Then use a loop to turn the dial right and finally use a loop to turn the dial back to the left 3 times. (The combination is 25, 16, 3). Then, pop open the latch, close the latch and return the dial to zero.

Hint: Use *Wait* to make the lock pause between each turn of the dial.

7-2 Exercises

5. *Frog and Ladybug*

Create a world with a frog (Animals) and a ladybug (Animals). Write an interactive program to allow the user to drag the ladybug around the scene. (Use a *let the mouse move objects* event.) As the ladybug is dragged around, make the frog chase after it by moving one hop at a time without colliding with the ladybug. If the user moves the ladybug within 2 meters of the frog, have the frog look at the camera and say "ribbit"—then end the animation.

6. *Bumper Cars*

Create a simulation of the bumper car ride (Amusement Park), where the cars move continuously around within the bumper arena. Add two bumper cars inside the arena. In this animation, each car should be moving forward a small amount until it gets too close to another car or to the wall, then turn the car a quarter of a revolution clockwise (to get a different direction) and continue moving forward. Use a switch (Controls) to stop and start the ride. As long as the switch is on, the ride should continue.

Hint: To avoid a car driving through a wall of the arena, a simple form of collision detection is needed. One way to check for a possible collision is to use the *distance to* function to compute the distance of the car to the arena. Remember that *distance to* is measured "center-to-center." In this world, a measurement from the center of the car to the center of the arena is exactly what you need. (When a car gets too far from the center of the arena, it will collide with a wall.) It is also possible to write a function that returns whether two cars are about to collide with one another. What should be done in this case?

7. *Stop and Start*
   Choose a ride object other than the carousel from the Amusement Park gallery that moves in a circular pattern (a round-and-round manner, like the Ferris wheel). Create a method that performs an animation appropriate for the ride object selected. Then, create a way to start and stop the ride using the *While something is true* event.

8. *Speed Control*
   Place a fan (Objects) in a new world. The fan has four buttons—high, medium, low, and off. Create a method that controls the speed at which the fan blades rotate, depending on which button is clicked. (You may want to use several methods instead of just one.) The blades should continue turning until the animation stops running or the user clicks the off button.

9. *Old-time Rock and Roll*
   Create a world with an old-fashioned phonograph (Objects) in it. Create methods to turn the crank and turn the record. Then, create the BDE control mechanism (Tips & Techniques 7) to call a method that plays the record at the same time the crank is turning.

10. *Wind-up Penguin*

    Create a world with a wind-up penguin. This is actually a penguin (Animals) with a windUpKey (Objects) positioned against its back. The key's *vehicle* property has been set to the penguin. In this world, make the penguin waddle (or walk) around the world continuously while its wind-up key turns.

7-2 Projects

1. *Drinking Parrot*

   A small toy popular with children is a drinking parrot. The parrot is positioned in front of a container of water and its body given a push. Because of the counterbalance of weights on either end of its body, the parrot repeatedly lowers its head into the water. Create a simulation of the drinking parrot (Objects). Use an infinite *Loop* statement to make the parrot drink.

   Hint: We used the blender object (Objects), pushed the base into the ground, and changed the color of the blender to blue to simulate a bucket of water.

2. *Tennis Shot*

   Create a tennis shot game with a kangaroo_robot (SciFi), a tennis ball, tennis net, and tennis racket (Sports). Position the tennis ball immediately in front of the robot on the other side of the net (from the camera point of view) and the tennis racket on this side of the net (from the camera point of view). The initial scene should appear as shown next.

Set up an event to *let the mouse move objects* (Tips & Techniques 5). In this game, the kangaroo_robot and the tennis ball move together left or right a random distance (use the World *random number* function) between −1 and 1 meter. Then the robot "throws" the ball across the net (the tennis ball moves up a random height and forward a given distance). The player will move the tennis racket to try to "hit" the tennis ball. A "hit" occurs when the tennis racket gets within 0.1 meter of the tennis ball. Actually, the tennis ball is virtual in this simulation and will go right through the racket even if the player manages to "hit" it. However, we will know when the player manages to "hit" the tennis ball, because the kangaroo_robot will wiggle his ears.

   The real challenge in writing this program is to figure out whether the player is successful in moving the tennis racket close enough to the tennis ball to hit it before it goes out of sight. To make this work, use a loop where each execution of the loop moves the tennis ball up and forward only a very short distance. Each time through the loop, check to see if the racket has gotten close enough to the ball to score a hit. As mentioned above, you will need to experiment to figure out the appropriate count for the loop so as to eventually move the ball forward out of sight of the camera. When the loop ends, have the kangaroo_robot turn left one-quarter revolution and move off the tennis court signaling that the game is over.

3. *Horse through a Hoop*

   The horse is in training for a circus act, in which the horse must jump through a large hoop (we used the torus from the Shapes folder). Create a world, as shown below, with a horse facing the hoop. Write a program to use a loop to have the horse trot forward several times and then jump through the hoop. When the horse gets close enough to the hoop to jump through it, have the horse jump through and then the world ends.

Your project must include a *trot* method that makes the horse perform a trot motion forward. A horse trots by turning the legs at the same time as the body moves forward. The leg motions can bend at the knee for a more realistic simulation, if desired. The loop calls the *trot* method.

4. *Juggling*

Create a world with an object that has arms (the picture below shows an ant) and three juggling balls. (A juggling ball is easily created by adding a sphere or a tennis ball to the world, resizing it, and giving it a bright color.) To juggle the balls, the object must have at least two arms and be able to move them in some way that resembles a tossing motion. Write a method to animate juggling the balls in the air. Use a loop to make the juggling act repeat five times, after which the juggling balls fall to the ground.

5. *Lighthouse Warning*

Set up a world that contains a lighthouse (Beach), a spotlight (Lights), a lightbulb (Lights), a stars skydome (Environments/Skies), and a number of boats (Vehicles), as seen in the image below. The lighthouse sits in the harbor to warn ships of shallow water. In this simulation, the light of the lighthouse is to rotate, as in real life. You should be able to see the sides of the boats illuminated as the light of the lighthouse swings around. Use repetitive world methods to continuously move each boat back and forth and rotate the spotlight. In *my first method*, make the world dark by setting the brightness property of the world's light to be 0. Then invoke the methods to create the lighting effect. Set the duration of the rotation to be 3 seconds or so.

Hint: To create a dramatic lighting effect in this animation, place a light bulb inside a spotlight and put both in the windowed area at the top of the lighthouse. Make both the lightbulb and the spotlight invisible (they will still give off light). The lightbulb and spotlight should rotate together to create a bright beam of light (set the lightbulb's vehicle property to be the spotlight).

6. *Carrier Landing*

Create a water world with a carrier in the ocean and a navy jet (Vehicles) in the air, as shown below. Write an interactive program to allow the user to use keyboard controls to land the jet on the deck of the carrier. Up, down, and forward controls are needed. Use a function to determine when the jet has landed (gotten close enough to the carrier's deck) and a *While* statement to continue the animation until the jet has landed.

7. *Moonwalk*

Write a program that will make the astronaut (Space) perform a moonwalk. The lunar lander (SciFi) and flag (Objects) are used to decorate the Space template scene.

To perform the moonwalk, the astronaut should turn right and then walk backward in a sliding sort of motion where one leg slides backward and then the other leg slides backward. The astronaut's entire body must move backward at the same time as the moonwalk leg motions are executed. Use a loop to make the astronaut repeat the moonwalk steps five times.

Summary

Loop and While were introduced in this chapter as control structures for repeating an instruction or block of instructions. A counted *Loop* allows you to specify exactly how many times a block of code will be repeated, and a *While* statement allows you to repeat a block of code as long as some condition remains true. The advantage of using loops is immediately obvious. Loops are fast and easy to write and also easy to understand. Of course, it is possible to write loop statements that are complicated. Overall, though, loops are impressive programming tools.

Important concepts in this chapter

- The counted *Loop* statement can be used to repeat an instruction, or a block of several instructions.
- A key component in a counted *Loop* is the count—the number of times the instructions within the loop will be repeated.
- The count must be a positive whole number or infinity. A negative value for the count would result in the *Loop* statement not executing at all!
- If the count is infinity, the loop will repeat until the program shuts down.
- A *Do in order* or *Do together* can be nested inside a loop; otherwise Alice assumes that the instructions are to be executed in order.
- Loops can be nested within loops.
- When a loop is nested within a loop, the inner loop will fully execute each time the outer loop executes once. For example, if the outer loop count is 5 and the inner loop count is 10, then the inner loop executes 10 times for each of the 5 executions of the outer loop. In other words, the outer loop executes 5 times and the inner loop 50 times.
- The *While* statement is a conditional loop.
- The Boolean condition used for entry into a *While* statement is the same as used in *If* statements. The difference is that the *While* statement is a loop, and the condition is checked again after the instructions within the *While* statement have been executed. If the condition is still true, the loop repeats.
- *If* statements can be combined with *While* statements. In some programs, a *While* statement is nested within an *If* statement. In other situations, an *If* statement may be nested within a *While* statement.

Chapter 8

Repetition: Recursion

...the kitten had been having a grand game of romps with the ball of worsted Alice had been trying to wind up, and had been rolling it up and down till it had all come undone again; and there it was spread over the hearth-rug, all knots and tangles, with the kitten running after its own tail in the middle.

This chapter introduces a third form of repetition known as recursion, in which a method (or a function) calls itself. This is an extremely powerful technique that greatly enhances the types of problems that can be solved in Alice. Recursion is often used where we do not know (at the time the program is written) the number of times a block of code should be repeated. (This is also true for the *While* statement, covered in Section 7-2.)

In Alice, there are two major situations where we do not know (even at runtime, when the program first starts to run) the count of repetitions. The first is when random motion is involved. As you recall, random motion means that an object is moving in a way that is somewhat unpredictable. In Section 8-1, we will explore the technique of writing methods where repetition is implemented with recursion.

In Section 8-2, we will look at a famous puzzle and present a solution using a second flavor of recursion. This form of recursion is useful when some complex computation is to be done that depends on an ability to break a problem down into smaller versions of the same problem (sub-problems). The solutions to the smaller sub-problems are used to cooperatively solve the larger problem.

8-1 Introduction to recursion

Recursion is a not a program statement with a special word that identifies it as part of the programming language. Instead, recursion is a well-known programming technique where a method calls itself. Recursion can be used to handle situations where the programmer does not know how many times the loop should be repeated. Examples in this section will show you how to use this technique.

A game-like example

To illustrate recursion, we will use a simple version of a horse race in a carnival game (Amusement Park). The initial scene is shown in Figure 8-1-1. Unlike a traditional horse race, where horses run around an oval-shaped track and each horse breaks to the inside of the track, horses in a carnival game move straight ahead in a mechanical track. In a carnival game, you win a prize if you pick the right horse. In this example, we won't worry about picking the right horse. We will simply have the winning horse say, "I won!!!" This is not a realistic end to the game—but it will serve the purpose of signaling the end of the race.

The problem is how to make this simulate a real carnival game, where the horses move forward again and again until one of them finally reaches the finish line. At each move, the

Figure 8-1-1. Initial scene for a three-horse race

horses move forward different amounts. To keep the game honest, each horse must have an equal chance of winning the race. This means that over several runs of the game, each horse should win about the same number of times as the other horses.

A possible solution is to randomly choose one horse to move forward a short distance. If none of the horses has won (gotten to the finish line), we will once again randomly choose one of the horses to move forward. This action (a randomly chosen horse moves forward a short distance) will be repeated again and again until one of the horses eventually gets to the finish line and wins the race.

An essential step is how to decide when the race is over. In this example, if one of the horses reaches the finish line, the horse wins the race and the game is over. An *If* statement can be used to check whether one of the horses has won. If so, the game is over. Otherwise (the *Else* part), we randomly choose another horse to move forward and do it all again. A storyboard for this animation could look something like this:

```
race

If one of the horses has won
        the winner says, "I won!!!"
Else
        randomly choose one horse and move it forward a small amount
        do everything again
```

In the storyboard above, the line "do everything again" means that the entire method should be repeated. How do we write a program instruction to "do everything again"? We simply have the method call itself! Let's modify the storyboard to show the recursive call:

```
race

If one of the horses has won
        the winner says, "I won!!!"
Else
        randomly choose one horse and move it forward a small amount
        call the race method
```

A close look at the modified *race* storyboard shows that the method is calling itself! This is known as recursion. A method that calls itself is said to be recursive. The effect of a recursive call is that the method will repeat. Repeated execution of a method may occur again and again until some condition is reached that ends the method. In this example, the condition that ends the recursive calls is "one of the horses has won."

Now, all we have to do is translate the storyboard into program code. To write the code for the race, we have three problems:

1. How to determine when the race is over.
2. How to randomly select one of the horses to move forward for each execution of the loop.
3. How to figure out which horse won the race and have it say, "I won!!!"

These problems can be solved using stepwise refinement, creating functions and/or methods to solve each.

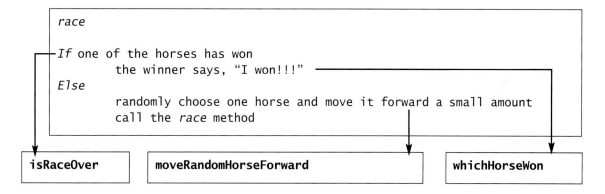

For now, let's pretend that the functions *isRaceOver* and *whichHorseWon* along with the *moveRandomHorseForward* method have already been written. (We will write them next.) If the functions and method were already written, we could write the *race* method as shown in Figure 8-1-2. The *If* part checks to see whether the game is over. If so, the game ends with the winning horse saying "I won!!!" Otherwise, the *Else* part kicks in and a horse is randomly selected to move forward a short distance. The last statement, *racehorseGame.race*, recursively calls the *race* method. The overall effect of the recursive call is repetition until some condition occurs that ends execution of the method.

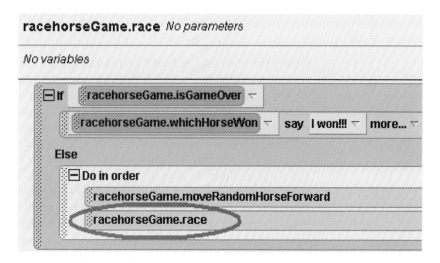

Figure 8-1-2. The *racehorseGame.race* method uses recursion (calls itself)

Now that you have the overall idea of how recursion works, we can look further at the details of implementing *isRaceOver, moveRandomHorse,* and *whichHorseWon.*

Determining when the race is over

Let's begin with the *isRaceOver* function. The race is over when one of the horses gets close enough to the finish line to be declared a winner. Either the race is over or it is not over—so the *isRaceOver* function should be a Boolean function (returns *true* or *false*). Within the *isRaceOver* function, we can make use of a built-in function. The question we will ask in the function is: "Is the finish line less than 0.5 meters in front of a horse?" The reason we have chosen 0.5 (rather than 0) is that Alice measures the distance between the horse and the finish line from the horse's center, not from the tip of its nose. In our example world, the horse's nose is approximately 0.5 meters in front of its center (a raceHorseGame has very small horses), so we use a value of 0.5 rather than 0. (If you try this world, you may resize the racehorseGame and find that this distance needs a slight adjustment.)

The function to determine if one of the horses has won is presented in Figure 8-1-3. A cascading *If/Else* control structure is used to check whether the game is over. If any one of the three horses is within the distance (0.5 meters) of the finish line, the function returns *true.* Otherwise, after all three horses have been checked and none is close enough to the finish line to end the game, the function returns *false.*

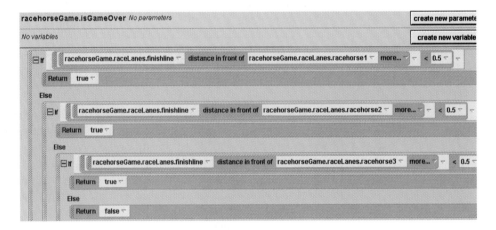

Figure 8-1-3. The *isGameOver* function

Random Selection

If the game is not over, we need to randomly choose a horse and move it forward a short distance. In this problem we need to give each horse a "fighting chance" to win the race. Let's use the world-level random selection function, *choose true (probability of true) of the time.* This function will return *true* some percentage of a total number of times (*probability of true* is a percentage). For example, saying "choose true 0.5 of the time" means that 50 percent of the time the function will return a *true* value, the other 50 percent of the time it will return a *false* value.

It seems reasonable to use a value of 0.33 (one-third) for *probability of true,* so that each horse will be chosen 33 percent (one-third) of the time. The other two-thirds of the time, that horse will not move. As shown in Figure 8-1-4, we start the random selection with the first horse, whose name is racehorse1. The racehorse1 will be selected one-third of the time. But, what if racehorse1 is not selected? Then the *Else*-part takes over and a selection must be made from racehorse2 or racehorse3. Once again, to decide which horse should move, *choose true (probability of true) of the time* is used. Figure 8-1-4 illustrates the code for the *moveRandomHorseForward* method.

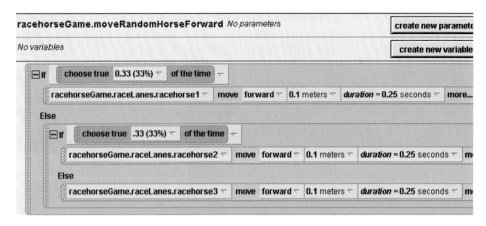

Figure 8-1-4. Randomly choose one horse and move it forward

Determining the winner

Each time the race method is executed, one of the horses moves closer to the finish line. Eventually one of the horses will get close enough to the finish line to win the race. This is when we need to determine which horse is the winner. We want to ask the question, "Did a horse get close enough to the finish line to win the race?" Once again, we use the distance (0.5 meters) of the finish line in front of the horse to check whether the horse is close enough to win. As in the *isGameOver* function, we can use a cascading (nested) *If/Else* structure to ask first about racehorse1, then racehorse2, and so on. If racehorse1 is not the winner, then we ask about racehorse2. If neither racehorse1 nor racehorse2 has won, we can assume that racehorse3 was the winner.

The *whichHorseWon* function, as illustrated in Figure 8-1-5, returns the horse object that has won the game. Note that it is impossible for two horses to cross the finish line at once as only one horse moves at a time, and we check for a winner each time one of the horses moves forward. The winning horse simply says, "I won!!!" We admit is not a very exciting end to a race, but at least it is easy to see which horse won.

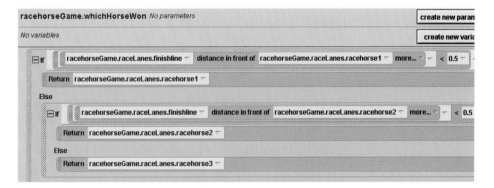

Figure 8-1-5. The *whichHorseWon* function

Testing the program

In any program where you are working with random numbers, it is especially important to do a lot of testing. Because of the random selection used in this program, different horses should win the race if the program is run several times. In this example, we ran the program 20 times and found the following very surprising results: racehorse1 won 7 times; racehorse2 won 3 times, and racehorse3 won 10 times! Something is very wrong. The results for racehorse1 are reasonable (it won about a third of the time). But racehorse2 didn't win nearly enough, and racehorse3 won far too often.

The problem is within the second (nested) random selection of which horse should move. We used 33% as the percentage of probability for choosing each horse. What we didn't think about was that if racehorse1 was not selected, then we have only two choices: racehorse2 or racehorse3. So, after racehorse1 has been eliminated, we should select racehorse2 to move 50 percent of the time to give racehorse2 an equal chance with racehorse3. The modified code is presented in Figure 8-1-6. Now, each horse wins approximately one-third of the time!

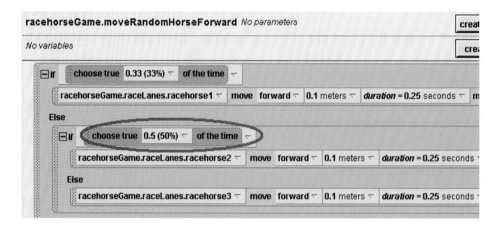

Figure 8-1-6. The corrected random-selection percentage

8-2 Another flavor of recursion

The concept of recursion, where a method calls itself, was introduced in Section 8-1. The example illustrated that recursion depends on a decision statement (*If*) that evaluates a condition. Depending on the results of that decision, a method may call itself. Each time the method is called, the same decision needs to be considered once more to determine whether another repetition will occur. This repetition may go on and on until, eventually, the tested condition changes and the method ends. In this section, we examine a second flavor of recursion. The goal here is to reinforce the concept of recursion by presenting a different kind of problem.

A second form of recursion

The second form of recursion depends on an ability to break a problem down into smaller and smaller sub-problems. The solutions to the smaller sub-problems are used to cooperatively solve the larger problem. As an analogy, suppose you have an emergency situation where you need $60, but you have only $10. So, you ask your best friend to lend you the rest ($50). Your best friend has only $10, but he says he will ask another friend for the remaining amount ($40). The story continues like this

You need $60 and have $10, so you ask a friend to borrow $50

Friend has $10 and asks another friend to borrow $40

Friend has $10 and asks another friend to borrow $30

Friend has $10 and asks another friend to borrow $20

Friend has $10 and asks another friend to borrow $10

Friend loans $10

Collectively, each friend lends $10 back up the stream of requests, and the problem of borrowing enough money is solved. (Of course, you now have the problem of paying it back!) Notice that each friend has a problem similar to your problem—but the amount of money each friend needs to borrow is successively smaller. This is what we mean by breaking the problem down into smaller and smaller sub-problems. When the smallest problem (the ***base case***) is solved, the solution is passed back up the line, and that solution is passed back up the line, and so on. Collectively, the entire problem is solved. To illustrate this form of recursion in terms of designing and writing a program, it is perhaps best to look at an example world.

Towers of Hanoi puzzle

The problem to be considered is the Towers of Hanoi, a legendary puzzle. In the ancient story about this puzzle, there are 64 disks (shaped like rings) and three tall towers. In the beginning, all 64 disks are on one of the towers. The goal is to move all the disks to one of the other towers, using the third tower as a spare (a temporary holder for disks). Two strict rules govern how the disks can be moved:

1. Only one disk may be moved at a time.
2. A larger disk may never be placed on top of a smaller disk.

Solving the puzzle with 64 disks is a huge task, and an animation showing a solution for 64 disks would take much too long to run! (In fact, assuming that it takes one second to move a disk from one tower to another, it would take many, many centuries to run!) However, we can use just four disks to illustrate a solution. Most people can solve the four-disk puzzle in just a few minutes, so this will allow you to quickly test for a correct solution.

In our solution to this puzzle, four disks (torus from Shapes folder) of varying widths have been placed on a cone (Shapes), as illustrated in Figure 8-2-1. The cones in the world will play the same role as towers in the original puzzle. Initially, four disks are on the leftmost cone.

Figure 8-2-1. The Towers of Hanoi

In setting up this world, careful positioning of cones and measurement of disks will make the animation easier to program. We positioned each cone exactly 1 meter from its nearest neighbor, as labeled in Figure 8-2-2.

Each disk is placed exactly 0.1 meter in height above its neighbor, as illustrated in Figure 8-2-3.

To make it easier to describe our solution to the puzzle, let's give each disk an ID number and a name. The disk with ID number 1 is disk1, ID number 2 is disk2, ID number 3 is disk3, and ID number 4 is disk4. The smallest disk is disk1 at the top of the stack and the largest disk is disk4 at the bottom. Also, let's name the cones cone1, cone2, and cone3 (left to right from the camera point of view). The goal in the puzzle is to move all the disks from the leftmost cone, cone1, to another cone. In this example, we will move the disks to the rightmost cone (cone3).

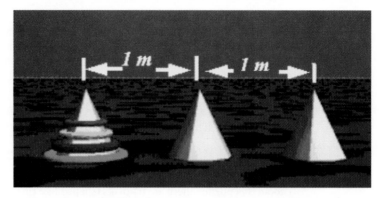

Figure 8-2-2. Each cone is 1 meter from neighboring cone

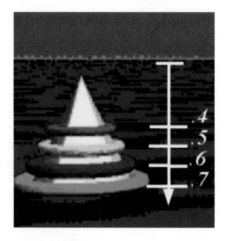

Figure 8-2-3. Each disk is 0.1 meter above its neighboring disk (measuring from top down)

A first attempt to solve the problem might be to use a while loop. The textual storyboard might look something like this:

```
While all the disks are not on the target cone
    Do
```

Unfortunately, it is not easy to figure out what needs to be done inside the "Do ." The problem can be solved using a *While* loop, but it takes much thinking and insight into the problem. Recursion makes the problem much easier to think about and solve, so we will use recursion.

Two requirements

We want to solve this puzzle for four disks using the second form of recursion, where the problem is broken down into smaller and smaller sub-problems. To use this form of recursion, two requirements must be met.

The first requirement is that we must assume we know how to solve the problem for a smaller sub-problem. Let's assume that we do know a solution for solving the problem for three disks. If we know how to solve the problem of moving 3 disks, it would be quite easy to write a program to solve it for 1 more disk (four disks). The following steps would work:

1. Move the three disks (imagining the solution for the puzzle with only three disks is already known) from cone1 to cone2. See Figure 8-2-4(a).
2. Move the last disk, disk4, from cone1 to cone3. See Figure 8-2-4(b). (Remember that this move is now safe, as all of the three smaller disks are now located on cone2.)
3. Move the three disks (again, imagining the solution is already known) from cone2 to cone3. The final result is shown in Figure 8-2-4(c).

The second requirement is that we must have a base case.   A base case is the simplest possible situation where the solution is obvious and no further sub-problems are needed. In other words, when we get down to the base case, we can stop breaking the problem down into simpler problems because we have reached the simplest problem. The obvious "base case" in the Towers of Hanoi puzzle is the situation where we have only one disk to be moved. To move one disk, we can just move it. We know that there are no smaller disks than disk 1. So, if it is the only disk to be moved, we can always move it to another cone!

Figure 8-2-4(a). After step 1

Figure 8-2-4(b). After step 2

Figure 8-2-4(c). After step 3

The towers method

Now that we have determined the necessary two requirements, we can write a method to animate a solution to the Towers of Hanoi puzzle. The method, named *towers*, will have instructions to move some number *(howmany)* of disks from a *source* cone (the cone where the disks are currently located) to a *target* cone (the cone where the disks will be located when the puzzle is solved). In the process of moving the disks from the source cone to the target cone, a spare cone (the cone that is neither source nor target) will be used as a temporary holder for disks on their journey from the source to the target.

To do its work, the *towers* method needs to know how many disks are to be moved, the source cone, target cone, and spare cone. To provide this information to the *towers* method, four parameters are used: *howmany, source, target,* and *spare.* Here is the storyboard:

---

towers

Parameters: *howmany, source, target, spare*

If howmany is equal to 1
    move it (disk 1) from the *source* to the *target*

Else

  Do in order
      call *towers* to move *howmany*-1 disks from *source* to *spare*
      (using *target* as *spare*)

      move it (disk # *howmany*) from the *source* to the *target*

      call *towers* to move *howmany*-1 disks from the *spare* to the *target*
      (using the *source* as the *spare*)

We know this looks a bit complicated; but it really is not too difficult. Let's break it down and look at individual pieces:

First, the *If* piece:

> if *how many* is equal to 1
>
> move it (the smallest disk) from the *source* to the *target*

This is simple. The *If* piece is the base case. We have only 1 disk to move, so move it! Second, the Else piece:

> *Else*
>
> (1) call *towers* to move *howmany*-1 disks from *source* to *spare* (using *target* as *spare*)
>
> (2) move it (disk # *howmany*) from the *source* to the *target*
>
> (3) call *towers* to move *howmany*-1 disks from *spare* to *target* (using the *source* as the *spare*)

All this is saying is:

1. Move all but one of the disks from the *source* to the *spare* cone.
2. Now that only one disk is left on the *source*, move it to the *target* cone. This is ok, because all smaller disks are now located on the *spare* cone, after step 1.
3. Now, move all the disks that have been temporarily stored on the *spare* cone to the *target* cone.

Notice that the *If* piece and the *Else* piece in this storyboard each have a sub-step that says "move it" (move a disk) from the source cone to the target cone. The *moveIt* sub-steps are highlighted in the storyboard below. Moving a disk from one cone to another is actually a combination of several moves, so we will need to use stepwise refinement to break down our design into simpler steps.

---

towers

Parameters: *howmany, source, target, spare*

If howmany is equal to 1
      move it (the smallest disk) from the *source* to the *target*

Else
  Do in order
      call *towers* to move *howmany*-1 disks from *source* to *spare*
      (using *target* as *spare*)

      move it (disk # *howmany*) from the *source* to the *target*

      call *towers* to move *howmany*-1 disks from the *spare* to the *target*
                (using the *source* as the *spare*)

---

moveIt:

Exactly what does the *moveIt* method do? *Move it* must lift the disk upward to clear the top of the cone it is currently on. Then, it must move the disk (forward or back) to a location immediately above the target cone. Finally, it must lower the disk down onto the target cone. Figure 8-2-5 illustrates a possible sequence of moves.

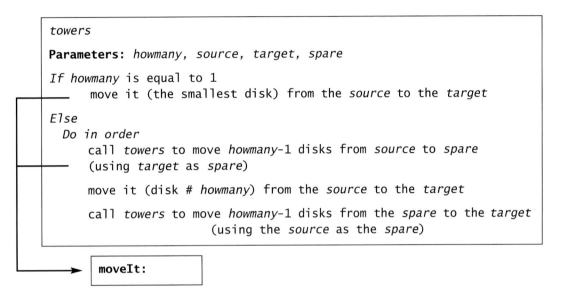

Figure 8-2-5. Moving a disk from source to target cone

To write the *moveIt* method, we need to use three parameters because it needs to know: (1) which disk is to be moved (*whichdisk*—the disk ID number), (2) the source cone (*fromcone*), and (3) the target cone (*tocone*). A storyboard for *moveIt* could be:

---

moveIt

Parameters: *whichdisk, fromcone, tocone*

Do in order
      Lift the disk up above the top of the *fromcone*
      Move it (forward or back) to a location above the *tocone*
      Lower the disk down onto the *tocone*

Two methods are to be written: (1) the *towers* method and (2) the *moveIt* method. Let's start by writing the *towers* method, as shown in Figure 8-2-6. The code is a straightforward translation of the storyboard.

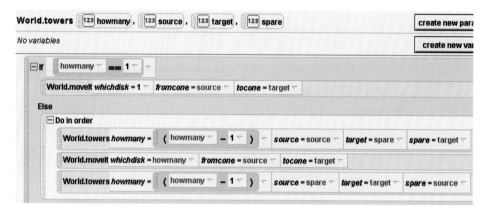

Figure 8-2-6. The *towers* method

The moveIt method

The first step in the *moveIt* method is to lift the disk up above the cone it is currently on. How high should the disk be lifted? Each disk is at a different initial height on the cone, so it will be necessary to raise each disk a different amount. In our example world, we made each disk 0.1 meters in height, so we need to lift disk1 approximately 0.4 meters, disk2 approximately 0.5 meters, disk3 approximately 0.6 meters, and disk4 approximately 0.7 meters to "clear" the cone. (Figure 8-2-3 illustrates the careful positioning of the disks on the source cone in the initial world.)

Now that we know the height to lift each disk, we can write the code to move a disk upward. Of course, the *moveIt* method needs to know which disk is to be moved. One possibility is to pass a parameter to the *moveIt* method that contains the ID number of the disk to be moved. If the disk ID is 1, move disk1, if the disk ID is 2, move disk2, and so on. We can use nested *If* statements to check on the ID number of the disk. When the correct disk is found, a *move* instruction can be used to lift it the appropriate amount. The storyboard (for the nested *If* statements) would look something like this:

```
If whichdisk is 1 then

   Move disk1 up 0.4 meters

Else
   If whichdisk is 2 then
         Move disk2 up 0.5 meters
Else
         If whichdisk is 3 then
               Move disk3 up 0.6 meters
         Else
               Move disk4 up 0.7 meters
```

The code in Figure 8-2-7 will accomplish this task.

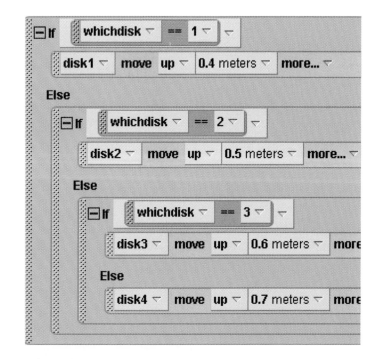

Figure 8-2-7. Nested *If* statements to select the disk to move upward

We thought about this for a while, realizing that the nested *If* statements might seem a bit awkward. We noticed that the distance each disk has to move up is 0.3 meters more than 0.1 * the ID number (*whichdisk*). Thus, a nifty mathematical expression could be used to move a disk upward. Using an expression to compute the distance would allow the storyboard to be just one step:

```
move the appropriate disk up 0.3 + 0.1 * whichdisk
```

Sometimes it is helpful to come up with an elegant idea like this one. We want to point out, however, that condensing the code into a more compact form may lead to other problems. In this case, using an expression to compute the distance leads us to a problem of how to write the statement. Notice that the one-statement storyboard uses the phrase "appropriate disk" because we don't know exactly which disk is to be moved. All we have is *whichdisk*—an ID number, not a name. Think of it like this: you have a name and a social security number. When someone talks to you, she says your name, not your social security number. Writing a *move* instruction is a similar situation. A *move* instruction uses the name of the object, not its ID number.

Conversion function

"How is Alice to be told the name of the disk object to be moved when only the disk ID number is known?" One solution is to write a conversion method that takes the ID number as a parameter and returns the appropriate name of the disk object to move. Such a conversion method can be written using a function. The *which* function is illustrated in Figure 8-2-8. In this code, each *If* statement includes an instruction containing the keyword *Return*. As you know, the *Return* statement sends information back to the method that called it. For instance, suppose *which*($i = 2$) is called; the information that will be returned is disk2. The *which* function provides a way to convert an ID number (the *whichdisk* parameter) to an object name. (We named the function *which* to make it easy to mentally connect the *which* function to the *whichdisk* parameter.)

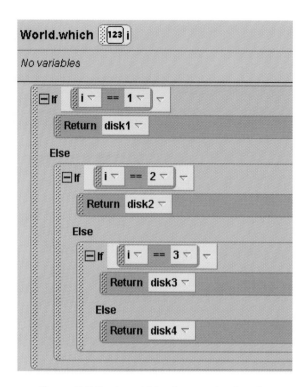

Figure 8-2-8. A world-level conversion function

An instruction can now be written in the *moveIt* method that calls the *which* function to determine which disk to move and uses a mathematical expression to compute the distance, as illustrated in Figure 8-2-9. In this instruction, $which(i = whichdisk)$ is a call to the *which* function. When executed, $which(i = whichdisk)$ will select the appropriate disk and return its name. That disk will then be moved upward the computed amount, as explained in the earlier expression.

Figure 8-2-9. Calling the function to determine which disk to move

Completing the moveIt method

Recall that the *moveIt* method is composed of a sequence of three movement instructions. So far, we have completed the first *move* instruction (highlighted in blue in the storyboard, below). Let's look at how to write the two remaining instructions.

```
moveIt

Parameters: whichdisk, fromcone, tocone

Do in order
        Lift the disk up above the top of the fromcone
        Move it (forward or back) to a location above the tocone
        Lower the disk down onto the tocone
```

For the second instruction, we want to move the disk *forward* or *backward* so as to position it immediately over the target cone. How far should the disk be moved? As previously illustrated (Figure 8-2-2), the cones are purposely positioned exactly 1 meter from one another. There are six possible moves, as shown in Table 8-2-1.

Table 8-2-1. Six disk moves from source cone to target cone

Forward moves	forward distance	Backward moves	forward distance
from cone1 to cone2	1 meter	from cone2 to cone1	−1 meter
from cone1 to cone3	2 meters	from cone3 to cone1	−2 meters
from cone2 to cone3	1 meter	from cone3 to cone2	−1 meter

Notice that moving forward a negative (−1 meter) distance is the same as moving backward 1 meter. After examining the six cases in detail, we see that the forward distance can be computed using an expression (*tocone − fromcone*). For example, to move a disk from cone1 to cone3, move it 2 meters $(3 - 1)$ forward. With this insight, an instruction can be written to move the disk to the target cone, as shown in Figure 8-2-10.

Figure 8-2-10. Moving the disk the appropriate amount forward/back

The last step in the *moveIt* method is to move the disk downward onto the target cone. This instruction should simply do the opposite of what was done in step 1. The complete *moveIt* method appears in Figure 8-2-11.

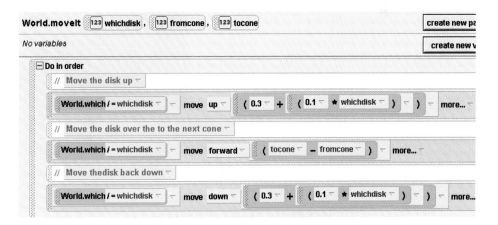

Figure 8-2-11. The code for *moveIt*

Now, with the *towers* and the *moveIt* methods completed, all that remains is to call the *towers* method when the world starts. A link in the Events editor can be used, as seen in Figure 8-2-12.

The second form of recursion (presented in this section) depends on the structure of a problem and its solution, breaking a problem down into smaller and smaller sub-problems. Many mathematicians (and computer scientists interested in logic) often prefer this form of

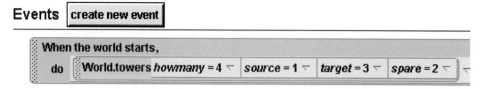

Figure 8-2-12. Calling the *towers* method

recursion because it is easy to show that the program does end—and that it ends with the correct solution. For example, with the Towers of Hanoi, we reasoned that we could:

> move 4 disks, if we can move 3 disks and then 1 disk (we know how to move 1 disk)
> move 3 disks, if we can move 2 disks and then 1 disk
> move 2 disks, if we can move 1 disk and then 1 disk
> move 1 disk (base case—we know how to move 1 disk)

Clearly, the problem has been broken down into smaller and smaller sub-problems. We know that the program will end, because we know that eventually the problem size will get down to the base case, which is moving one disk.

Tips & Techniques 8
Camera and Animation Controls

The camera controls in the Alice scene editor, as in Figure T-8-1, allow you to move the camera position at the time an initial scene is being created. Of course, the camera controls are not available while the animation is running. In this section we look at a technique for controlling the movement of the camera at runtime. Also, we offer a tip on how to use the speed multiplier to speed up (or slow down) an animation at runtime.

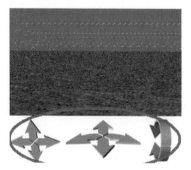

Figure T-8-1. Camera navigation controls in the scene editor

Setting the point of view

One way to move the camera around a scene is to create one or more dummy objects that mark locations where the camera will be used during the animation. A dummy object is invisible and can be used as a goalpost—a target object to which the camera will move during the animation. Once a dummy object is in place, an instruction can be created to set the camera *point of view* to the *point of view* of the dummy object. At runtime, the *set point of view* method effectively moves the camera to the dummy object (similar to a *move to* instruction), and the camera viewpoint is now from that location.

This technique is best illustrated with an example. You may find it helpful to sit at a computer and try this out as you read the description. Figure T-8-2 shows an initial scene with the

Figure T-8-2. Camera front view

camera pointed at a skateboarder (People). The skateboard and the rail-ramp can be found in the SkatePark folder on the CD or Web gallery. From our perspective (as the person viewing the scene), the camera is allowing us to look at the scene "from the front."

We want to be able to move the camera around to view the skater's actions "from the back" of the scene while the animation is running. To prepare for this action, let's create a couple of dummy objects for the front and back viewpoints. First, drop a dummy object at the current location of the camera. To do this, click the **more controls** button in the scene editor, as in Figure T-8-3.

Figure T-8-3. The more controls button

The interface expands to show additional controls, including a **drop dummy at camera** button, seen in Figure T-8-4.

A click on the drop dummy at camera button creates a dummy object as a goalpost at the current location of the camera. The dummy object is added to the Object tree, as shown in Figure T-8-5. Alice automatically names dummy objects as dummy, dummy2, etc. In this example, we re-named the dummy object as frontView (a meaningful name makes it easy to remember).

The next step is to reposition the camera to view the scene from the back. One technique that seems to work well is to drag the camera's forward control (the center camera navigation arrow) toward the back of the scene. Continue to drag the forward control and allow the camera to move straight forward until the camera seems to move through the scene. When the camera seems to have moved far enough to be on the other side of the scene, release the mouse. Select the camera in the Object tree and select a method to turn the camera one-half revolution, as in Figure T-8-6.

Figure T-8-4. The buttons for camera control with dummy object

Figure T-8-5. Dummy object is added to the Object tree

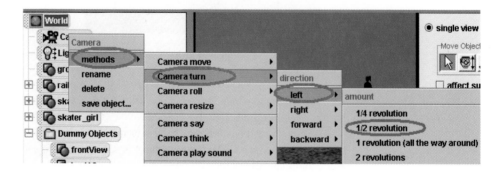

Figure T-8-6. Move camera to back of scene and then turn it around one-half revolution

The camera should now be facing in the opposite direction and you should be able to see the scene from the back. Click once more on the drop dummy at camera button. We renamed the dummy marker as backView. Two dummy objects should now be in the Object tree, frontView and backView. To return the camera to the front view, select frontView from the dropdown menu of the **move camera to dummy** button (see Figure T-8-4).

Now instructions can be written to move the camera at runtime. Select camera in the Object tree and then drag the *set point of view* instruction into the editor. Select the particular dummy object for the point of view. Figure T-8-7 illustrates how to create the instruction.

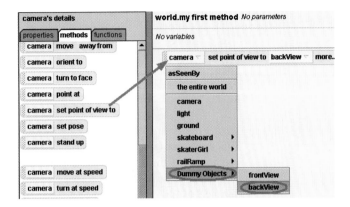

Figure T-8-7. Creating a *set point of view* instruction

A sample instruction is shown below. At runtime, this instruction will move the camera to backView and the camera's *point of view* will be from that location.

Controlling the runtime speed

As you gain experience in programming with Alice, your animations will become more and more complex and the runtime longer and longer. Naturally, this means that testing your programs takes longer because the animation takes a while to run through the sequence of actions to get to the most recent additions.

A great way to "fast forward" through the actions you have already tested is to use the Speed Multiplier that appears in the Play window, as seen in Figure T-8-8.

Figure T-8-8. The speed multiplier

The Speed Multiplier is a slide bar with a thumb. You can grab the thumb with the mouse and slide it left or right while the animation is running to control the speed of the animation. (Sliding the thumb has no effect if the animation has stopped.) To return the animation to normal speed, simply drag the thumb all the way to the left.

Note: The speed multiplier affects only the speed of the animation. If a sound is being played, the sound is not affected by the speed multiplier (that is, the sound does not play faster).

Exercises and Projects

8-1 Exercises

1. *Modify the Horse Race*
   The horse race (Amusement Park) example presented in Section 8-1 randomly selected one horse at a time and moved it forward until one of the horses won the race. Another solution is to move all three horses forward at the same time, but to move each a random distance. Modify the horse race program to use this solution to the problem.

2. *Butterfly Chase*
   Use recursion to make the white rabbit (Animal) chase a butterfly (Animals/Bugs). The butterfly should fly to a random, nearby location (within 0.2 meters in any direction). The white rabbit, however, must always remain on the ground (rabbits do not fly). Each time the butterfly moves, use *turn to face* to make the rabbit turn toward the butterfly and then move the rabbit toward the butterfly 0.5 meters. When the rabbit gets close enough, have him catch the butterfly in his net (Objects).

   Hint: To move the butterfly to a random nearby location, you can adapt the *randomMotion* method presented in Tips & Techniques 6. It is necessary to keep the butterfly from flying too high or too low. (The butterfly could disappear below the ground or fly too high, so that the rabbit would never get close enough to catch it.) To limit the up-down direction of the butterfly's movement, use an *If* statement to check the butterfly's *distance above* the ground and then move the butterfly up or down accordingly. The butterfly's distance above the ground should always be within the range of 0 (ground level) and 1 (meter above the ground).

3. *Midas Touch 1*
   In the story of the Midas Touch, a greedy king was given the gift of having everything he touched turn to gold. This exercise is to create a simulation of the Midas Touch. In the initial scene shown below, a woman is facing a candy cane (Holidays). (Use *turn to face* to make this alignment.) Write a recursive method, named *checkCandy*, that checks whether the woman's right hand is very close to the candy cane. If it is, the woman should touch the candy cane. After she touches the candy cane, the candy

cane turns to gold (color changes to yellow). If the woman is not yet close enough to the candy cane to be able to touch it, she moves a small distance forward and the *checkCandy* method is recursively called.

4. *Midas Touch 2*

   Create a second version of the MidasTouch1 world. This new version will be interactive. The idea is to allow the user to guide the movement of the woman toward a candy cane. To make this a bit more challenging, the woman should NOT be facing the candy cane in the initial scene. This will require the *checkCandy* method be modified so that whenever the woman is close enough to the candy cane to touch it, she first turns to point toward the candy cane before bending over to touch it.

   Use the left and right arrow keys to turn the woman left or right. Create two methods: *turnRight* and *turnLeft*. The methods should turn the woman 0.02 revolutions to the right or left when the user presses the right or the left arrow key. These methods will allow the user to guide the woman toward a candy cane.

   Hint: It is possible that the woman will wander out of the range of the camera. There are two possible solutions. One is to make the camera point at the woman each time she moves. The other is to make the camera's vehicle be the woman.

8-2 Exercises

5. *Towers of Hanoi*

   Create the Towers of Hanoi puzzle as described Section 8-2. When you have it working, modify the event-trigger link that calls the *towers* method so that it moves the disks from cone1 to cone2 (instead of cone3).

6. *Towers of Hanoi Modified*

   We do not need to pass around the spare cone as a parameter. The spare cone is always

   $$6 - fromcone - tocone.$$

   Modify the towers method to use this new approach.

7. *On the Hour*

   Place a cuckoo clock (Objects) in a new world. The idea of this animation is to have the cuckoo clock keep time (not in real time, of course). The minute hand should go around on the face of the clock (perhaps one complete revolution should take about 30 seconds in real time) and the pendulum should swing back and forth. When the minute hand has made one revolution (from 12 back to 12 on the face of the clock), then the hour hand should advance to the next hour, the doors should open, and the cuckoo bird (on the clock arm) should come out and chirp once. Then the bird should retreat inside the clock and the doors should close until the next hour has gone by. "All is well" as long as the clock is running—which should continue until the user stops the animation. Use a recursive method to implement the animation.

8-2 Projects

1. *Why Did the Chicken Cross the Road?*
   A popular child's riddle is, "Why did the chicken cross the road?" Of course, there are many answers. In this project, the chicken (Animals) has a real sweet-tooth and crosses the road to eat the gumdrops (Kitchen/Food) along the way.

   Write a game animation where the player guides the chicken across the road to get to the gumdrops. Cars and other vehicles should move in both directions as the chicken tries to cross to where the gumdrops are located. Use arrow keys to make the chicken jump left, right, forward and back. Use the space bar to have the chicken peck at the gumdrop. When the chicken is close enough to the gumdrop and pecks, the gumdrop should disappear.

   A recursive method is used to control the play of the game. If the chicken gets hit by a vehicle, the game is over (squish!). The game continues as long as the chicken has not managed to peck all the gumdrops and has not yet been squished by a vehicle. If the chicken manages to cross the road and peck at all the gumdrops along the way, the player wins the game. Signal the player's success by making 3D text "You Win" appear or by playing some triumphant sound.

2. *Reversal*
   In the world below, the row of skeletons (Spooky) is guarding the gate (Spooky). Every so often in this world, the row of skeletons is to reverse order. This project is to animate the reversal using the second form of recursion. The storyboard goes something like the following:

```
reverse

If the row of skeletons not yet reversed is more than one then
    reverse the row of skeletons starting with the second skeleton (by recursively
                calling reverse)
    move the head skeleton to the end of the row
```

   The base case is when there is just one skeleton in the row (that has not yet been reversed). Of course, a row of 1 skeleton is already reversed! The recursive case (for n skeletons, where n is larger than 1) says to first reverse the last $n - 1$ skeletons and then move the first skeleton to the end of the row.

   Implement the Skeleton reversal storyboard given above. The program you write should be quite similar to the Towers of Hanoi program, including the *which* function.

3. *Never Ending Slide Show*

This project makes use of the technique of changing the skin of an object (Tips & Techniques 3). In this world, you are to create a never-ending slide show. Set up a new world with a square (Shapes) as the screen, the slide projector on a table (Furniture on CD or Web), and a lightbulb (Lights) in front of the screen, as shown in the image below left. The lightbulb is for the purpose of lighting up the screen (simulating light from the projector). Then, make the lightbulb invisible by setting its *isShowing* property to *false*.

For an added sense of realism, start with the world's light on and them dim the light before turning on the projector. The slide show in your project must display at least three different slides. Numbering the slides and using an *If* statement may help you create a method to change slides. Between each slide, the screen must go blank, the projector light must flicker (change the color of the light), and the slide projector's tray of slides must rotate. (The blank slides below show the screen going blank between one slide and the next.) The slides are to change continuously (meaning once all three have been seen, the show should go back to slide 1 and start over). The sequence of images is a sample slide show. (The cat pictures are of Muffin, one of our graduate student's cats.)

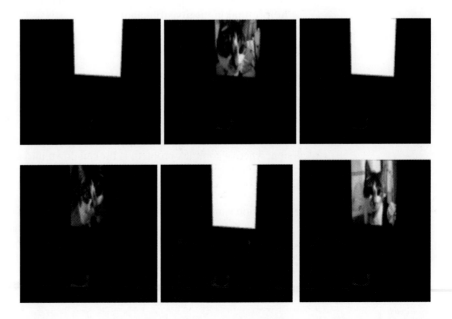

4. *Click-a-Cow*

   Let us design a game where the goal is to click on an object that is appearing and then disappearing on the screen. If the user successfully clicks on the object while it is visible, some visual action should happen so the user will know he/she has managed to "click" the object with the mouse. In our sketch of a storyboard below, a cow (Animals) is the object and a windup key (Objects) is used to signal success. (Of course, you can creatively choose a different object and a different way to signal the fact that the user has clicked on the object.)

   We assume that the cow and wind-up key have been added to the world and both have been made invisible by setting their *isShowing* property to *false*. A storyboard for a method, *check*, will look something like this:

```
If the wind-up key is not visible

        Move the cow to a random location on the screen
        Make the cow visible
        Wait a short period of time, say 0.25 seconds
        Make the cow invisible
        Move the cow off the screen
          (perhaps by moving it down 10 meters so the user can no longer click on it)
        Recursively call check
Else

        Have the cow say, "Thanks for playing"
```

When the user finally manages to click the mouse on the object, a method should be called that signals success. In our example, the wind-up key would become visible. Once the key is visible, the game ends.

Hint: The most challenging part of this project is to move the object to a random location on the ground (perhaps between −3 and 3 in the forward-back and right-left directions). Also, you will find it helpful to experiment with a *Wait* instruction to find out how long to wait while the object is visible (not too fast, not too slow) before making it invisible again.

Summary

This chapter introduced the concept of using recursion as a mechanism for repetition. Recursion is a powerful tool for building more complex and interesting worlds.

The horse race example in this chapter demonstrates a kind of recursion where more executions of a section of program code are "generated" each time the result of the previous decision is true. The famous Towers of Hanoi puzzle is an example of a second flavor of recursion, where a complex problem is broken down into simpler and simpler versions.

Important concepts in this chapter

- Recursion is most useful when we cannot use a *Loop* statement because we do not know (at the time we are writing the program) how many loop iterations will be needed.
- Recursion occurs when a method calls itself.
- Recursion enables a method to be repeatedly called.
- Any recursive method must have at least one base case, where no recursive call is made. When the base case occurs, the recursion stops.

- When you use recursion, you generally do not also use a loop statement (*Loop* or *While*). Instead, an *If* statement is used to check a condition, and the decision to recursively call the method depends on the value of the condition.

A comparison of repetitions

Chapters 7 and 8 presented three ways for accomplishing repetition in a program: *Loop*, *While*, and recursion. You might ask, "Which one should I use, and when?"

The choice depends on the task being completed (the problem being solved) and why you need the repetition. If you know how many times the repetition needs to be performed (either directly or via a function), the *Loop* statement is generally easiest. In most programming that you do, you will want to avoid infinite loops. In animation programming, however, an infinite *Loop* statement can be used to create some background action that continues to run until the program is shut down.

Otherwise, use the *While* loop or recursion. Some programmers prefer *While* and others prefer recursion. Put two programmers in the same room and they are likely to disagree over this issue. The underlying difference between the two is how you think about solving a problem. We say, "Try both." Some problems are easier to solve with a *While* loop and others are easier to solve with recursion. With experience, you will discover which works best for you. The important thing is that you learn to write code that uses repetition.

Part IV
Advanced Topics

Chapter 9

Lists and List Processing

"The time has come," the Walrus said,

"To talk of many things:
Of shoes—and ships—and sealing-wax—
Of cabbages—and kings–"

This chapter will explore a different aspect of programming—that of organizing objects or information of the same type into a group. Up to now, worlds typically contained only a few objects. Programs were written to make each individual object carry out specific actions, sometimes acting alone and sometimes coordinated with other objects. But what if you wanted to create an animation where 20 soldiers were marching in a parade, all performing the same marching steps? You could certainly create a marching method for a new class of soldier and then instantiate 20 soldiers in the world. To make each soldier perform the marching steps, though, you would have to drag the marching instruction into the editor at least 20 times (once for each soldier)! One way to make this programming situation less tedious is to collect all the objects into an organizing structure. Then you can write program code either for all the objects as a group or for the individual objects, as before.

In programming, we call such an organizing structure a data structure. This chapter introduces a data structure known as a list. Section 9-1 begins with a demonstration of how to create a list. We then look at how to iterate through the list. (We have used the word "iterate" before—when we were talking about repetition.) To "iterate through a list" means to do the same thing repeatedly for all the items in a list.

Section 9-2 illustrates another use of lists, that of searching through a list to find an item that possesses a certain property. Searching through a list is similar to going shopping for a new pair of jeans. You walk down the aisle where all the jeans are hanging on the rack and look at each to find the pair with just the right size and color.

9-1 Lists

A list is one of the most popular ways to organize information. We use lists in our everyday lives. For example, you might have a grocery list or a list of homework assignments. Programmers use lists to organize objects and information about objects in their programs. Examples of specialized lists can be found in thousands of software applications. In Alice, a list (generally) contains items of a similar type. (For example, we might want a list of objects or a list of colors.) In this section we will look at how to create a list and then how to iterate through the list, to look for a particular item or to take some action with each item in the list.

Creating a list

In the initial scene shown in Figure 9-1-1, five rockettes (People) have been added to the world. The rockettes are famous for their holiday dance routines. We want to create an animation where

233

the rockettes will perform the kick-step from one of their dances. In a kick-step routine, the dancers each perform a kick, one after the other down the line. Then, they all perform the same kick-step at the same time. This is an example of an animation where a list can be used to organize objects to act as a group.

Figure 9-1-1. The rockettes

Before a list can be used in a program, the list must be created. Five rockette dancers have been added to the scene and positioned to form a dance line. Just adding the objects to the world and then positioning them next to one another, however, is not enough to create a list.

To actually make a list, a list variable must be created (to give the list a name) and then the objects (already in the world) must be added to the list. To create a list variable, select the properties tab for the World and then click the **create new variable** button, as shown in Figure 9-1-2. (The list is created at the world-level rather than at the class-level because it will contain several different objects.)

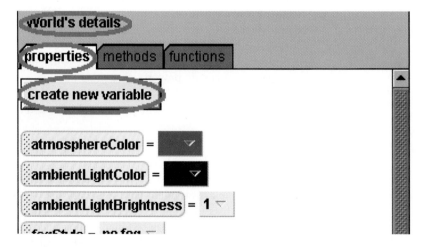

Figure 9-1-2. Creating a list variable

When the **create new variable** button is clicked, a popup dialog box allows you to enter the list variable name, as shown in Figure 9-1-3. In this example, we used the name *dancers* and selected its Type as *Object*. The key action here is to check the box marked **make a List**. Then you can click the button labeled new item to add an object to the list. In the example shown in Figure 9-1-3, the new item button was clicked five times to enter each rockette. Finally, click the Okay button. The list variable name can now be used in instructions where we want to have the dancers perform as a group.

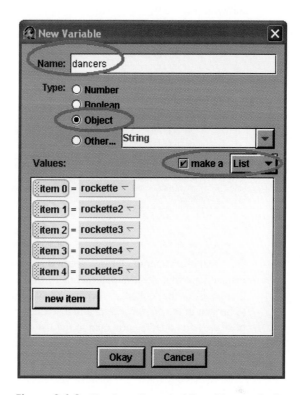

Figure 9-1-3. Naming a list and adding objects to the list

For all in order—Iterating sequentially through a list

A useful operation that can be done with a list is to iterate sequentially through it. This means that each item in the list will be instructed to perform the same instruction, one after the other. This is like a mail delivery person walking down the street and placing mail in each mailbox. Iteration through a list is sometimes called "walking" or "traversing" a list.

Alice provides a special *For all in order* statement that works with one item at a time from a list. As an example, let's have each rockette, from left to right, kick up her right leg as part of the dance routine. The storyboard is shown below. The *kickUpRightLeg* method consists of several simpler actions.

```
For all dancers in order
   item_from_dancers kickUpRightLeg
```

```
kickUpRightLeg

Parameter: whichRockette

Do in order
   Do together
     whichRockette right thigh turn back
     whichRockette right calf turn forward
     whichRockette right calf turn back
```

Now we can translate the design into a world-level method named *World.kickUpRightLeg*, where the *whichRockette* parameter acts as a placeholder for an item from the *dancers* list. (At first glance, we might think the *kickUpRightLeg* method should be a class-level method. However, several different objects may be used in the *dancers* list.) The *kickUpRightLeg* method is shown in Figure 9-1-4.

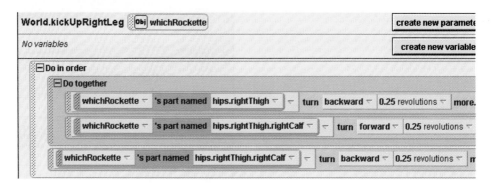

Figure 9-1-4. World-level *kickUpRightLeg* method

An object parameter in a method requires that you perform more than one step to create instructions that use the parameter. In this example, we want to move parts of the right leg (subparts) of the rockette. Alice has no way of knowing which kind of object is actually going to be sent in to *whichRockette* and also does not know whether the object has a right leg. (Suppose we had added a snowman to the list of *dancers*. Sending in a snowman to *whichRockette* would be a problem, because snowmen do not have right legs, or any legs for that matter!) What all this means is that we must use a *part named* function to specify the exact subpart of *whichRockette* is involved in the *turn* instructions.

As an example, let's look at the steps we used to create the first turn instruction in *kickUpRightLeg*.

1. Create an instruction to turn one of the rockettes backward 0.25 revolutions.

2. Then, drag in the *part named* function for the rockette and drop it on top of the rockette tile. The result should look like this:

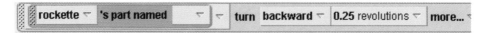

3. Click to the right of part named and enter the exact name of the part (Alice is case sensitive, so type it correctly). Now, we have this:

4. Now, drag the *whichRockette* parameter tile down to drop it on top of the rockette. The final instruction should look like this:

Now that the *kickUpRightLeg* instruction has been written, a *For all in order* statement can be used to create the animation. The *For all in order* tile is dragged into the editor, and the expression *World.dancers* is selected as the name of the list, as illustrated in Figure 9-1-5.

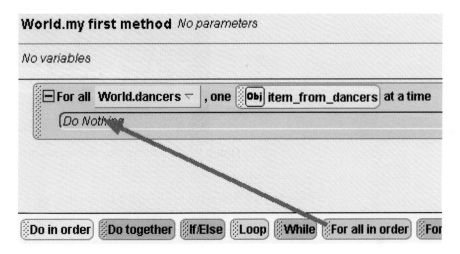

Figure 9-1-5. The *For all in order* tile

An instruction is written inside the *For all in order* statement to call the *World.kickUpRightLeg* method, as illustrated in Figure 9-1-6.

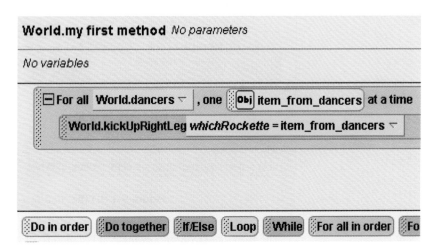

Figure 9-1-6. Calling *kickUpRightLeg* with *item_from_dancers* as the argument

When the program is run, each item from the *dancers* list is sent as an argument to the *kickUpRightLeg*method, one at a time. Each dancer kicks up her right leg one after the other, down the dance line. The screenshot in Figure 9-1-7 was captured after the first two rockettes have already kicked their right leg in the air and the third rockette has just started to do so.

For all together—Iterating simultaneously

Alice also provides a statement named *For all together* to make all the objects of a list perform the same action at the same time. This is called "iterating through a list simultaneously." One way to think of *For all together* is that it is similar to a multi-way telephone conference

Figure 9-1-7. Running the dance animation using *For all in order*

call—everyone who is connected to the conference call is on the phone line at the same time and everyone can talk and interact at the same time.

In any dance group, the dancers perform some steps sequentially and others at the same time. Let's have all the rockettes kick up their right leg at the same time. To do so, drag the *For all together* tile into the editor, as shown in Figure 9-1-8.

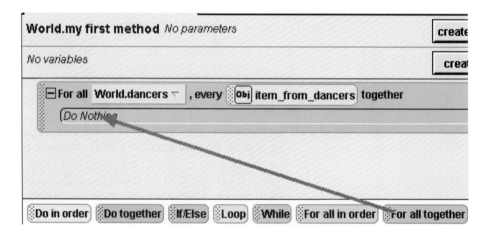

Figure 9-1-8. The *For all together* tile

The *World.kickUpRightLeg* method is called from within the *For all together* statement. The resulting instruction is shown in Figure 9-1-9.

Figure 9-1-9. Calling *kickUpRightLeg* in a *For all together* statement

Now, when the code is run, the dancers all kick up their right legs at the same time, as illustrated in Figure 9-1-10.

Figure 9-1-10. Running the dance animation using *For all together*

9-2 List search

Internet search engines are a great invention for helping us locate Web pages. For instance, imagine you are looking for a video that tells the story of Caesar and Cleopatra. You connect to a search engine (such as Google™) and enter "Caesar and Cleopatra." In a few short seconds, a list of Web page links appears on your web browser. Now, you do a list search—you read through the items, one item at a time, and look for a Web page that has exactly what you want. A list search is a common list operation used in programming. Its purpose is to iterate through a list of items, one item at a time, and check each one to see if it has exactly what we are looking for. In this section we will explore how to do a list search in Alice.

Simulation using a list search

As an example of a list search, imagine a popular carnival game named "Whack A Mole." In this game, the player picks up a hammer and whacks at a mole-like puppet that pops up here and there out of a box. Points are scored each time the player whacks a mole.

Figure 9-2-1 shows the initial world for the game. A WhackAMole game booth has been added to a world. Twelve moles have been added and placed inside the game, one below each hole (out of sight in Figure 9-2-1—except for the mole in a popped-up position). The WhackAMole game booth and moles are from the Amusement Park gallery. Finally, two cylinders (named totalScore and playerScore) have been added in the background to act as a primitive visual scoreboard. The cylinders are from the Shapes gallery. The totalScore cylinder, representing the total (or target) score, is grey and is positioned on the ground. The playerScore cylinder is yellow and is positioned so that its top is just under the surface of the ground (out of sight in Figure 9-2-1). The playerScore cylinder represents the current score. Of course, at the beginning of the game the player's score is zero—which is why the top of the playerScore cylinder is initially at ground level.

The idea for the game is for a mole to randomly pop up and down. The player tries to mouse-click on the mole before it goes back down. Each time the player succeeds, the playerScore cylinder is raised, indicating an increase in the player's score. Once the entire playerScore cylinder has been raised above ground level, it will then be the same height above ground as the totalScore cylinder. At this point, the player has won the game, and the moles should cease popping up and down. Figure 9-2-2 shows a screen capture of the game during execution. The top of the yellow playerScore cylinder is approaching the top of the grey totalScore cylinder, showing that the player is doing well in the game. (You may want to peek ahead to Chapter 10 to see how a more conventional scorekeeper could be constructed.)

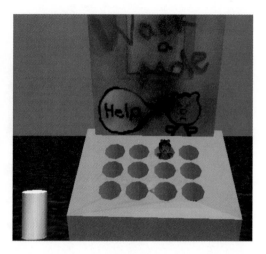

Figure 9-2-1. Initial scene for WhackAMole game

Figure 9-2-2. Scorekeeping columns at runtime

In designing a solution to this problem, two subtasks need to be considered. The first is to set up a loop that continues to pop (raise and lower) moles randomly while the game is in progress. The second is to increase the player's score each time the player manages to actually click on one of the moles that pops up. In storyboard form,

---

Event: *When the world starts*
Response: *World.myFirstMethod*
  While the *playerScore* column is not yet completely above ground
       pop (and lower) a random mole

Event: User clicks mouse
Response: *World.score*
  If mouse was clicked on one of the moles
       Do together
       move the *playerScore* column upward
       play a pop sound (sound is optional)

First subtask—game in progress

When the world starts, the game should immediately begin. As you know, Alice automatically executes *World.my first method* when the world starts. Taking advantage of this automatic execution, the code for starting the game and keeping it in progress will be written in *World.my first method.*

A *While* loop can be used to provide continuous action in the game. While the player-Score column has not yet moved above the ground (meaning that the player hasn't yet won the game) calls will be repeatedly made to a *popMole* method. So, we need a method to pop up a mole. We have twelve moles, so we will use a parameter *whichMole* to represent one of them. The method is illustrated in Figure 9-2-3.

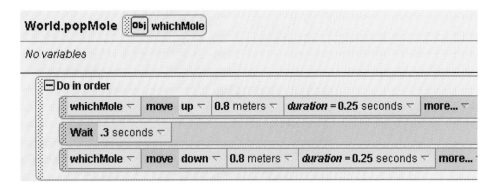

Figure 9-2-3. The *popMole* method

Of course, the first thing to do after this method is written is to test it. (We don't have to wait until the program is written!) Just call the method from *World.my first method.* Whichever mole is passed to *whichMole* is the mole that pops up. The popup action makes the mole move up, stay up for 0.3 seconds, and then move back down.

Now we need to figure out how to pass a random mole to the *popMole* method. Our solution is to organize the moles into a list structure and then randomly select a mole from the list. A list of moles is created, as previously described in Section 9-1. The name of the list variable in this example is *moles*—not a very creative name, but it has the advantage of being obvious!

Now that the *popMole* method has been written (Figure 9-2-3) and the *moles* list created, the code for keeping the game in progress can be written in *World.my first method,* as in Figure 9-2-4. To send a random mole from the list to the *popMole* method each time it is called, we dragged the mole list into the parameter tile and then selected *random item from list* from the popup menu. When this code is run, a random mole from the list is passed as an argument to the *popMole* method each time the while statement is repeated.

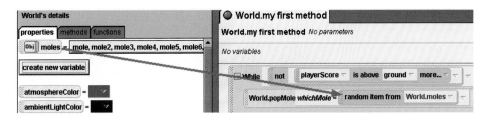

Figure 9-2-4. Repeatedly calling *popMole*

Wait a second! When the code shown in Figure 9-2-4 is tested, it keeps playing and playing and playing. The *While* loop is supposed to end when the playerScore column moves up above the ground. Of course, the playerScore column does not move upward because we have not yet written the code to make that happen. Our program is not yet complete ... we have one more step to accomplish.

Second subtask—scoring

A score method needs to be written to visually display the player's success in the game. Each time the player actually clicks the mouse on a mole that pops up, the playerScore column should be raised. The *score* method is shown in Figure 9-2-5. The object clicked by the mouse will be sent to the *clicked* parameter. In this method, a *For all in order* statement is used to iterate through the list of moles. Each mole is checked to determine whether it is the object clicked. This is where the list search takes place! If one of the moles in the list is the object clicked, the player's score is increased (by raising the playerScore column), and the mole that was clicked makes a popping noise.

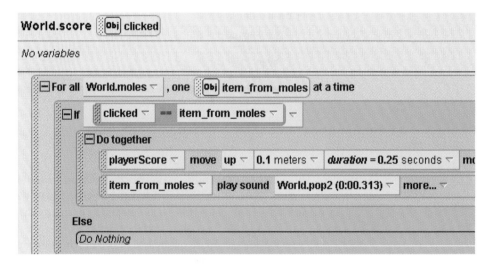

Figure 9-2-5. The *score* method

Critical to scoring is the event *When the mouse is clicked on something*. To use this event, a *When the mouse is clicked on something* event is created. Then the *World.score* method tile is dragged into the editor and dropped on top of <Nothing>. From the popup menu, we selected *object under the mouse cursor* as the argument for the *clicked* parameter. The result is shown in Figure 9-2-6.

In response to the mouse being clicked on something (anything), the *score* method is called. This event notifies Alice the mouse has been clicked, and Alice can then determine what object is under the mouse cursor. The object under the mouse cursor will be passed to the *clicked* parameter for the *score* method.

Figure 9-2-6. Creating the event

Of course, it is possible that the player clicked too soon or too late and the object under the cursor was the top of the WhackAMole game booth (because the mole had disappeared back underneath). The player may move the cursor too quickly and click on the grass or the sky. In such situations, the search for a mole that has been clicked fails, so the player's score is not increased and no pop sound is made.

In summary, the important concept illustrated by the WhackAMole example is that of searching a collection of items to determine whether one of them has a particular property. Other techniques for searching can be used, but the overall idea is the same. In this example, the collection of items is a list of moles. The search is conducted using a *For all in order* statement to iterate through the list. The *For all in order* statement goes through each mole in the list and checks whether one of them has been clicked by the player.

Tips & Techniques 9
Poses

As you know, each Alice object has a center that marks its location. You may also have intuitively realized that an Alice object has the ability to remember the position of its component parts. We call the set of positions of the component parts a pose. You can think of a pose in the same way that a fashion model strikes a pose or a ballerina assumes a classic pose beside the ballet bar (Objects). Figure T-9-1 illustrates a ballerina (People) in a pose known as "first position." The ballerina's body is upright, the arms are outstretched, the feet are positioned with the heels together, and each foot is turned outward.

Figure T-9-1. The ballerina pose in first position

Suppose a program is written to have the ballerina begin in a first-position pose and then perform several ballet movements. Once the animation has been played (and the arms and legs of the ballerina are now in different positions), a click on the Restart button will cause the ballerina to resume her initial location and pose, so that the animation can play again.

You can use the scene editor to arrange an object in other poses and ask the object to remember them. Use the mouse and object methods to position the body parts of the object into the desired pose. Then click on the **capture pose** button in the object's Details panel and enter a name for the pose. Figure T-9-2 illustrates the capture of an *onToe* pose for the ballerina.

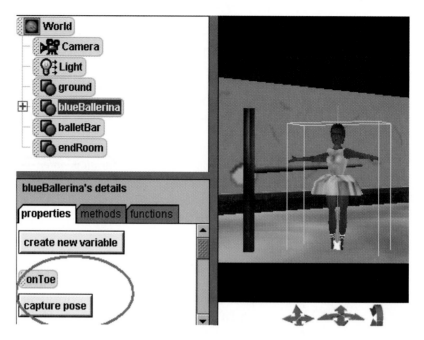

Figure T-9-2. Capturing an *onToe* pose

Now you can write instructions to make the ballerina assume the pose during an animation. To create an instruction using a pose, drag the pose tile into the editor, as illustrated in Figure T-9-3.

A few words of caution about poses: resizing an object may have an unpredictable effect on poses. For this reason, we recommend that capturing a pose be the last step in creating an initial world. Also, we suggest avoiding poses if objects are being resized during the animation.

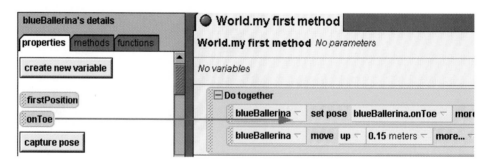

Figure T-9-3. Creating an instruction to have an object assume a pose

Exercises and Projects

9-1 Exercises

1. *The Wave*

   This exercise is to practice using *For all in order*. Create an animation that simulates some sports fans doing "the wave"—a popular stadium activity. Create an initial scene where a coach, student1, skaterGirl, and randomGuy2 (People) are standing on the field in the stadium (City). All four of these people have the same subpart structure. Then create a list made up of the people objects in the scene. Use the *For all in order* statement to animate each person raising his or her arms to simulate "the wave."

2. *Military Drill*

   This exercise is to practice using *For all together*. Create a world with five soldiers (People) on the edge of the carrier (Vehicles). The idea is to make the soldiers walk "in step" from one end of the carrier to the other. An initial world is shown below. Create a list variable, named *platoon*, made up of the five soldiers. Use the *For all together* statement to conduct a military drill with the soldiers.

3. *Spring Flowers*

   If you have a copy of that world created in Chapter 5, Exercise 13, you can revise that world. Otherwise build the world using the a box (Shapes) and flowers (Nature). Five flowers (your choice) are hidden inside the box.

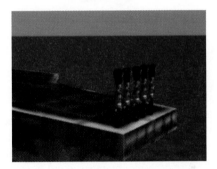

   (**Hint:** The flowers can be hidden inside the box by using the mouse to position them out of sight.)

   Create a list, where each flower is one item of the list.

   (a) Make each flower "grow" upward (out of the flowerbox) one at a time using *For all in order*.

   (b) When you have that working well, create a second version where all flowers grow out of the flowerbox at the same time, using *For all together*.

9-2 Exercises

4. *Earthquake*

   Geologists who study earthquakes often use simulations of earthquake motions to study shifts in the earth's crust. Simulated earthquake motions can be useful when seismographic recordings are unavailable or are difficult to obtain. For example, earthquakes in the ocean depths are not measured easily. In this exercise, you will create a simulation of earthquake motions. The world is created using four mountainous structures (four Island2 objects from the Environments folder). Arrange the island objects close together, in various positions, to create a mountain range, as shown below.

   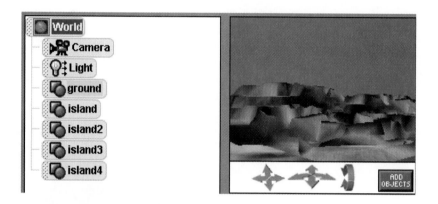

   Make a list consisting of the four mountain objects (made with the island objects). Create an animation where each of the islands in the list undergoes a "shake." A shake is a move in a random direction by a random amount. The animation should occur for each mountain structure in order and then for all mountain structures together. Experiment with different limits for the randomly generated amount of movement.

5. *Ship Motion*

   To create a realistic animation of ships at sea (Vehicles), ships must appear to move as if responding to the motion of the waves. A response amplitude operator (RAO) ship-motion approach is commonly used by animators. Create a simulation of ship motion with a world containing four ships. Make a list of the four ship objects. Animate all ships moving at the same time but by different amounts. Use a randomly generated RAO to determine the amount of movement in a random direction for each ship in the list. Because the ships are moving with the waves, the movements tend to be symmetrical. That is, a forward (left, up) movement is followed by a backward (right, down) movement in approximately the same amount. Use a loop to continue the motion simulation until the user stops the animation.

6. *Modify the WhackAMole game*

One possible modification to the WhackAMole game is to play it until the user has whacked all of the moles. To make this adjustment, change the color of a mole in the list to red whenever it is whacked. Allow the mole to be raised only if it is not already red. The game ends when all moles have been whacked!

9-2 Projects

1. *Halloween Treasure Hunt*

In this game, a ghost (Spooky) is out for a treasure hunt on Halloween night. The haunted house (Amusement Park) has been littered with tombstones (Spooky). Under each tombstone is a treasure. When the ghost gets close to a tombstone, the tombstone falls over and the treasure is revealed. The ghost's task is to visit all the tombstones and reveal all the treasures. Unfortunately, skeletons (Spooky) are patrolling the grounds—walking back and forth near the tombstones to protect the treasures. If the ghost gets too close to a skeleton, he will vaporize and the game ends (and the ghost will have to wait until next Halloween night to find the treasures).

Create an animated game for the Halloween Treasure Hunt. Use a list to store 10 tombstones. The tombstones are all around the haunted house (screen shot shows only the front side). Allow the user to use the keyboard arrow keys to move the ghost around the grounds of Phantom Manor. Make the camera follow the ghost so he is always in sight. Do not worry about the ghost moving through an object—he is a ghost! As each tombstone gets visited, change its *opacity* property from *1* to *0*. If the ghost manages to visit all the tombstones (all of them have an opacity of 0), the game is over and the ghost has won. If the ghost encounters a skeleton at too close a range, the game is over and the ghost will vaporize into thin air.

2. *Monty*

A famous mathematical problem (the Monty Dilemma) goes something like this:
Suppose you're on a game show, and you're given the choice of three doors. Behind one door is a car, behind the others, toy monkeys. You pick a door, say number 1, and the host, who knows what's behind the doors, opens another door, say number 3, which has a toy monkey. He says to you, "Do you want to pick door number 2?" Is it to your advantage to switch your choice of doors?

One way to find an answer to this question is to create a simulation of the game where the objects are placed randomly behind the doors. Play the game 25 times where you do not switch and 25 times where you do switch. Keep track of your success rate when you switch and your success rate when you do not switch. Then you will know the answer to the question!

To set up the initial world, add three doors (Furniture), a car (Vehicles), and two toy monkeys (Animals) to a new world. Position the car and the two monkeys behind the

three doors, as shown above. Each door should be 2.5 meters to the left (or right) of its neighbor door. Make the door positioned in front of the car the vehicle for the car and then do the same for each monkey and its respective door. (When the door moves, the object behind will move with it.) Also create a 3D text object that asks the player to "Select a Door." Make the text object invisible by setting its *isShowing* property to *false*.

To program the game, make a list containing the three doors. When the animation begins, randomly pick two doors and swap them. Use a method called *swap* that takes two doors as parameters. Swap the two doors by having them move 2.5 meters in opposite directions.

Important: Two doors should swap only if they are different (a door cannot swap places with itself). Repeat the swap ten times. (The idea is to make it difficult for the player to know what object is behind what door.)

Display the 3D text to ask the player to select a door. After the player clicks on one of the doors, pick another door that hides a monkey and open that door. Then ask the player whether he/she wants to switch the choice. If the object behind the door (selected by the player) is the car, the player has won. Open the door and declare the player a winner. Otherwise, the player has lost. Use sound or 3D text to indicate the win or loss.

3. *Frog Crossing the Pool*
   Add a rectangle (Shapes) to a new world and change its color to blue. This will serve as a swimming pool. Add 7 circles (Shapes) to the world—5 yellow along the long side of the pool (each 1 meter apart), 1 green at the nearest side, and 1 red at the far edge. The yellow circles are lily pads that float back and forth across the pool. Add a frog, and place it on the green circle. The goal is to make the frog jump from lily pad to lily pad until it gets all the way across the pool. If the frog lands on the water (not on a lily pad) the frog sinks into the pool and the game is over. If the frog jumps all the way across the pool and lands on the red circle at the far edge, the player wins.

   Your program must place the 5 yellow circles in a list. Write a method that uses an infinite loop to repeatedly move each of the 5 yellow circles in the list across the pool and back at different speeds. (The easiest way to do this is to pass a random number to the method to specify the duration for the circle to move across the pool.) Create event handling methods that have the frog jump forward 1 meter if the player presses the ↑ key, move left if the player presses the ← key, and move right if the player presses the → key. Connect each event handling method to an event.

Summary

In programming, many different kinds of organizing structures can be used to create a collection of objects or information about objects. Each kind of structure offers different capabilities or features. In Alice, lists are used as organizing structures (data structures). A list is a collection of several items of the same type (such as *Object* or *Color*).

In this chapter we looked at creating a list as well as iterating through a list. Alice provides two mechanisms for iterating through a list: sequentially (using *For all in order*) and simultaneously (using *For all together*). The *For all in order* iteration is similar to "walking" (or traversing) through each item in the list, one at a time. The *For all together* iteration is like setting up a multi-way telephone conference call—everyone is on the line at the same time. The *For all in order* statement is similar to *Do in order* in that actions are performed in sequence, and the *For all together* statement is similar to *Do together* in that actions are performed simultaneously. A common application of lists is searching for an item in a list. A list search walks through each item in the list, one at a time, until we find the one we want.

Important concepts in this chapter

- A list is a collection of items.
- The items in a list all have the same type (such as object). In Alice, objects in a list do not all need to be instances of the same model. For example, a list containing five rockettes is fine. A list containing three rockettes and two snowwomen is also fine, as both of these are the same type—*Object*.
- A list can be iterated through either sequentially or simultaneously.
- If a list contains objects, and each object is to perform some action, the list item is often passed as a parameter to a method, where the object performs the action.

Chapter 10

Variables and Revisiting Inheritance

*"Must a name mean something?" Alice
asked doubtfully.
"Of course it must," Humpty Dumpty
said with a short laugh: "My name
means the shape I am. ..."*

This chapter introduces the concept of mutable variables and revisits classes and inheritance, as used to create new classes. A mutable variable is a piece of storage that holds onto a value (a piece of information) while a program is running. We say it is mutable because we can change the value as things happen during program execution.

In Section 10-1, mutable variables are introduced as properties that can be changed at runtime using a *set* instruction. We look at how to add new properties to an object (as class-level variables). The object and its new properties can be saved out in a new class. An instance of the new class has all the old properties of the original class but also has the new properties. You have seen this technique before (in Chapter 4), where we defined new methods for an object in the world and then saved out the object as a new class.

In Section 10-2, an array visualization is created. An array is a structure that organizes a collection of items. Each item is located in a certain position in the array structure. In working with an array, we use an index variable to keep track of the position of each item in the array.

10-1 Variables

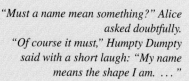

From Alice's perspective, a mutable variable is a property that can be directly changed using *set* (or some other methods, as will be shown below). The word "mutate" means "to change," and we use "mutate" to describe what happens when a property is changed. For simplicity, we often drop the word "mutable" and just say "variable."

What makes mutable variables worth learning about? They allow you to keep track of changes. In the same way that we need to track the balance of money in a checking account or the amount of gasoline in the tank of a car, we often need to keep track of changes in position, color, opacity and other properties of objects in our programs. In a game, we might want to keep track of the number of times the player has put a basketball through the hoop or how much time is left on the clock. The mutable variables in our examples are class-level variables, designed to keep track of a property for a specific kind of object. But, we are getting ahead of ourselves. Let's begin with a quick recall of properties of objects and how properties relate to state. Then, we can look more closely at mutable variables.

Recall: properties and state

As you may recall, a class model in Alice defines properties for its own kind of object. Each object (as an instance of a class) gets its own set of properties, illustrated in Figure 10-1-1. Properties store information about the object. For example, in Figure 10-1-1, the *vehicle* of the basketball object is student and isShowing is *true*.

Figure 10-1-1. Properties of a basketball

An object's property values are the information we know about the object. We call this set of information the state of the object. Instructions in our programs generally change the state of the object. For example, a *move* instruction changes an object's *position* and a *turn to face* instruction changes its *orientation*. Some of the state can be changed directly, using a *set* method (available by dragging a property tile into the code window). For example, the *color* property of the basketball is set to orange in Figure 10-1-2. You have probably used a *set* method to change *opacity, isShowing,* and other properties of objects in programs.

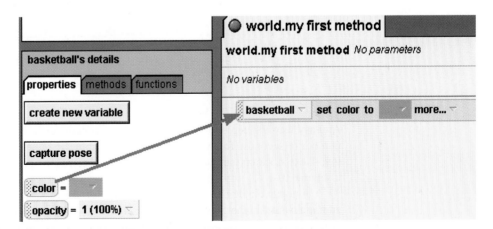

Figure 10-1-2. Using a *set* instruction to change the *color* property

Using class-level variables

New variables can be added to the properties list for an object. Then, if the object is saved out and given a new name, a new class is created. This new class will have all the properties of the original class and new properties as well. In programs and projects presented in previous chapters, we used a similar technique of designing and creating new classes by writing new class-level methods that extend the capability of an existing object. Then we saved out the object with its new methods as a new class. The new class inherits all the properties and behaviors of the original class, but now has additional capabilities.

A newly added variable is NOT directly visible in our world. Although variables have no visible representation when a program is running, they are sometimes quite useful as another way to extend a class's capabilities. This concept will be illustrated by means of two examples.

Example 1: A timer

A common component in games is a timer. A timer is used to keep track of how much time the player has left to play the game. For example, in a basketball game a timer (clock) begins with 12:00 minutes at the beginning of each period. As the game is played, the timer counts down to 0:00. When the timer reaches 0:00, the period ends. Another common component of games is a scorekeeper. A scorekeeper is similar to a timer, but it increases the score when a player scores a point (or points).

In this example, we will construct a timer that counts down in seconds. Figure 10-1-3 shows a world with a timer object. The timer is actually a 3D text object, displayed in the lower left of the scene. The string stored in the 3D text object has been set to 0.0 (to indicate that the timer is inactive). Our task is to set the timer to an initial number of seconds for a game (say 10.0 seconds) and then count down the seconds remaining in a game. The number of seconds remaining will be displayed and will be updated with each passing second.

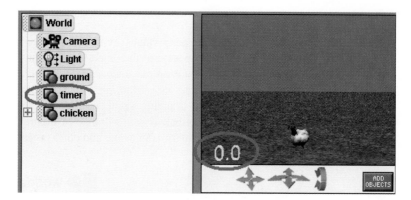

Figure 10-1-3. A timer using 3D text (initial string is 0.0)

Creating a class-level variable

An easy way to keep track of the number of seconds left is to use a variable that stores the number of seconds. To create a class-level variable, first click the timer object in the Object tree. Next, click on the properties tab and then the **create new variable** button, as illustrated in Figure 10-1-4.

A popup dialog box allows you to enter a name for the variable, select its type, and give it an initial value. In the example shown in Figure 10-1-5, we named the variable *timeLeft*, set its type to be Number, and gave it a default value of *0*. Any number could be used—we arbitrarily chose 0 as a reasonable example.

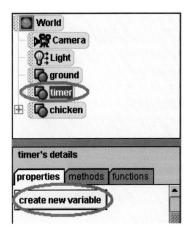

Figure 10-1-4. The create new variable button

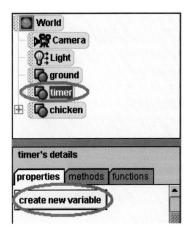

Figure 10-1-5. Creating a new variable *timeLeft*

Because the timer has a default *timeLeft* of 0 seconds, it would be helpful to create a parameterized method that can be used to initialize the timer to some number of seconds appropriate for any game. A class-level method is created named *initialize*. A storyboard for the *initialize* method is:

```
initialize

parameter: amountOfTime

timeLeft is set to a value specified by amountOfTime
```

The code for the initialize method is shown in Figure 10-1-6. The *set* instruction is created by dragging the *timeLeft* variable into the editor and selecting *amountOfTime* as the value.

The next step is to create a method that causes the timer to count down by seconds and update the 3D text to display the new time with each passing second. A simple storyboard for a *countDown* method is:

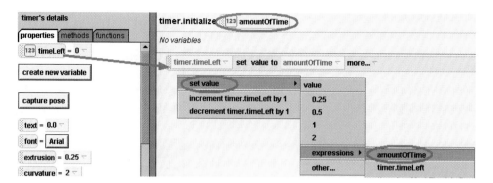

Figure 10-1-6. Creating an instruction to set *timeLeft* in the *initialize* method

```
countDown

Do in order
  While timeLeft is greater than 0
    Do in order
    update the 3D text to show the remaining number of seconds
    decrease timeLeft by 1
  update the 3D text to display 0 seconds
```

You may be puzzled by the last line of the storyboard. Think about it like this: the *While* statement runs again and again, as long as the value of *timeLeft* is greater than 0. When the value of *timeLeft* becomes 0, the *While* statement ends and the 0 does not get displayed! We added the last line to display the 0, thereby showing that the time on the clock has run out.

Now, the storyboard is translated into the corresponding code in the *countDown* method for the timer. First, a *While* statement tile is dragged into the editor and then the World function (a > b) is dragged in as the condition, as shown in Figure 10-1-7. We selected *timer.timeLeft* as the value for **a**. (Recall that the variable *timeLeft* stores a number value, as set by the *initialize* method.) To complete the condition (a > b), select *other* as the value for **b**. A popup number pad is used to enter 0 as the value for **b**.

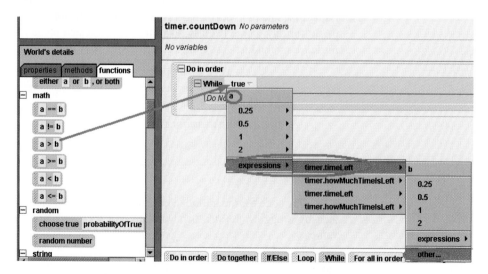

Figure 10-1-7. Creating the condition in a *While* statement

The resulting code is shown below.

Instructions can now be written within the *While* statement. First, a *Do in order* block is dragged in and then an instruction is created to update the 3D text display to show the remaining time. Select the *timer* 3D text object in the Object tree and then drag its *text* property tile into the editor. Select the default string from the popup menu, as shown in Figure 10-1-8.

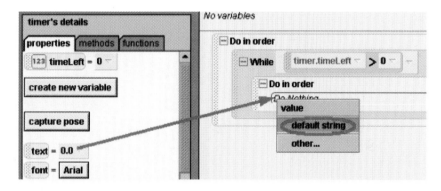

Figure 10-1-8. Dragging the *text* property into the editor to create a *set* instruction

The *default string* is just a placeholder. We want to replace the default string with the number of seconds remaining. The problem is that the value stored in the *timeLeft* variable is a Number but we want to display it as a 3D text string. To solve this problem, a World-level function can be used to convert a Number to a string. Select World in the Object tree and then click on *functions*. Drag the *what as a string* function over the *default string* tile and select *timeLeft* from the popup menu, as illustrated in Figure 10-1-9.

Figure 10-1-9. Dragging the *what as a string* function into the editor

The code created, thus far, is shown below. Notice that the duration of this instruction is 0 seconds, meaning that updating the 3D text string is done instantaneously.

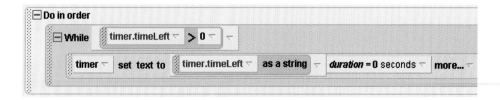

Now, the count down instructions can be created. One way to do this is wait 1 second and then decrease the value stored in *timeLeft* by 1 second, as illustrated in Figure 10-1-10. As with the *set* instruction, the *decrement* instruction has a *duration* of 0 seconds. Because we used a *Wait* 1 second instruction and made the other instructions occur in 0 seconds, we can be sure the timer decreases 1 second.

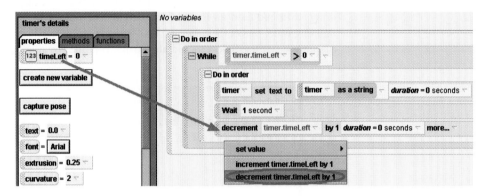

Figure 10-1-10. Decrementing *timeLeft* by 1

Finally, the last statement is added to display 0 seconds on the clock after the *While* statement ends. The completed code is shown in Figure 10-1-11. Notice that the last line of code is created outside the *While* statement, to display 0 seconds.

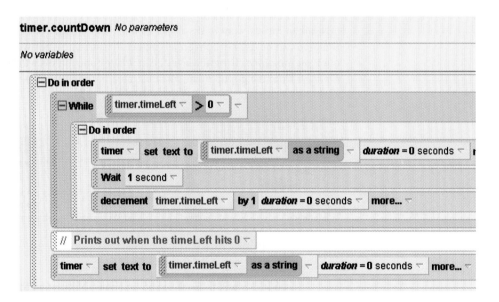

Figure 10-1-11. The *countDown* method

To demonstrate how the timer is used, we created the code shown in Figure 10-1-12. First, *timeLeft* is initialized to 10 seconds, by passing 10 as the argument to the *amountOfTime* parameter. Then, a *Do together* block is used to play a game while the timer counts down.

The critical technique in using the timer is to control the length of time the player is allowed to play the game so that when *timeLeft* decreases to 0, the game is over. This means

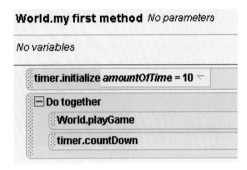

Figure 10-1-12. Code to play a game at the same time as the timer counts down

the *playGame* method must be able to find out how much time is left on the clock. We created a class-level function *howMuchTimeIsLeft* for the timer, as shown in Figure 10-1-13. This function allows the *playGame* method to check the time left on clock, as needed.

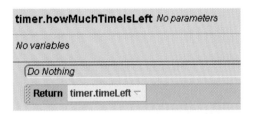

Figure 10-1-13. The timer's *howMuchTimeIsLeft* function returns the value of *timeLeft*

The *playGame* method is created using a *While* statement that makes use of the *how MuchTimeIsLeft* function in its conditional expression, as illustrated in Figure 10-1-14. The code in this example is not really a game—just a demonstration of some code that repeats until the time left on the clock reaches zero. Nonetheless, it illustrates how a block of game instructions can be controlled by the timer.

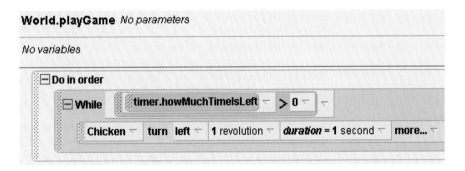

Figure 10-1-14. Simple example of using the *timer* to control a game

A more complex example: Tracking the steering of a car

Consider an interactive world that simulates steering (driving) a car. In this example we will use a convertible corvette from the Vehicles folder in the gallery. The challenge is to create an animation where the user can steer the corvette, perhaps to drive along city streets, or as part of a racecar game, where the player needs to steer along the road and avoid obstacles.

Figure 10-1-15 illustrates an initial scene, with a city terrain (City) and a corvette added to an initial world.

Figure 10-1-15. An initial scene

We want to allow the user to steer the car using the left, right, up, and down arrow keys. Alice has a built-in event *Let the arrow keys move <object>* but this does not work the way a steering a car works in the real world. Using the built-in event, the left arrow moves the car left sideways and the right arrow moves the car right sideways—not a very realistic motion. The corvette has front-wheel drive, so its front wheels should turn right and left in response to a right or left arrow key press, and the corvette should move forward and back up in response to an up or down arrow key-press.

To design and write the program code for this animation, it is important to understand that the left and right arrow keys will be used to steer the car left and right and the up and down arrow keys move the car forward or back. (In other words, the left and right arrow keys do not move the car—they only turn the steering wheel.) This is true in a real car, as well; turning the steering wheel left or right does not actually cause the car to move. You must press the gas pedal and put the car in gear to make it move forward or back. So, think of the left and right arrow keys as steering and the up and down arrow keys as a gear/gas mechanism that moves the car forward or back. Four class-level methods will be needed: turning left and right and moving forward and back.

One problem we need to figure out is how to keep track of which way the front wheels have been turned. This is needed because when the corvette moves and the wheels have been turned right or left, the corvette should move and turn right or left at the same time. Also, we need to keep track of how much the wheels have been turned. For example, if the wheels have been turned sharply to the left, a move forward should be sharply toward the left. We can create a class-level variable, *direction,* that will track the amount the wheels have been turned and whether they have been turned right or left, using a linear scale, as shown in Figure 10-1-16.

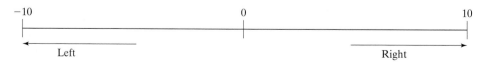

Figure 10-1-16. Linear scale for tracking the amount the car has turned left or right

The *direction* variable value will begin at 0, meaning that the wheels are aligned straight ahead with the front of the car. If the direction is 0 and the up arrow is clicked, the car will move straight. When the left arrow key is clicked, the *direction* will be decremented by 1 (decrementing subtracts 1 from the current value). When the right arrow key is pressed, the *direction* will be incremented by 1 (incrementing adds 1 to the current value). In other words, a direction value < 0 means the wheels are turned to the left, and a *direction* value > 0 means the wheels are turned to the right.

As with real cars, you can turn the steering wheel only just so far. We arbitrarily chose a linear scale of -10 to $+10$. This means the direction variable can store a minimum value of -10 and a maximum value of 10. The minimum value limits how far left, and the maximum value limits how far right the car can turn.

Now, we can design the methods to make use of the *direction* variable for steering and moving the corvette. The four storyboards are shown below. The left and right arrow storyboard design is to keep track of how much the wheels have been turned by incrementing or decrementing the *direction* value. The condition of the *If* statement for the left arrow ensures that the direction will never be less than -10 for a left turn and never greater than 10 for a right turn.

Event: left arrow

Response:
If direction > -10
   Decrement direction by 1

Event: right arrow

Response:
If direction < 10
   Increment direction by 1

Event: up arrow

Response:

Do together
  corvette move forward 1 meter
  corvette turn direction * 2/360

Event: down arrow

Response:

Do together
  corvette move backward 1 meter
  corvette turn direction * 2/360

The design of the up arrow storyboard is to move the corvette forward 1 meter and at the same time turn the corvette based on the value of the direction. The down arrow storyboard does the same thing, but in reverse. Each turn of the steering wheel is 2 degrees. (A complete revolution is 360 degrees, so 2 degrees is 2/360 of a revolution. A maximum value for a direction of 10 would correspond to 20 degrees, a reasonable turn of the steering wheel in a fast-moving corvette.)

Implementation

The first step in writing the code is to create the *direction* variable. Then the methods can be written to make use of the variable. To create the class-level variable, select the corvette in the Object tree, and then its Properties tab. Click on the *create new variable* button. Then, enter the name *direction* and select Number as its type with an initial value of 0, as illustrated in Figure 10-1-17.

The simplest methods to write are those to steer the wheels *right* and *left*. The *corvette.right* method is illustrated in Figure 10-1-18 and the *corvette.left* method in Figure 10-1-19. In each method the *direction* variable has been used twice. The first occurrence is in the *If/Else* statement—if the wheel has turned right less than 10 times, it is okay to turn it further to the right. The second occurrence of the *direction* variable is in the increment (for *corvette.right*) and the decrement (*corvette.left*) method calls. The *forward* and *backup* methods are illustrated in Figures 10-1-20 and 10-1-21.

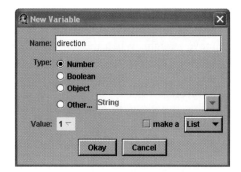

Figure 10-1-17. Creating the corvette's class-level variable

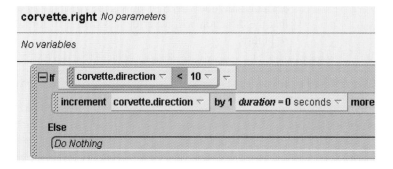

Figure 10-1-18. The *corvette.right* method uses the *direction* class-level variable

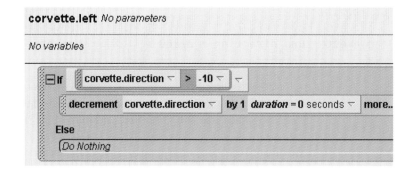

Figure 10-1-19. The *corvette.left* method

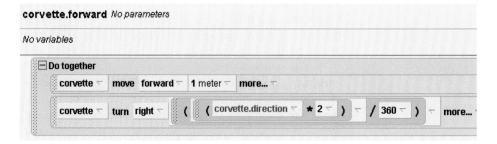

Figure 10-1-20. The *corvette.forward* method

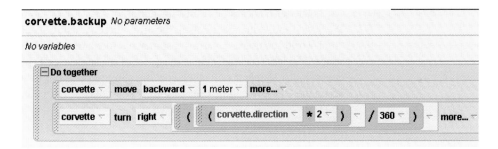

Figure 10-1-21. The *corvette.backup* method

You may have noticed that the *forward* and *backup* methods only use a *turn right* instruction. The reason a *turn left* instruction is not needed is that the direction variable stores negative values for a left turn. A negative direction for the *turn right* method will cause the corvette to turn left instead of right.

Using the steerable car

Now that the methods have been written, we are ready to use the methods to steer the car. This means that we must set up events so the → key turns the wheels turn right, the ← key turns the wheels left, the ↑ moves the car forward, and the ↓ moves the car backward. Figure 10-1-22 shows the necessary events.

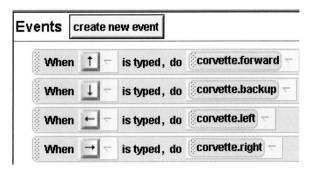

Figure 10-1-22. Events to link arrow keys to event-handling methods

To use the corvette in other worlds, rename it (we chose the name steerableCorvette) and save out as a new class. An instance of the new *steerableCorvette* class will have its own *direction* variable and *right, left, forward*, and *backup* methods.

10-2 An array visualization using an index variable

In Section 10-1 we used variables to extend the properties of objects as defined in a class. In this section, we make use of variables to help with organizing information. An array is a structure for collecting and organizing objects or information of the same type into a group. The individual objects in an array are its elements. An array uses an index variable to keep track of where each element is positioned (located) in the array. An array is generally created to hold a certain number of elements and its size (number of elements the array can hold) does not change while the program is running.

In Alice there are two kinds of arrays: (1) arrays created using a built-in array data structure (similar to a list in Chapter 9) and (2) array visualization objects. Arrays created using a built-in array can be collections of any type of data or objects. An array Visualization object contains only visual Alice objects (of type Object). The purpose of array visualization is to demonstrate what arrays are and what actions can be performed with them.

The term access describes the action of "getting at" an individual element of the array. We access individual elements in the array directly, using special array operations. Let's use a "real-world" analogy. An array is somewhat like a music CD. The CD contains a collection of songs. The label on the CD lists the order of the songs. A CD player will allow you to use a location index to select (access) a specific song to play. For example, if you want to play song #5 on the CD, you can just select song #5 and play it. (Of course, you can also play the entire CD from beginning to end, if you wish.)

Creating an array

To create an array, we begin by adding several objects to a world. (Just adding the objects to a world does not create an array, but it is the first step.) Next we add an instance of the array Visualization class (in the Visualizations folder of the local gallery). The Array Visualization class defines properties and actions for an object especially designed to represent an array structure. (Arrays are not actually visible objects. We created this visual representation to make it easy to show you how an array works.) The last step is to add each object to the array structure. The objects become elements of the array.

To demonstrate the steps in creating an array, let's say that we want to create an array of bugs, using five different bugs (from the Animals collection in the gallery). (You may find it helpful to sit at a computer and try these steps as you read.) First, we select five different kinds of bugs and add an instance of each to the world. Figure 10-2-1 shows a world with a beetle, mantis, scarab, bee, and ladybug (Animals/Bugs).

Figure 10-2-1. Five bugs—not yet elements of an array

Now add an instance of the ArrayVisualization class to the world. The ArrayVisualization class is in the Visualizations folder in the local gallery, as seen in Figure 10-2-2.

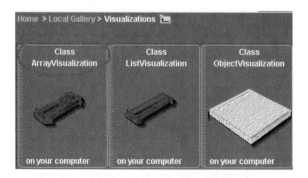

Figure 10-2-2. The ArrayVisualization class

A dialog box pops up, where you can add each object to the array, as seen in Figure 10-2-3. A click on the new element button creates an entry named *item0* in the editor. Click on <None> and select the object to be added to the array, as in Figure 10-2-4.

Figure 10-2-3. The initialize array popup box

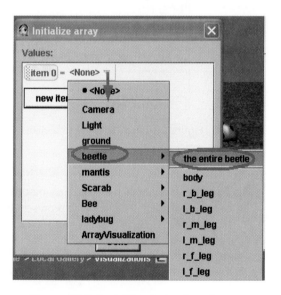

Figure 10-2-4. Adding the beetle to the array

As each bug is added, it moves into its position in the array. Note that arrays start at location 0. This step is repeated for each of the bugs. Figure 10-2-5 shows the completed array.

We number the locations in the array 0, 1, 2, 3, and 4. The location number is known as an ***index***. The beetle is in location 0, and we say it is "at index 0." Likewise, the mantis is at index 1, the scarab at index 2, and so on. (If you look closely, you can see the index number in the blue box under each bug in Figure 10-2-5.) An important note about elements in an array: an individual element cannot be in two locations at the same time! In other words, do not add the same instance of a class to two different places in the array. For example, the mantis cannot be in position 1 and also in position 3. Of course, you could have two different mantis instances (mantis and mantis2), and both could be in the array (at different locations).

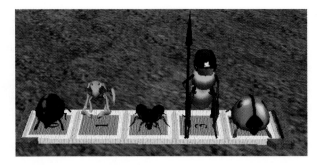

Figure 10-2-5. The completed array—bugs are now elements in the array

The arrayVisualization structure has a variable named *elements* that contains a listing of all the objects that have been added to the array, as illustrated in Figure 10-2-6. The order of the elements in the *elements* variable matches the order of the objects in the arrayVisualization structure. The *elements* variable keeps track of the location of each object in the array.

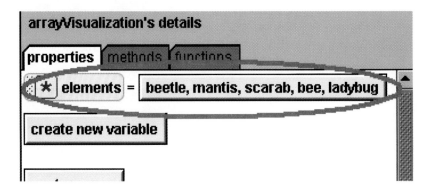

Figure 10-2-6. The *elements* variable maintains a listing of ordered elements in the array

Accessing an individual element in an array

To access an individual element in a particular location in the array, some special notation has been developed. For example, to represent the element at index 0 (in this example, the beetle), we can specify: *"item 0 from arrayVisualization."* The index of elements in an array provides a way to access individual elements. Let's write an instruction to make the bee (at index 3) spin around. We begin by selecting the arrayVisualization object in the Object tree, and we drag its *turn* method into the editor, as shown in Figure 10-2-7.

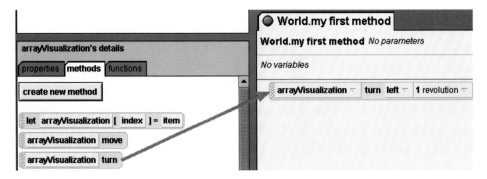

Figure 10-2-7. Creating an arrayVisualization instruction in the editor

But wait a minute! This instruction will turn the whole arrayVisualization structure around. This is not what we intended. What we really want is the element at index 3 to spin around. The instruction must be modified to access the specific element at index 3. This is where we can use the *elements* to specify the index of the element we want. Drag the *elements* tile into the editor and drop it in place of arrayVisualization in the *turn left* instruction. From the popup menu, select the index 3, as shown in Figure 10-2-8.

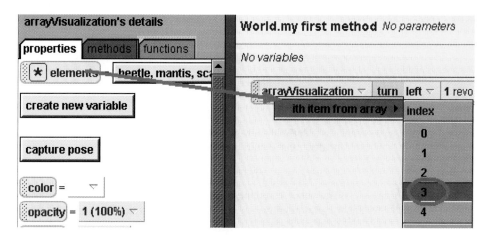

Figure 10-2-8. Modify the instruction to select the element at index 3

The resulting instruction is shown in Figure 10-2-9.

Figure 10-2-9. Accessing element 3 (the bee)

Accessing a random element in the array

What if we wanted to spin a randomly selected element in the array? In this case, all we need to do is select a random index and then spin that element. The instruction above can be modified to use a randomly selected index. All that needs to be done is drag the World's *random number* function tile into the editor and drop it in for the index, as shown in Figure 10-2-10.

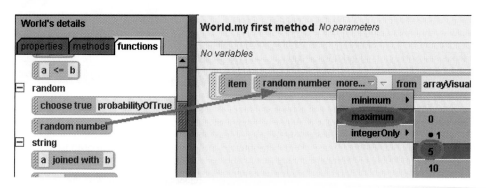

Figure 10-2-10. Random selection of an element in the array

The *minimum* value for random number is 0 by default. We selected a *maximum* of 5 (to generate numbers between 0 and 4). Then, we set the *integerOnly* option to *true*, as shown in Figure 10-2-11, to ensure the index value will be a whole number.

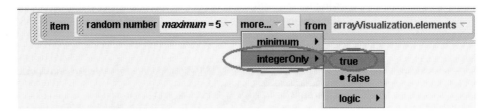

Figure 10-2-11. Selecting *integerOnly* for the *random number* function

Now that the statement is complete, the program can be run to test the statement. Repeated runs should make different bugs in the array spin around.

Swapping elements in an array

The act of changing the order of elements in an ordered group is a well-known mathematical operation known as permutation. For example, a permutation of the group of numbers (1, 2, 3) is (2, 1, 3). We can illustrate a permutation by swapping elements in an array. To show how this is done, let's swap the beetle (at index 0) with the mantis (at index 1) in our array of bugs.

To perform a swap, we use a temporary location where we can move one of the elements out of the way. The second element can take the position vacated by the first element. Then the first element can move into the position the second element just abandoned. A temporary holding space can be created by adding an instance of the ObjectVisualization class to the world. (The ObjectVisualization 3D model is found in the Visualizations folder of the local gallery.) Figure 10-2-12 shows an objectVisualization instance, as added to the bug array world.

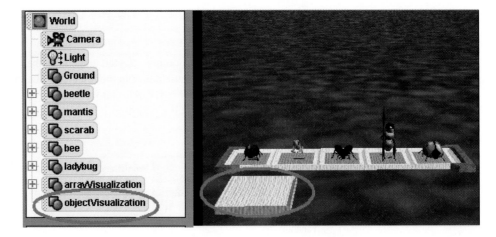

Figure 10-2-12. A temporary holding space

With a temporary holding space now available in the world, a method can be designed to perform the three steps in a swap. Two number parameters will be needed to identify the index position of the elements to be swapped. The *indexOne* parameter will be the index of the first element and *indexTwo* the index of the second element. A storyboard for the method could be:

```
swap
Parameters: indexOne, indexTwo
Do in order
  relocate element at indexOne to objectVisualization temporary location
  relocate element at indexTwo to indexOne
  relocate element from objectVisualization to indexTwo
```

The only thing left to do is translate the storyboard into program code. The curious thing about this storyboard is that the three steps within the *Do in order* do not use *move* instructions. The term relocate is used to indicate that more is involved than just moving an object from one place to another. A special *let* instruction is used relocate an element in an array. The *let* instruction moves the element and also updates the *elements* variable to keep track of the change in location index.

To write the code for this method, first we need to relocate the element at *indexOne* to the objectVisualization temporary location. Select objectVisualization in the Object tree, click on its methods tab, and drag the *let* instruction into the editor. In the popup menu, select arrayVisualization. This process is illustrated in Figure 10-2-13.

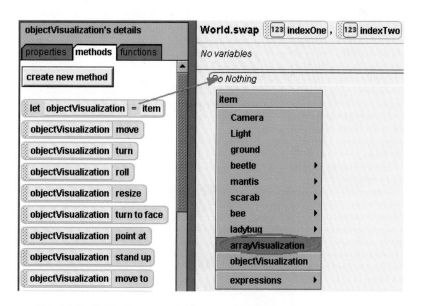

Figure 10-2-13. Drag in *let* instruction and select *item* from popup menu

Of course, we do not want the entire arrayVisualization structure to move into the temporary location, so we use the arrayVisualization's function *the value at* to select an element from the array. The *indexOne* parameter is selected as the index location. Figure 10-2-14 shows the result.

Figure 10-2-14. A *let* instruction to relocate an element to the temporary holding space

Finally, create the instructions to relocate the elements in the array. This is done by dragging the *let* instruction for the arrayVisualization into the *swap* method and selecting the *indexOne* and *indexTwo* parameters, as needed. Figure 10-2-15 shows the completed *swap* method.

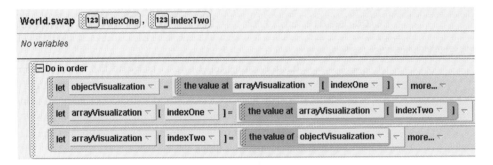

Figure 10-2-15. Complete *swap* method

To test the program, create an instruction to call the *swap* method. Pass in the position of the two elements to be swapped. For example, calling the *swap* method, as shown in Figure 10-2-16, swaps the beetle (at index 0) with the mantis (at index 1). Figure 10-2-17 illustrates the beetle and the mantis in swapped positions.

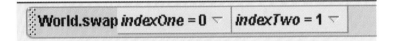

Figure 10-2-16. A call to the *swap* method

Figure 10-2-17. A permutation of the bug array

As the beetle and mantis are swapped around, the *elements* variable is automatically updated. Figure 10-2-18 shows the *elements* variable before and after *swap* is run.

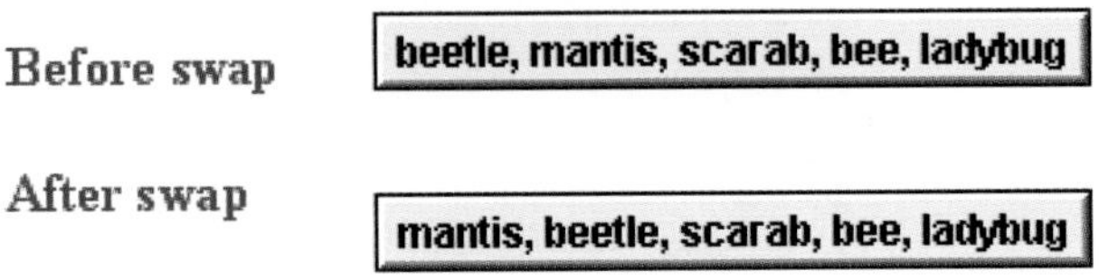

Before swap   beetle, mantis, scarab, bee, ladybug

After swap   mantis, beetle, scarab, bee, ladybug

Figure 10-2-18. Elements *swap* locations and the *elements* variable is updated

Walking through an array

Although arrays are well known for providing an ability to access individual elements in any order, it is also possible to walk through (iterate through) an array. Begin at the beginning of the array (location 0) and access each individual element in successive locations in the array. One way to write program code to walk through an array is to use a *Loop* statement. A click on the **show complicated version** button (in the *Loop* statement) makes the loop count variable (named *index*) visible. We can use the *index* variable not only as a counter for the loop but also as an index to successive elements in an array.

As an example, let's walk through our bug array and make each bug turn right one revolution. That is, the beetle will turn around and then the mantis will turn, then the scarab, and so on. The program code is:

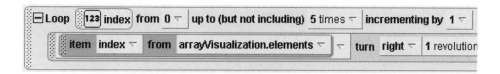

The loop executes five times—the loop count (index) starts at 0 and increases by 1 each time (0, 1, 2, 3, 4). The first execution of the loop, the index is 0 and the beetle (at index 0) turns one revolution. The second execution of the loop, the index is 1 and the mantis (at index 1) turns around, and so forth. Eventually, each element in the array is accessed in succession.

Tips & Techniques 10
Debugging with *Watch* and Text Output

Throughout this text, we have encouraged an incremental development process. Write a method and test it (by running the animation) and then write another method and test it—and so forth until the entire program is completed. We have also encouraged you to test interactive programs by trying different combinations of user input. Testing is a crucial part of program development. At each juncture, you can see the actions of the objects as the instructions are executed. In this way, you may find bugs in your program. This debugging process helps in building confidence that a program will work as expected each time it is run.

In this chapter we have introduced the concept of variables that store a value that can change as the program executes. The elusive thing about variables is that the values are changing "behind the scene"— somewhere in the murky depths of memory chips inside the computer. Variables are somewhat "magical" because, unlike the active objects we see in an animation, running the program does not allow us to view what is going on with the value stored in a variable. In this section, we look at two techniques that allow you to see variables in action as an animation runs: creating a watch and printing text.

Creating a watch

Creating a *watch* is like hiring a private investigator to snoop on someone. The "private eye" sets a "tail" on that person and keeps a constant watch on his/her activities. In Alice, a *watch* creates a small window where the value in the watched variable is constantly displayed at runtime. Every time the value changes, it is immediately updated in the *watch* window.

As an example, let's create a *watch* on the *direction* variable used in the corvette steering example presented in this chapter. To create a *watch*, right-click on a variable and select *watch this variable*, as illustrated in Figure T-10-1.

After a *watch* has been created, a run of the animation is displayed in a split window. One panel displays the animation while another panel displays the value of the watched variable. You may recall that the *direction* variable is used to track the amount the corvette's steering

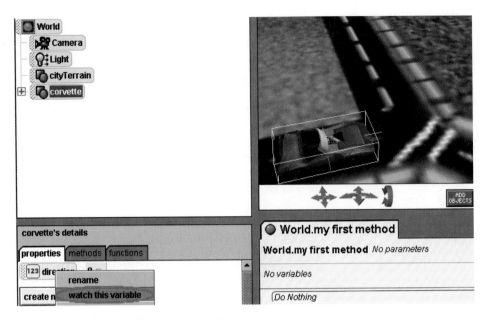

Figure T-10-1. Creating a *watch* on a variable

wheel has been turned left or right. The *direction* amount is then used to guide the movement of the corvette. In Figure T-10-2(a), the value stored in *direction* is 0, and the corvette moves straight ahead. In Figure T-10-2(b), the value stored in *direction* is −2 and the corvette is steering toward the left. Viewing the *direction* value and the resulting motion of the corvette in the animation confirms that the animation is working as designed.

Text output

The *print* instruction in Alice is another way to keep an eye on the value stored in a variable at runtime. As with the *watch* feature, the print instruction causes the animation to be displayed in a split window. One panel displays the animation, while another panel displays output in a text console.

As an example, let's modify the steering corvette program to use *print* instructions to display the value in the corvette's direction variable. In this program, the *direction* variable is incremented each time the right arrow key is pressed and decremented each time the left arrow key is pressed. All that needs to be done is to add a *print* instruction to the *corvette.right* and *corvette.left* methods. Figure T-10-3 illustrates dragging a *print* instruction into the *corvette.left* method. From the popup menu, we selected *object → expressions → corvette.direction*.

The modified *corvette.left* method is shown in Figure T-10-4. A *print* instruction is also created for the *corvette.right* method. After the *print* instructions are created, a run of the animation and a text console are displayed in a split window. The first left or right arrow press causes the text console to appear. Thereafter, the mouse can be used to activate/deactivate the text console. Clicking the mouse on the animation panel activates the text console; moving the mouse elsewhere on the screen deactivates the text console. A sample run is illustrated in Figure T-10-5. (On some machines, the runtime window must be resized to make it large enough to view the text console.)

If the text console is active, each left arrow or right arrow key-press causes the value stored in the *direction* variable to be displayed on the next line in the text console. In this way, a text console provides a history of the changes in a variable's value.

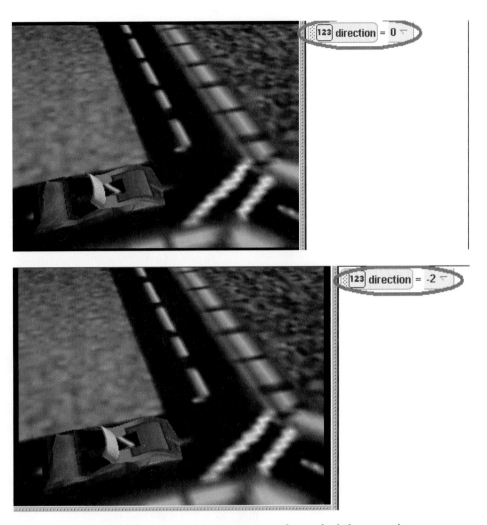

Figure T-10-2. (a) and (b) Screen captures of a *watch* window at runtime

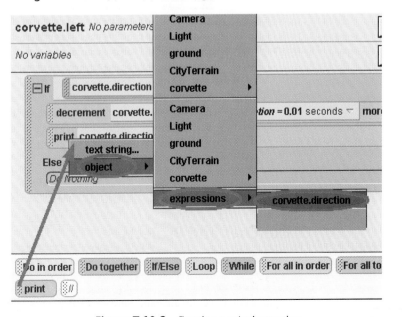

Figure T-10-3. Creating a *print* instruction

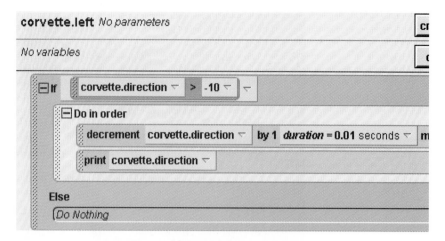

Figure T-10-4. The modified *corvette.left* method

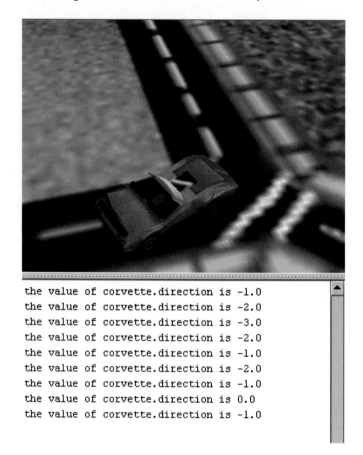

Figure T-10-5. Runtime text console

Exercises and Projects

10.1 Exercises

1. *Scorekeeper*

   If you have not already done so, recreate the WhackAMole game from Chapter 9 Section 2. Replace the visual scorekeeper with a 3D text scorekeeper. The scorekeeper should work just like the timer example demonstrated in Chapter 10 Section 1 except that the scorekeeper increases the score by 1 each time the player successfully clicks on a mole. The player wins when the score gets to 10. What changes do you have to make to the WhackAMole world to allow the use of a 3D text object as a scorekeeper?

2. *Spanish Vocabulary Builder*
   Exercise 11 in Chapter 6 was to build a simple version of a Spanish vocabulary builder. The initial scene for the vocabulary builder is shown below. This exercise was extremely limited. Here, you are to expand the capabilities of the vocabulary builder world to use three different animals (use a list). Position all the animals in the center of the scene and make them all invisible. Create 3D text words for each of the three animals and display all three words.

   Create a class-level variable, called *myWord*, for each animal. The variable should store the Spanish word for that animal. Write a program that randomly selects one of the objects to be visible. Then allow the user to click on a 3D text word. If the user clicks on the correct word, have the animal say something in Spanish (such as "Si, si!") to indicate that the correct word was selected. Wait a few seconds and repeat. The program should run in an infinite loop, continuing to play until the user stops the program.

3. *Binary Switches*
   Digital electronics is based on the use of high and low currents to represent binary values. A high current flowing through a circuit represents the digit 1 and a low current the digit 0. Thus, a single circuit represents a single **bi**nary digit (a **bit**). A nibble is a combination of four circuits (4 bits) put together to represent numbers in base 2 (binary numbers). A byte is eight circuits (8 bits).
   As a review, let's compare our base-10 number system to the base-2 number system. A base-10 number is created using digits 0 through 9. The following example breaks down the base 10 number 5932:

$$10^3 \qquad 10^2 \qquad 10^1 \qquad 10^0$$
$$5 \qquad\quad 9 \qquad\quad 3 \qquad\quad 2$$
$$(5 * 10^3) + (9 * 10^2) + (3 * 10^1) + (2 * 10^0)$$
$$(5 * 1000) + (9 * 100) + (3 * 10) + (2 * 1)$$
$$5000 + 900 + 30 + 2$$
$$= 5932$$

Like base-10 numbers, the first column from the right represents 2^0 or 1, the second column represents 2^1 or 2, the third 2^2 or 4, and the fourth 2^3 or 8. Here is an example of how the base 2 number 1001 is converted to its base 10 equivalent:

$$2^3 \qquad 2^2 \qquad 2^1 \qquad 2^0$$
$$1 \qquad \ 0 \qquad \ 0 \qquad \ 1$$
$$(1 * 2^3) + (0 * 2^2) + (0 * 2^1) + (1 * 2^0)$$
$$(1 * 8) + (0 * 4) + (0 * 2) + (1 * 1)$$
$$8 + 0 + 0 + 1$$
$$= 9$$

This exercise is a simulation of a byte of computer memory. Create a world with four switches, each with an *onOff* Boolean variable. Above each switch, insert 3D text for the number 0, and centered above these, four 0s. Then add an additional 0, as shown below. Create an event handling method to set the 3D text above a switch to 0 when the switch is off (down) or to 1 when the switch is on (up).

The top-level 3D text digit is to be the base-10 representation of the binary number represented by the zeros and ones below it. Write a method called *findResult* that converts the base-2 number represented by the switches to a base-10 number and change the top-level 3D text to this base-10 number each time a switch is clicked and switched. The easiest way to make this work is to create a number variable for each 3D text object that represents the digit value to which its text is set. Also, modify the on-off event handling method so that in addition to changing the 3D text above it to 0 or 1, it also sets its value variable to the corresponding 0 or 1 and then calls the *findResult* method.

Hint: Use the following formula: $(a * 8) + (b * 4) + (c * 2) + (d * 1)$, where *a, b, c,* and *d* represent the 0s and 1s in the appropriate columns. In the World's functions under *String* you will find the option <*what*> *as a string.* This will convert the integer result to text that can be displayed by the base-10 3D text.

4. *Steerable Car with Rotating Tires*
   Create the interactive car world, as demonstrated in this chapter. Once you have the program working so the car can be steered, modify the program to rotate the tires as the car moves forward or back. The phrase "rotate the tires" means that each wheel will turn to simulate the motion of tires as the corvette travels. (The number of times each tire must turn around is computed using the same technique as described for rolling a ball in the world presented in Chapter 6.)

5. *Steerable Car with Shifting Gears*

   This is a second modification for the steerable car. Give the car the ability to shift gears, thereby increasing or decreasing its speed. Make sure that the speed can never go below 0 and is given a reasonable maximum limit. Add events and event handlings so that when the user presses 'F', the car's speed is increased (the car goes faster), and when the user presses 'S', the car's speed is decreased (the car goes slower). (This may mean that the car's forward and backup methods will both need modification.)

10.2 Exercise

6. *All Possible Permutations*

   A permutation is a rearrangement of a set of objects. For example, a permutation of the numbers 1, 2, 3 could be 2, 1, 3 or it could be 2, 3, 1. How many possible permutations are there?

   Create an array containing three 3D text number objects, as shown below. Write the *swap* method as illustrated in Chapter 10, Section 2. Then write a program that calls the *swap* method to show the numbers moving around to create a permutation of the numbers. Call the *swap* method with different parameters so that all possible permutations can be seen.

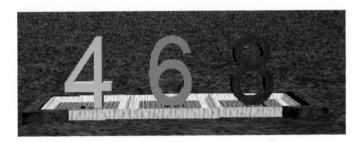

Projects

1. *A Flight Simulation Game*

   The goal of this project is to create a flight simulation game, where the player must steer a seaplane (Vehicle) and fly through ring targets. Two rings (torus from Shapes folder) are floating in the water and a third is suspended on a pole (cylinder from Shapes folder) from the deck of a boat (Vehicles). The scene below shows an initial world. You may find your experience with the flight simulator (Chapter 5) helpful in providing ideas for writing this more sophisticated game.

Use a billboard to provide instructions on to how to play the game. The player should click on the billboard to make it go away (become invisible) and start the game. The seaplane is constantly moving forward. The two sailboats are moving forward and back between the rings. To keep the plane from flying out of range of the camera, the camera's vehicle may be set to be the plane—or you may wish to move the camera every time the plane moves. The player should be able to steer the plane right, left, up and down. To steer the plane, you may wish to use the *while key is pressed* event.

Write a method to check whether the plane has moved through one of the rings (gets within a small distance of the ring). If the plane has moved through a ring, the ring should be made invisible. (This method should be called from within an infinite loop.) Write a function that checks to see if all the rings are invisible. (You could use a list of rings.) The function should return *true* if all the rings are invisible, and *false* otherwise.

To win the game, the player must steer the seaplane through all three rings. Provide some way to tell the player he has won (perhaps display 3D text saying the player has won.) If the plane gets too close to one of the sailboats, the player loses. Give the player three tries to win the game (use a class-level variable for the plane to track the number of tries).

Extra: Add one or more of the following features: (a) require the player to fly the plane through the rings within a certain period of time, (b) allow the player to control the speed of the plane, (c) use four or five rings instead of three, to make the game more challenging.

2. *A Horse Race Game*
(This carnival style horse race is a variation of the horse race example presented in Chapter 8, but you can easily write the program here without having studied Chapter 8.)

Unlike a traditional horse race, where horses run around an oval-shaped track and each horse breaks to the inside of the track, horses in a carnival game move straight ahead in a mechanical track. Start a new world and add an instance of the Race-HorseGame (Amusement Park) and three circles (Shapes). Position the circles near the start line of each racetrack, as shown in the initial scene below.

In a carnival game, you win a prize if you pick the winning horse. In this game, the player will pick the horse by clicking one of the circles at the beginning of the track. For example, if the player clicks on the green circle, the player picks the horse in the nearest track. Create a class-level Boolean variable named *isClicked* for each of the circles. The *isClicked* variable should be *false*. When the player clicks on the circle, change *isClicked* to *true* and start the game.

When the game begins, use a *Do together* to move all three racehorses forward a short random distance. This action should be repeated until one of the horses gets to the finish line and wins the race. You can use either a *While* loop (Chapter 7) or recursion (Chapter 8) to repeat the action until the race is over.

An essential step is to know when the game is over. Write a function named *isGameOver* that asks: "Is a horse within 0.5 meters of the finish line?" We suggest 0.5 rather than 0 meters because the distance between the finish line and the horse is measured from the horse's center, not from the tip of its nose. (You may need to adjust this distance, depending on how much you resized the raceHorseGame object in setting up the initial scene.)

Write a function named *whichHorseWon* that returns the horse that is closest to the finish line. When the loop ends, determine whether the player picked the winning horse (use the circles' *isClicked* variable). If the player has selected the winning horse, display the message "You won!" If not, display "Try again!" Because of the random distances used in this program, different horses should win the race if the program is run several times.

3. *Car Race*

   Create a world containing an obstacle course, either using the city terrain or perhaps enlarging the stadium. Add a steerableCar object (using the SteerableCar class, as created in Exercises 4 and 5 or the one demonstrated in this chapter). If the car hits an obstacle, the speed should be reset to 0, and perhaps the car should be backed up some distance. Using the timer from Section 1 of this chapter, allow the user to steer the car for 30 seconds. A user who has completed the course within 30 seconds wins a prize (perhaps by making some object visible or playing a victory song). If the user has not completed the course by the end of the 30-second period, an appropriate 3D message should appear—something like "Better luck next time!"

Summary

In this chapter we reviewed the use of properties to store information about an object in a world. We call this state information. Then we introduced the term mutable variable to describe those properties that can be changed at runtime. The mutable variables we presented were class-level. Class-level variables keep track of information about a specific object.

We added a new class-level variable to an object and then saved out the object and its new variable to create a new class. This is a form of inheritance similar to the technique used in previous chapters, where we defined our own methods and saved out the object and its new methods as a new class. The difference is that previously we extended a class by adding behavior (methods), while in this chapter we extend a class by adding state information.

An array visualization was created to illustrate the concept of an array structure. In Alice, an arrayVisualization object has a built-in *elements* variable that tracks the index (position) of each element in the array.

Important concepts in this chapter

- Mutable variables can be useful for extending the capabilities of a class.
- Like class-level methods, class-level variables are saved out with the object and reused when instances of the new class are added to other worlds.
- An array structure organizes a collection of elements. Each element is located in a particular position in the array.
- An array index variable is used to refer to the location of an element in the array.

Chapter 11
What's Next?

"Would you tell me, please, which way I ought to go from here?"

"That depends a good deal on where you want to get to," said the Cat.

We expect that many students who are using this book as a text will decide to take another course in programming. If you are one of these people (and we sincerely hope you are), you will need to make a transition from Alice to another programming language.

As we write this book, the most likely language you will learn next is Java, C++, or C#. These are all object-oriented languages. This is great, because the Alice programming language has a distinct object-oriented flavor. Alice does, however, differ in some ways from the so-called "real-world" languages. The reasons for the differences are clearly the underlying goals of the languages. Java, C++, and C# are designed for general-purpose programming of workhorse applications in a world of commerce, internet communication, and scientific research. Alice was designed to achieve two very different goals: (1) to provide a programming environment for 3D graphic animations, and (2) to provide a high-impact visualization tool that can enjoyably be used for learning to write computer programs.

It is not within the scope of this book to introduce another programming language. What we can do, however, is summarize the concepts you have learned with Alice that prepare you to learn another language. Also, we can point out a major change you will encounter as you move from Alice's drag and drop editor to a text editor, where details of writing a statement in a program become important. This chapter will demonstrate a feature of Alice that will help you make that change.

Fundamental concepts

One advantage of learning to program with Alice is that the concepts you learn in writing an Alice animation are the same fundamental concepts used in real-world languages. For example, the steps in writing a program in Alice are the exact same steps using in writing programs in Java. (We will use Java in our examples in this chapter. Everything we say about Java could easily be applied to C++ and C#, as well.) To write a program in Java, you would follow these steps:

1. Read: Each programming project begins with a description of what is to be done. For animation programs, we have called this a scenario because it describes an initial scene as well as the problem or task. In Java, programming tasks also begin with a description of a problem to be solved or a task to be performed. Large projects begin with a very detailed description, called a specification.

2. Design: Although simple programs require only small amounts of planning, large and more complex programs require that some thought be put into how the program will be written. One design technique you have learned is a textual **storyboard**, which is much like a to-do list. Another technique you have learned is **stepwise refinement**, which allows you to start thinking about the overall process and progressively break the steps down into simpler and simpler actions. These same design techniques are commonly used in planning Java programs. Other techniques can be used, as well. But, the overall idea is the same—plan before you begin writing code.

3. Implement: Writing program code takes some organization in an object oriented language such as Java. Classes and methods must be written. Objects must be instantiated. Methods must be called and arguments sent to parameters. The control statements used in the program code are decisions (*If/Else*), loops (*For* and *While*), and recursion. Execution can be sequential or simultaneous. As you have learned to program in Alice, you have gained experience and understanding of these concepts.

4. Test: Testing is one thing we definitely respect as part of the programming process. No doubt you have discovered that testing often reveals a bug in a program. Then the program has to be revised, which sends us back into the design and implementation steps. This is OK. No one is expected to sit down and write perfect code on the very first try. In fact, we often learn from our mistakes!

A major change

A major change you will encounter is the move from using Alice's drag-and-drop editor to a text editor. To write a program in Java, for example, you will use a simple text editor and type in your program. Figure 11-1-1 shows a simple Java program, as written in a text editor. Although we are not trying to introduce how to program in Java, a quick explanation of the program will be helpful. A Java program is made up of one or more class descriptions, where properties (variables) are declared and methods are defined. This example has one class, named *SimpleProgram*. In the *Simple Program* class, one method, *main*, is defined. In this very simple example, the only statement in the *main* method is to print a line (*println*) of text: "This is a simple Java program!" (Java does have graphics—but are much more complicated to use than graphics in Alice.)

```
public class SimpleProgram {

  public static void main (String [] args) {
    System.out.println("This is a simple Java program!");
  }
}
```

Figure 11-1-1. A simple Java program, as written in a text editor

As you look at this Java program, you may realize that moving from a drag-and-drop editor to a text editor involves more than just typing the program instructions (as compared to simply dragging in the instruction tiles). As you write the program statements, you will need to type various symbols such as curly brackets, parentheses, commas, quotes, and semicolons. Also, you will use some Java words such as *public, static,* and *void*.

Syntax

The symbols and words you saw in the simple Java program above are part of the **syntax** of the Java programming language—the rules about how a Java statement can be written. All languages, both human and computer, have rules about how to write statements. Statements must begin with certain kinds of words, which are followed by other kinds of words, which are followed by other kinds of words, and so on. Furthermore, punctuation marks such as commas, quotes, semicolons, and parentheses are sprinkled liberally throughout. For example, in the English language we can write a statement:

The panda moves forward 1 meter.

The statement begins with a capitalized word and ends with a period. The noun phrase of the statement ("The panda") is followed by the verb phrase ("moves forward"). To write a statement like this:

forward 1 panda the moves meter

is an error because the order and punctuation do not follow the rules. Figure 11-1-2 illustrates the syntax of a typical statement in Alice. The tiles and colors give visual clues to the different parts of the statement.

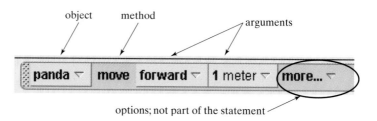

Figure 11-1-2. Syntax of a typical Alice statement

Syntax rules can be frustrating because you have to learn where all the punctuation marks go and the order in which the words must be positioned. In Alice, the editor for writing statements is purposely designed to reduce the frustration for beginning programmers. You drag and drop the parts of a statement into the editor, and it enforces the rules of the language, so you have not had to worry about syntax errors.

Syntax switch

To help you prepare for learning a real-world language (such as Java), you can turn on a Java-style switch in Alice. The style switch is a setting in the **Edit/Preferences** menu. To turn on Java-style, first selecting Edit from the main menu bar at the top of the Alice interface and then the Preferences menu item. In the General tab of the Preferences menu, select the *Java Style* option, as illustrated in Figure 11-1-3. The style switch acts as a toggle

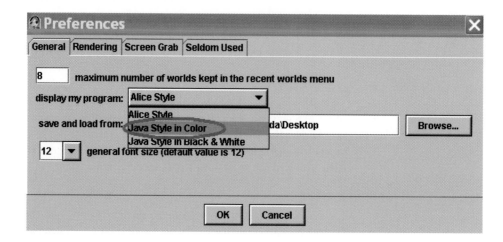

Figure 11-1-3. Select *Java Style* to turn on the Java-style switch

switch that can be turned on and off to suit the programmer's preferences. To return to the default Alice-style display, simply set the style switch back to the *Alice Style* setting.

Technical Note: On your computer, setting the style switch may require that Alice be shut down and then restarted for the switch setting to take effect.

Once the syntax switch has been set, statements in the editor are more detailed and include symbols and words like those that appear in a Java program. The statement from Figure 11-1-2 is displayed using Java-style in Figure 11-1-4.

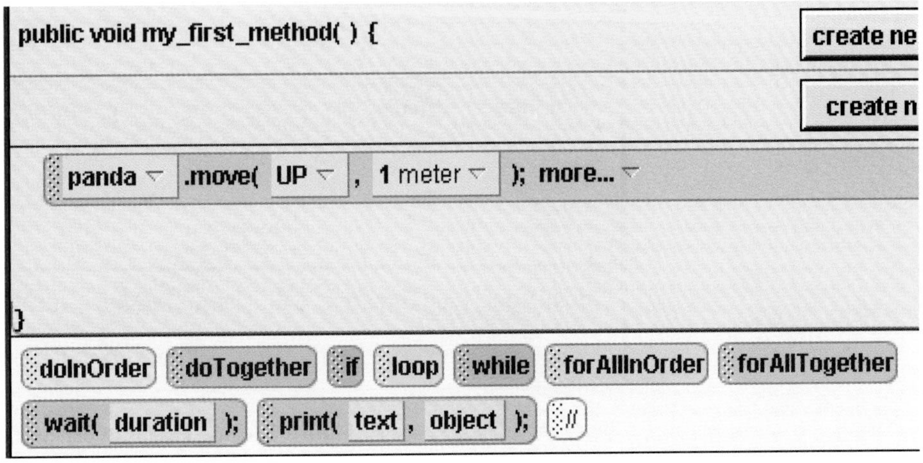

Figure 11-1-4. A statement in Java-style syntax

Syntax details

Let's take a look at some of the details of Alice instructions displayed using Java-style syntax. First look at the method signature, circled in Figure 11-1-5. A ***method signature*** always begins a method definition in a Java program. The name of the method contains no blank spaces.

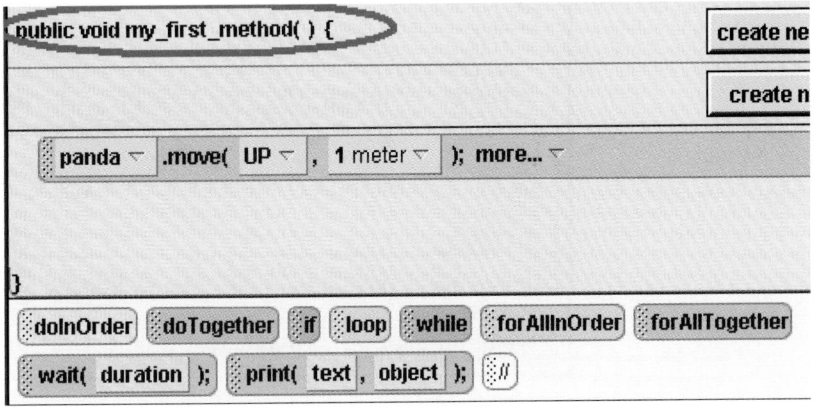

Figure 11-1-5. A method signature begins a method

Alice's *my_first_method* is similar to the *main* method in Java—it is the first method executed when the program runs. The word *public* means that it can be called from anywhere.

(In Alice, all methods are public.) The word *void* means that it does not return any information. In other words, it is NOT a function that sends back some information to a calling method.

A second detail to notice is the use of punctuation symbols. We have circled some punctuation symbols in Figure 11-1-6. A dot (.) has been placed between the object named *panda* and the method named *move*. The arguments are enclosed in parentheses and separated by commas *(UP, 1 meter)*, and the entire statement now ends with a semicolon (;). This is exactly

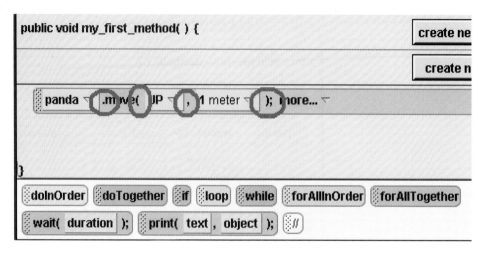

Figure 11-1-6. Details of punctuation

how these punctuation symbols are used in Java statements. Finally, notice that two curly brackets have been added to enclose statement(s) within the method, as circled in Figure 11-1-7. As you know, a method is a block of code (possibly several instructions), and blocks of code in Java are marked by enclosure in matching curly brackets.

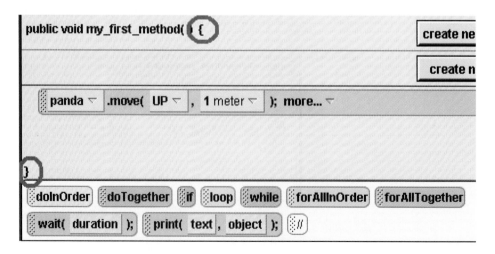

Figure 11-1-7. Curly brackets enclose a block of code

You can look at the Alice programs you have already written to get an idea of what similar statements would look like in Java. This will give you a head start in learning Java or another programming language.

Appendix

Appendix A: Using Alice

The purpose of this tutorial-style self-paced exercise is to help you learn the basics of using Alice. We suggest you work through these exercises with a friend. You'll have fun together, and you'll be able to help each other work through any parts you might find confusing. If at any point you get lost or stuck, go back to the beginning of the section, reload the world and try again. You can't hurt anything and you will lose only a few minutes of work.

Part 1: Running virtual worlds in alice

In this part, you will work with two worlds (FirstWorld and DancingBee—found on the CD that accompanies this text). You will also create and save your own new world.

Whenever you see text printed like this, specific instructions are given about what to do.

How to Start Alice: Alice can be started in one of two ways:

1. **Click the icon on the desktop of your machine. (See Figure A-1-1 on next page.)**
2. **Or, use the windows search utility to find and click on the "Alice.exe" startup file.**

Alice may take a minute or two to load.

In some installations, the Alice startup may display a choice dialog box, shown in Figure A-1-2. If you decide you no longer wish to see this dialog box each time you start Alice, uncheck the box in the lower left corner of the dialog box, labeled "Show this dialog at start." (Note: Some academic computer network systems restore each computer to a primary image with a reboot. We advise that you do not uncheck the box if your computer is part of a network system.)

Click on the Templates tab and select a "grass" world as the initial scene. Then, click on Open. Alice starts with an empty world. In the World View window, you should see the green grass and blue sky initial scene, shown in Figure A-1-3. If this is not the case, consult the instructions at www.alice.org on how to troubleshoot your installation of Alice.

World 1: A first animation

Let's start by opening a world.

Select the File menu at the top of the Alice window and then choose Open World as shown in Figure A-1-4.

Alice opens a dialog box for opening a world file. **Click the Textbook tab to view text examples, as shown in Figure A-1-5.**

Alice

Figure A-1-1. Alice shorcut icon on the desktop of your computer

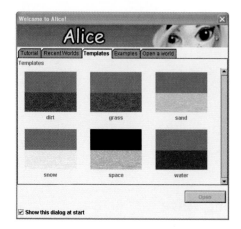

Figure A-1-2. Startup dialog box

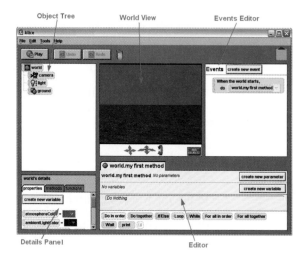

Figure A-1-3. The Alice interface

Figure A-1-4. File open world menu

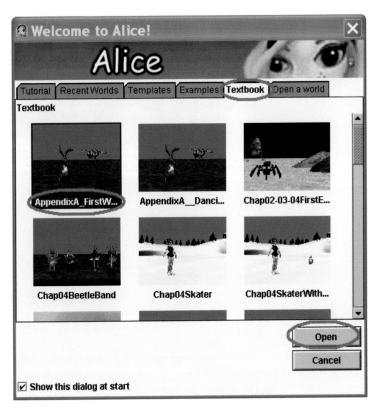

Figure A-1-5. Opening AppendixA_FirstWorld from Textbook examples in the dialog box

Select AppendixA_FirstWorld and click the Open button. The bee and hare objects are displayed in the world that opens, as shown in Figure A-1-6. The Object tree lists the objects in the world.

Click Play to run the world.

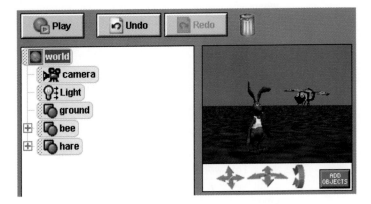

Figure A-1-6. Play button at top, Object tree on left, First World initial scene on right

Take a close look at the controls at the top of the animation window (Figure A-1-7). Some buttons, such as **Pause** and **Restart,** are obvious. The **Take Picture** button will take a single snapshot of the animation and save it as a graphic image file. (A popup menu allows selection of a location for saving the file.) The **Speed** slide control allows you to adjust the speed of the animation.

Figure A-1-7. The animation window

Of course, the speed of the animation is affected by the capabilities of your computer hardware. A helpful hint is that the size of the window in which the animation runs (the **World Running** window) affects the speed of an animation. If your animation is running too slowly, make the window smaller. (Grab the lower right corner of the window with the mouse and drag the window to the size you want.) After the window size is changed, Alice will remember it the next time you play an animation.

Close the animation window for the FirstWorld (use a mouse-click on the X at the upper right of the animation window or click the Stop button).

World 2

World 1 (FirstWorld) is a "movie" style of animation. A movie runs from beginning to end while you, as the human "user," view the animation. Let's look at a world that is interactive where you can make choices as to how the animation works.

Use File → Open World to open the dialog box.
In the dialog box, select Textbook and then AppendixA_Dancing Bee, as shown in Figure A-1-8.
Click Play.

Then, try each of the two choices (keys can be pressed in any order):

1. Press the up arrow key
2. Press the space bar

When you have finished viewing the animation, close the window.

This world uses the same initial scene as in the first world, viewed above, but the program has been changed to be an interactive, event-driven animation. Pressing the up arrow key creates an event. Alice responds to the up arrow event by making the hare jump. Pressing the space bar creates a different event. Alice responds to the space bar event by making the bee perform a pirouette in flight. This world is an example of an interactive, event-driven animation.

Summary

Here's a recap of what we just covered with Worlds 1 and 2. If you're not comfortable with any of these topics, go back to the start of this section and go through it again.

Figure A-1-8. Select AppendixA_Dancing Bee world

- How to **Start** Alice
- How to **Open** a saved world
- How to **Play** a world
- How to **Stop** a world
- Running interactive worlds with events and responses

World 3: Creating and saving your own new world

Figure A-1-9. Select New World from the File menu.

Click on the File menu in the upper left-hand corner of Alice. Select "New World" as shown in Figure A-1-9. Then select the snow template for an initial scene.

Saving a world

Each time a new world is created, it is a good idea to save the world. Then, if the computer crashes or loses power (it can happen, even on the best of machines!), your work will be safe to reload when the computer is rebooted. A world can be saved to any one of several different locations (desktop, file server space, disk, or a memory stick). If a disk is to be used, we recommend that a zip disk or memory stick be used rather than a floppy disk (the size of the world may be more than a floppy disk can hold). The example below shows directories on a zip disk, but other storage devices should work just as well.

Go to File → Save World As.

This brings up a Save World dialog box that lets you navigate to the location where the world will be saved, as shown in Figure A-1-10.

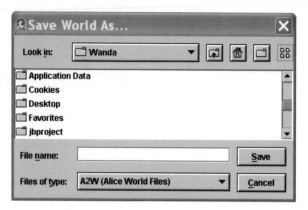

Figure A-1-10. Save World dialog box

Navigate to the folder (directory) where you plan to save your world, as shown in Figure A-1-11. We recommend that you create a folder named **AliceWorlds** where you will save all your animations.

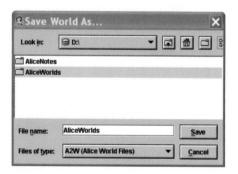

Figure A-1-11. Select a folder where the world be saved

Make up a name for your world—we recommend a single word name, such as Snow-manExercise, that uses upper- and lowercase characters. **Enter the name for your world and then click the Save button, as shown in Figure A-1-12.**

Figure A-1-12. Enter a file name and click **save**

Your world will be saved with the **.a2w** extension (an Alice version 2 world).

As you work on your world, Alice will periodically prompt you to save your world. We recommend that you save the world every half hour or so. Alice automatically makes back-up copies of your world when you save it. The folder is named **"Backups of ...."**

Adding objects to the world

Click on the Add Objects button in the lower right of the World view window, as shown in Figure A-1-13.

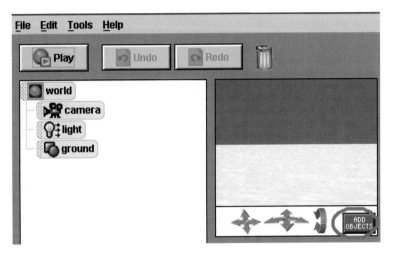

Figure A-1-13. Add Objects button

Alice opens the Scene Editor. A visual directory to the Local and Web Galleries is provided for access to 3D models. A **Search Gallery** button allows you to search for a particular kind of object. (See Appendix B for more details on searching for an object.)

> **Important Note:** The Local Gallery is a sampler, containing an assortment of 3D models. The CD and Web galleries contain thousand of models. See the next section of this tutorial for instructions on how to use the Web Gallery. The CD Gallery folder will only be displayed if the Alice CD is in your machine. Examples, exercises, and projects in this text use 3D models from both the Local Gallery and the Web Gallery. If you are looking for a particular model in the Local Gallery and cannot find it, try looking in the online Web Gallery at www.alice.org.

Click on the Local Gallery folder, as shown in Figure A-1-14.

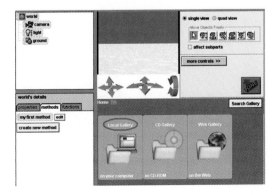

Figure A-1-14. Local Gallery folder

Note: The Gallery is organized into collections—for example Animals, Buildings, and People.

Click on the people thumbnail picture, as shown in Figure A-1-15.

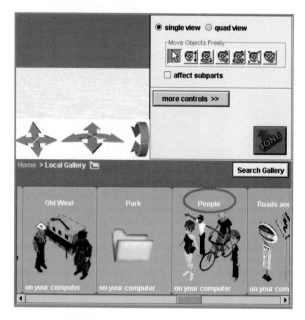

Figure A-1-15. The People collection of 3D models

Click on the Snowman.

Click add instance to world. You can also add an object to the world by using the mouse to drag and drop the object into the world, as shown in Figure A-1-16.

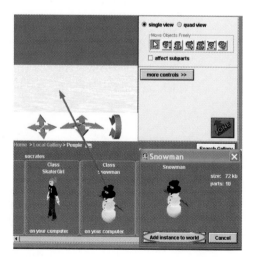

Figure A-1-16. Two options: drag and drop or click to add an an object (instance)

Note: Drag and drop works relative to the ground. If the ground is deleted from a world, the drag and drop technique cannot be used to add an object to the world.

Using the web gallery (optional)

If your computer is attached to the internet, you may wish to use the Web Gallery, as shown in Figure A-1-17. The online gallery provides many more models than are available in the Local Gallery.

Figure A-1-17. The Web Gallery folder

Note: The models in the Web Gallery may take longer than the models on the CD to load, depending on the speed of your connection.

Follow the same procedure as outlined above to add a snowman object from the online People collection of 3D models.

Mouse controls in the scene editor

Drag the snowman around the scene with the mouse. Then click Undo, as shown in Figure A-1-18.

Figure A-1-18. The Undo button

This illustrates an important point—you don't have to worry about messing things up. Use Undo to get back to a previous position.

On the far right of the scene editor is a toolkit of buttons that allow you to select the way the mouse moves an object in 3D space. By default, the horizontal (left-right, forward-back) movement is selected.

One at a time, select each of the mouse control buttons and experiment with the snowman using that control, as shown in Figure A-1-19.

For your reference, Figure A-1-20 identifies the actions of the mouse control buttons. The default button, labeled "Horizontal," allows the mouse to move an object left, right, forward, or back in the scene.

Figure A-1-19. Mouse control toolkit.

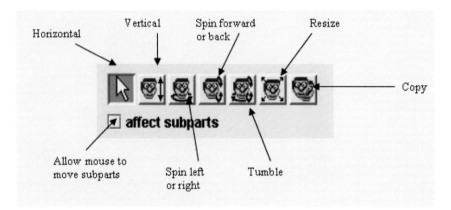

Figure A-1-20. Mouse control buttons

Moving subparts of objects

The mouse movement controls are automatically set to move an entire object. If you check the **affect subparts** box, the mouse can be used to control the movement of subparts, rather than the entire object.

Check the "affect subparts" box and use the vertical mouse control to move the snowman's hat, as shown in Figure A-1-21.

Figure A-1-21. Affect subparts is checked

Be sure to uncheck the "affect subparts" box before going on!

Experiment with the copy and delete:

1. **Use the Copy mouse control button (see mouse control reference above) to create a second snowman. Then, click on the snowman.** This creates a second snowman object (in the same location).

2. Actually, a copy is somewhat like a ghost of the original object—not completely independant. In most worlds, we prefer to add new objects. **Delete the second snowman—right-click on the second snowman and choose Delete from the popup menu.**

3. **Finally, click the mouse cursor in the mouse control buttons to stop copying objects.**

Note: If the ground is deleted in a world, new objects can only be added using the "Add instance" button (rather than a drag-and-drop action).

Add a snowwoman object to the world.

The world will now have two objects, a snowman and a snowwoman, as shown in Figure A-1-22.

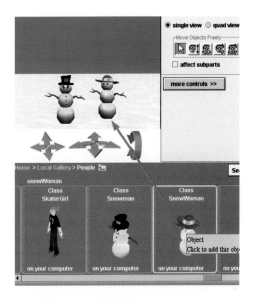

Figure A-1-22. Snowman and snowwoman

Using quad view

We would like the snowman and snowwoman to stand side-by-side and face one another. The scene editor can be used to arrange the two objects.

Select "quad view" in the editor, as shown in Figure A-1-23.

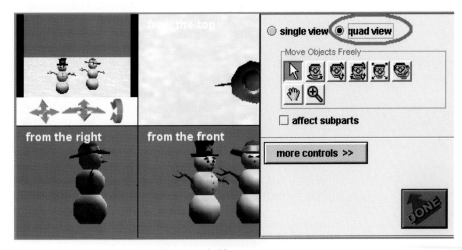

Figure A-1-23. Quad view panes

The world view window changes to a four-pane **quad view.** The four panes show Camera, Top, Right and Front viewpoints. Note that the vertical mouse control button is no longer available because the **Front** and **Right** panes automatically have vertical movement. The toolbox now displays a second row of mouse control buttons, containing a scroll and a zoom button, as labeled in Figure A-1-24.

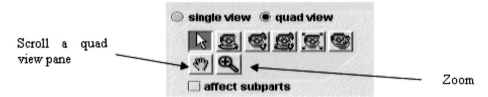

Figure A-1-24. A second row of mouse controls

In the quad view shown above, the snowwoman is partially out of sight in the Top view. (Your world may appear somewhat different than ours.) The scroll tool can be used to reposition the viewpoint in a pane. As shown in Figure A-1-25, we used the scroll control to reposition the Top view pane.

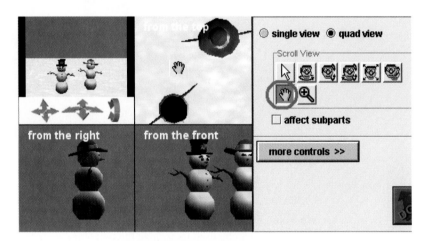

Figure A-1-25. Using the scroll tool

Another useful feature is the zoom tool. The zoom tool can be used to zoom in or out in a pane. As shown in Figure A-1-26, we have used the zoom tool to zoom out in the pane that shows the view from the top.

Figure A-1-26. Using the zoom tool

Use the mouse to arrange the two objects side-by-side.

A side-by-side position can be recognized when one object (more or less) hides the other in the Right view (see circled Right view pane in the Figure A-1-27).

Figure A-1-27. Right view pane

Use the mouse to arrange the objects facing one another.

The facing position is recognized in the Top and Front views, as shown in Figure A-1-28.

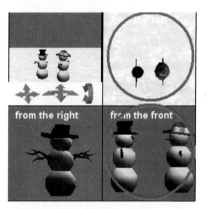

Figure A-1-28. Top and Front view panes

Click **single view** to return to a single pane in the scene editor, as shown in Figure A-1-29.

Figure A-1-29. Single view

Using ctrl and shift keys with mouse-object movement

Although the mouse control buttons offer several options for moving and posing objects in a scene, it is sometimes more convenient to use keyboard controls with the mouse. Pressing and holding-down the Ctrl key allows you to use the mouse to turn an object around in a spinning motion. Pressing and holding-down the Shift key allows you to use the mouse to move an object up and down.

Moving the camera

In setting up a scene, the camera viewpoint allows us to adjust what the user will be able to see in the animation. It may be helpful to think of the camera as a remote-controlled airborne device that hovers in mid-air over the scene. By moving the camera, we change our view of the world.

The blue controls at the bottom of the scene editor window are the camera controls, as shown in Figure A-1-30.

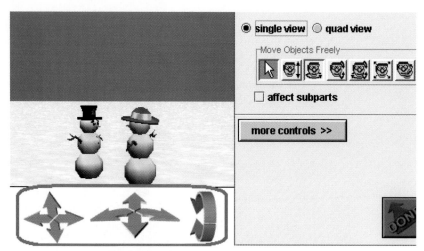

Figure A-1-30. Camera navigation controls

Click and drag on the camera controls to get an idea of what each camera control does.

You can always use Undo to return to a previous camera position.

Arranging many objects in an initial scene

When many objects are to be in the scene, adding objects one at a time and arranging them around the scene can be time consuming. The reason is that not only are you moving objects, you are also moving the camera around the scene. After several such moves, a new object might not be in view of the camera when it is first added to the scene. This means you may spend a lot of time with the camera controls trying to find newly added objects and arranging objects in the scene.

We recommend that all objects for the world be added to the scene immediately upon creating the world. Then use the mouse and camera controls to arrange objects in the scene. This simple process saves a lot of time and makes setting up the initial scene much easier. Figure A-1-31(a) on the next page shows a new world where many objects have been added, all clustered near the center of the world. Figure A-1-31(b) shows the objects rearranged in the scene.

Summary

Here's a recap of what you just learned with World 3. If you're not comfortable with any of these topics, go back to the beginning of this section and try it again.

Figure A-1-31. (a) All objects near center of world (b) Objects rearranged in the scene

- How to make a new world
- Saving a world
- Adding objects to the world
- Using mouse controls (in the scene editor)
- Using mouse controls for subparts of objects
- Deleting an object
- Using quad view
- Camera movement
- Arranging objects in a scene

Part 2: Using popup menus to create an initial scene

In Part 1, you used mouse controls to arrange objects in a scene. In this part, you will learn how to use methods to work with objects in setting up a scene.

Alice provides a number of built-in instructions that can be used to adjust the size and position of objects in a scene. These instructions are called methods. To illustrate their use, let's work with a new world where methods will be used to set up the scene (in addition to the mouse controls you learned to use in Part 1 of this Appendix).

To begin this section, first use File → New **World to start a new world. Select the grass template world. Click on the Add Objects button to set up your initial scene, as shown in Figure A-2-1.**

Add a happy tree and a frog to the new world.

The frog can be found in the Animals folder of the Local Gallery. The happy tree is in the Nature folder.

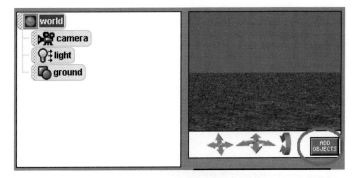

Figure A-2-1. Add Objects button

As seen in the Figure A-2-2, the frog is a bit small and it seems to fade into the grass, making it somewhat difficult to see. This situation is great for camouflaging the frog from its enemies but is not so good for an animation. You can use a *resize* method to make the frog larger.

Figure A-2-2. The frog is too small

Right-click on *frog* in the Object tree.
Select the method "*frog resize*" and select 2 as the amount as shown in Figure A-2-3.
This will make the frog 2 times as big as its current size.

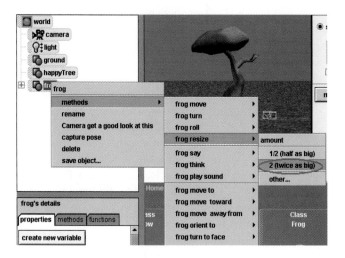

Figure A-2-3. Resize the frog, twice as big

Note: Resizing an object may have some unexpected results. An object standing on the ground may sink into the ground. **Reposition the object using the mouse, as needed.**

The *turn* method makes an object turn in a given direction (forward, back, left, right) by a given amount (in revolutions). An object moves relative to its own sense of direction (orientation).
Use a method to turn the frog left 1/4 revolution, as shown in Figure A-2-4.
The *roll* method rolls an object left or right.
Use a roll method to roll the tree left 1/4 revolution, as shown in Figure A-2-5.
The *stand up* instruction makes an object's vertical axis line up with the vertical axis of the world. In other words, the object stands up!
Use a stand up instruction to put the tree back into an upright position, as shown in Figure A-2-6.

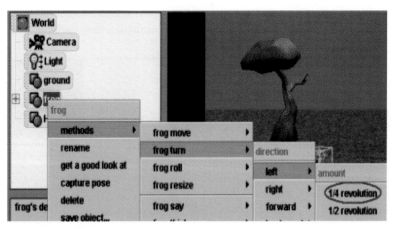

Figure A-2-4. Turn the frog left 1/4 revolution

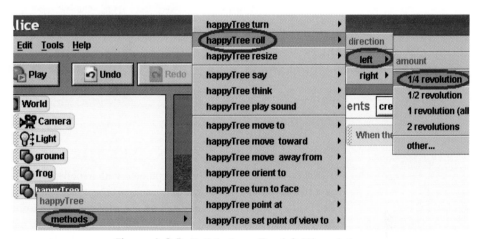

Figure A-2-5. Roll the happyTree left 1/4 revolution

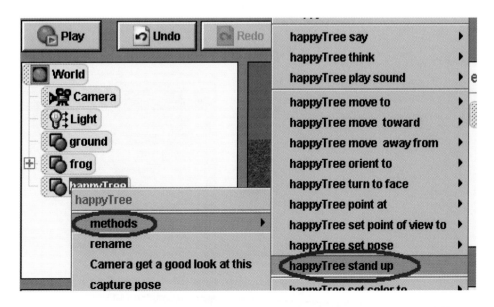

Figure A-2-6. Make the happyTree stand up

The *turn to face* method makes an object turn to look toward another object. **Use turn to face to make the frog face the tree, as shown in Figure A-2-7.**

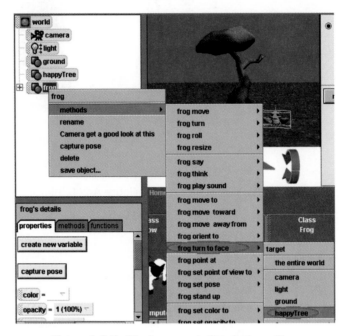

Figure A-2-7. The frog turns to face the happyTree

Using methods with object subparts

Subparts of an object can be manipulated with a method, by clicking on the subpart in the Object tree and then right-clicking the subpart to get the popup menu. **To view a list of the subparts of an object, first left-click on the plus box to the immediate left of the object in the Object tree.** Figure A-2-8 shows the frog's subparts in the expanded Object tree. One of the frog's parts is its jaw—and the tongue is a subpart of the jaw. (Parts can have parts, which can have parts, and so on ....)

Select the frog tongue and a method to move the tongue forward "Other" amount, as shown in Figure A-2-9. A number pad pops up where you can select the amount. **Enter .05.** (This is an arbitrary value—try different values until you get a satisfactory effect.)

Figure A-2-8. Frog parts

The frog sticks its tongue out, as shown in Figure A-2-10.

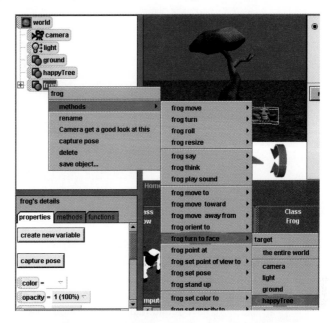

Figure A-2-9. Move the frog's tongue forward

Figure A-2-10. The frog's tongue sticks out

Get a good look at this object

The right-click popup menu for an object displays a menu containing several items. In this tutorial, you have used *methods*. Other menu items (*rename, capture pose,* and *save object*) are explained, as needed, in example programs in the text. One item in the menu is different from others in the menu. The *methods, rename, capture pose, delete,* and *save object* items are all designed to act on the object. But, *Camera get a look at this* is a camera method. When you select *Camera get a good look at this* from the menu, the camera zooms in to display a close-up view of an object. You can use Undo to return to the previous view.

Use *"Camera get a good look at this"* to get a close-up view of the frog, as shown in Figure A-2-11.

(If another object is between the camera and the object, and blocks the camera view, use Undo and move the camera or the object.)

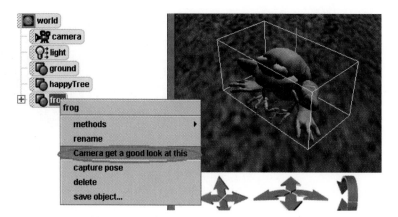

Figure A-2-11. *Camera get a good look at this*

A comparison of motion controls

In Part 1 of this tutorial, you experimented with mouse motion controls. In Part 2, you worked with methods. In both cases, you were positioning objects to set up an initial world scene. You may be wondering, "Which kind of motion control is best—mouse controls or methods?"

We have found that mouse motion control (in the scene editor) is very good for placing an object in an approximate location, but the popup menu methods are needed for exact alignment. The scene editor (especially the quad view) is great for positioning objects relative to one another. It is quite easy to add an object to a world and then use the mouse to move and rotate it approximately to the location we would like. If we make a mistake, we can simply undo our actions (or even delete the object) and try again. While the approximate positioning of an object is easy to do with the mouse, its exact positioning (we find) is a bit more challenging. For example, trying to position one object on top of another is difficult to do with the mouse. Getting them approximately on top of one another isn't too difficult, but placing them exactly is tough to do with the mouse. Methods, however, give good alignment. In setting up world scenes, the best strategy is to use a combination of methods and mouse motion controls.

Appendix B: Managing the Alice interface

Searching the gallery

Often, you may want to find an object, say a ball, but not know where to find the 3D model for it in the gallery. You can search the gallery for a particular kind of object. **Click the Search Gallery button, as shown in Figure B-1-1.**

You can search either your Local Gallery or the Web gallery at www.alice.org (assuming your computer is connected to the internet). You should always search your Local Gallery first, since this search will be much faster. **When the search prompt is displayed, as in Figure B-1-2, enter the name of the model (or part of the name) you are searching for, and then click on the Search! button next to the text box.**

If you do not find what you are looking for, you search www.alice.org, as illustrated in Figure B-1-3. The first time you search www.alice.org, your search may take a couple of minutes (depending on the speed of your internet connection). Additional searches will be much faster.

Creating your own people models

The galleries provide over a thousand 3D models for use in building your worlds. Alice is not a graphics model builder, but two special people-building utilities (hebuilder and shebuilder) are available in the People folder of the local gallery, as seen in Figure B-1-4. **A click on hebuilder or shebuilder will bring up a people builder window (Figure B-1-5), where you**

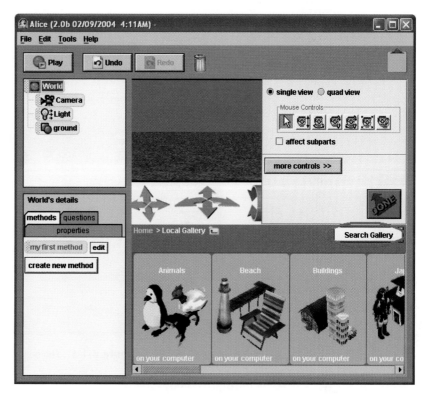

Figure B-1-1. Search the Gallery

Figure B-1-2. Entering a name for an object

Figure B-1-3. Search the Web gallery at www.alice.org

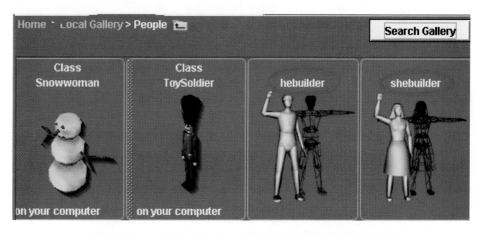

Figure B-1-4. The hebuilder and shebuilder model building utilities

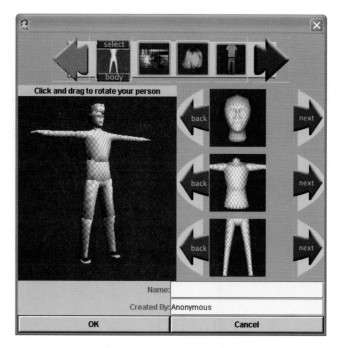

Figure B-1-5. The hebuider

can select the desired body type, hair, skin color, eyes, and clothing. When you have completed your selections, click on OK to name the object and add it to your world. Alice automatically defines a *walk* method for the person object that you build. This is an advantage, because a *walk* method is difficult to write on your own.

Copy and paste: clipboards

Suppose a particular sequence of animation instructions is something that you would like to copy and paste. This is where a clipboard is useful. **To copy a sequence of instructions, click on the left side (on the small dots) of the block of instructions you would like copied.** This action selects the instructions to be copied. (Note: Selecting a *Do in order* or a *Do together* statement selects all the instructions within it.) **Then use the mouse to drag the instructions to the clipboard.** Figure B-1-6 illustrates dragging instructions onto the clipboard from the editor.

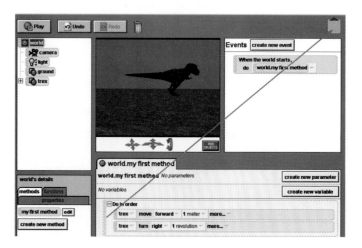

Figure B-1-6. Dragging instructions to the clipboard

Once instructions have been copied to a clipboard, the clipboard changes color (white). The color change is a visual clue indicating that copied instructions are now on the clipboard. **Now that the clipboard contains instructions, you can use the mouse to drag the selected instructions from the clipboard into the editor to create a new copy of those instructions elsewhere in your program, as illustrated in Figure B-1-7.** You now have two copies of the instructions in the editor. (You can delete the old instructions by dragging them to the waste basket.)

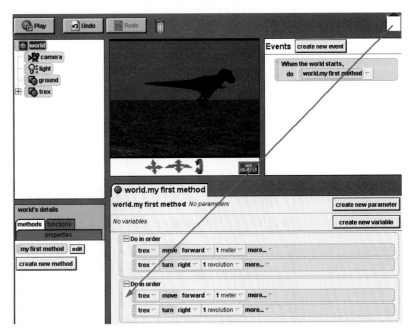

Figure B-1-7. Drag instructions from the clipboard into the editor

Note that a clipboard can hold only one set of instructions at a time. If instructions were previously copied to the clipboard, copying a new set of instructions to the same clipboard will overwrite (destroy) what was already there. As originally installed, Alice displays only one clipboard. The number of clipboards can be increased by selecting the **Edit** menu and then the **Preferences** menu item. In the **Seldom Used** tab of the Preferences window, modify the number of clipboards, as in Figure B-1-8.

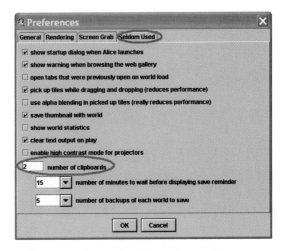

Figure B-1-8. Increasing the number of clipboards

Deleting code

What if you make a mistake or want to change some code that you have created? The easiest way to remove a line of code is to **drag it to the wastebasket at the top of the Alice window.** An entire block of code can be deleted by dragging the block to the wastebasket, as illustrated in Figure B-1-9.

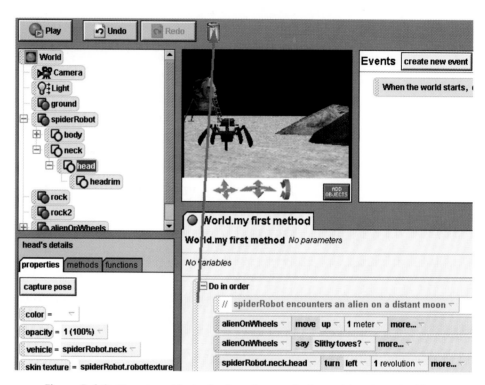

Figure B-1-9. Dragging a block of code to the wastebasket to delete the entire block

If you want to remove a *Do together* or *Do in order* block but keep the lines of code, **right click on the block and select** *dissolve*, **as seen in Figure B-1-10.** The lines of code will be promoted one level and the previously enclosing block will be erased, as shown in Figure B-1-11.

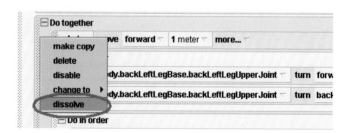

Figure B-1-10. Selecting *dissolve* to remove the *Do together* block

Printing: Exporting program code to an HTML file

You may wish to print the code from one or more of your program methods. First, be sure the world is open in Alice. **Then, to print a method from your program, click on the File menu and select the Export Code For Printing menu item, as shown in Figure B-1-12. In the**

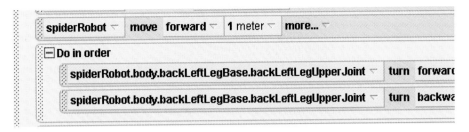

Figure B-1-11. After *dissolve*, the *Do together* block has been erased but the instructions remain

Figure B-1-12. Selecting the *Export Code For Printing* menu item

Print dialog box, select the name of the method (or methods) to be printed, the folder where the document is to be stored, and your name. Then click the **Export Code** button, as illustrated in Figure B-1-13. The code in the selected methods will be exported to an HTML document, which can be printed from your browser.

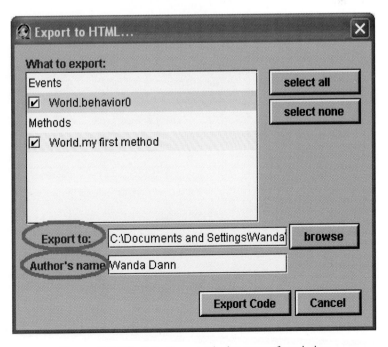

Figure B-1-13. Selecting a method to export for printing

Web display: Exporting a world

Exporting a world for display on a Web page is an excellent way to show off your creativity. First be sure the world is open in Alice. **To export a world, click the File menu and then select the Export As A Web Page menu item, illustrated in Figure B-1-14.**

Figure B-1-14. Selecting the *Export As A Web Page* menu item

A **Save World for the Web** dialog box allows the entry of a title, width and height of the world window to be displayed in a browser, and a location where the Web files will be saved, as illustrated in Figure B-1-15. (The location in the Save Location box cannot be a URL.) A click on the Save button causes Alice to save three files to the directory you select: the usual .a2w file, an .html file, and a Java archive (.jar) file.

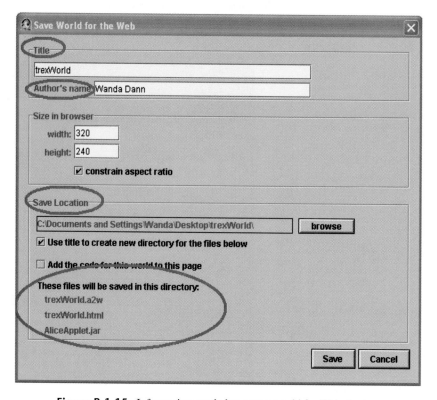

Figure B-1-15. Information needed to save a world for Web display

To allow others to view your world via the internet, you must store the three files on a Web server. All three files must be in the same directory. The first time someone downloads a page, it will take a few seconds (depending on the speed of their internet connection) because of the size of the Java archive file. (If the computer does not have a Java enabled browser or Java 3D or Java Media Frameworks, the web page will prompt the user to download a plug-in from the Java website, maintained by *Sun Microsystems®*). Thereafter, a page will download quickly.

Export to movie

At the time of this publication, this feature has not yet been implemented. We expect it may be implemented by the time you are reading this book. Check the www.alice.org website for updates.

Index